100 THINGS
CARDINALS FANS
SHOULD KNOW & DO
BEFORE THEY DIE

Derrick Goold

TRIUMPH
B O O K S

Library of Congress Cataloging-in-Publication Data

Goold, Derrick.
100 things Cardinals fans should know and do before they die / Derrick Goold.
    p. cm.
Includes bibliographical references.
ISBN 978-1-60078-755-3
    1. St. Louis Cardinals (Baseball team)—Anecdotes. 2. St. Louis Cardinals (Baseball team)—Miscellanea. I. Title. II. Title: One hundred things Cardinals fans should know and do before they die.
    GV875.S74G68 2012
    796.357'640977866—dc23
                                    2012002835

This book is available in quantity at special discounts for your group or organization. For further information, contact:

Triumph Books LLC
542 South Dearborn Street
Suite 750
Chicago, Illinois 60605
(312) 939-3330 | Fax (312) 663-3557
www.triumphbooks.com

Printed in U.S.A.
ISBN: 978-1-60078-755-3
Design by Patricia Frey
All photos courtesy of AP Images

To Ian, our very own Wonderboy,
and to beautiful Erika, my 4-for-4 day

Contents

Foreword by Stan Musial

Being able to play major league baseball for a living was an opportunity that I have forever cherished. But the chance to play major league baseball in St. Louis for the St. Louis Cardinals was a privilege that has me forever humbled.

I first put on a major league uniform in September 1941, and before I ever took a swing, I knew I wasn't just putting on a jersey with two birds and a bat. I was wearing a tradition. I was accepting a responsibility. By the time the Swifties arrived in the 1940s, the Cardinals' identity had been established decades before by Rogers Hornsby and the 1926 champions and by those beloved characters in the Gas House Gang. There was a Cardinals way to play, and we knew it was a pretty good way to win, too. That tradition guided all of us, and my teammate Red Schoendienst helped pass it along to Lou Brock and Bob Gibson and then on to Ozzie Smith and Willie McGee. Even the players today wear that same jersey with the same appreciation for the past and the great Cardinals who came before them.

Putting on the St. Louis Cardinals uniform means a player is accepting the expectations of history.

The Cardinals spirit is more than the records, however, more than the ballparks, and even more than the championships. Any history is hollow without the people. What makes the Cardinals the Cardinals are the people who have played for the team, like Ken Boyer, the people who have owned the team, like Gussie Busch, and of course the people who have lived and rooted for the team, like you. Baseball is more than a pastime here, it's a passion. I fed off the fans as a player, and my days are brightened by them still. Any story of the Cardinals must begin, end, and involve the fans, like this book does.

I've had the pleasure of traveling all over and seeing the best of every city I visit, and it takes only one trip to Busch Stadium to remind me that to know St. Louis you have to know the Cardinals.

To know the Cardinals, you have to know the people.

That was true before I ever came around. It was true when I played. And it is true today. It's all the red that greets you in every corner of the city on days the Cardinals are home. It's the Cardinals-Cubs rivalry. It's October baseball. It's that next rookie putting on the Birds on the Bat and feeling how tradition fits for the first time. It's better than a triple, and my knee tells me I had enough of them to know.

It was a thrill to play for the Cardinals for 22 years.

But the real honor is to be a Cardinal for life.

—November 2009

Introduction

Even back when they called Sportsman's Park home, a weekend series was part geography lesson for the Cardinals. Hall of Famer Red Schoendienst remembers walking to the neighborhood stadium with teammates and weaving through fields of parked cars, the expanse of the Cardinals' fan base revealed by the license plates. The Cardinals would count the cars from Arkansas, from Oklahoma, from Tennessee, sometimes from all eight of Missouri's contiguous states and often from further afield, such as Mississippi and Indiana. In the decades that followed, the club's reach would extend, and license plates would give way to letters, with broadcasters receiving postmarks from Gulf Coast to West Coast and provinces in Canada, thanking them for KMOX's muscular signal that made St. Louis, fittingly, the gateway for baseball's western expansion. In the age of the Internet, all teams belong to the world, and Mike Shannon, the voice of the Cardinals, hears from listeners in West Point, Beijing, and Jamaica, and once granted a birthday-wish request from London. He was recognized in Greece and stopped in Vatican City—because a priest had received word a Cardinal was visiting.

The only thing that can match the depth of the Cardinals' history, which is arguably the most decorated in the National League, is the breadth of the Cardinals' fan base. It was baseball's westernmost and southernmost club for most of its impressionable years. Generations of fans continue to flock to Cardinals games, if not actually as they did when Schoendienst would count cars then virtually by tuning in or logging on. In 2009, when the 80th All-Star Game came to town, Cardinals Hall of Fame shortstop Ozzie Smith said it was a world audience's chance to see that "this is a baseball mecca."

"This is a special organization," Shannon said. "You had the Gas House Gang and then you had Musial, and then you had the

1960s. There has always been winning and there has always been a Hall of Famer. So, you knew you went from the 1930s to the 1940s, zip through the '50s, won again in the '60s and into the '80s, and now in the 2000s we're winning again. The fans are always rewarded, the history is carried on, and there's always some reason to listen or watch. Almost everywhere you look there's greatness in this organization."

Attempting to distill the volumes of Cardinals history into a list of 100 moments that define the franchise would be foolish. Stan Musial alone has exponentially more highlights than that. A list of the top 100 best players might capture the continuous lineage of Hall of Famers—which is nearly seamless from Roger Bresnahan arriving in 1909 to manager Tony La Russa, a candidate for Cooperstown, retiring after 2011—but it would miss the cult heroes who mean as much to the fan base as the immortals. No, a representative list of 100 things every Cardinals fan should know and do has to be more than a recitation of history, more than a bound highlight reel. It should celebrate the fans as well as the franchise.

Think of this book, organized into 100 vignettes and a scattering of sidebars, as a road map for Cardinals Nation. Follow it in order, or take a route all your own.

Of course, there are entries about all 11 World Series championships, just as every player with a retired number is represented, from Ozzie Smith's No. 1 to Bob Gibson's No. 45. Landmark games are noted, from the Dean Brothers' dynamic doubleheader (No. 18) to Adam Wainwright's Game 7 curveball in the 2006 National League Championship Series (No. 7), from Albert Pujols' three-homer World Series game (No. 5) to Musial's five-homer day (No. 95). So, too, are the moments that may have been paved over or pushed back from the main road, such as Cy Young's role in Cardinals history (No. 4), Bake McBride's early-morning gallop (No. 74), and Mike Laga's famous foul ball (No. 86). There are sites to see (Low A affiliate Quad Cities, No. 76), places that should be visited (Trinket City, No. 32), and instrumental Cardinals to know (George Kissell, No. 60).

Like any good guide who has had the opportunity to see and experience the underpinnings of history, my hope is to offer a new look at familiar sights while also making new sights look familiar. That goes for the urban legends (the origin of the Redbird logo, No. 19), the legendary (David Freese and the comeback Cardinals, No. 11), and certainly the legends (Lou Brock, No. 20).

Former Cardinals third baseman Scott Rolen once said the thing that enriches St. Louis and Cardinals fans is "the history and the way they have of celebrating baseball itself." The Cardinals are more than a club, they are a public trust. They bridge generations and they bind regions. This 100-step guide aims to capture more than the history of the Cardinals by providing snapshots of what makes them the Cardinals. St. Louis is home to thriving amateur baseball, boasts attendance at Major League Baseball's traveling FanFest that eclipsed New York's record, and has twice owned the Guinness World Record for longest time spent playing baseball, set each time by 40 locals. The Cardinals nourish those deep roots for a city that, in many ways, is defined by its cherished pastime.

"As a player, you feel like royalty," said Joe Torre, who won the MVP as a Cardinal in 1971. "It's something very special to be there. Once you're a Cardinal, that never leaves you. Baseball in St. Louis is very sacred."

The first stop on any trip along the bond between these fans and their franchise is where this tour starts. Come along, it's just up ahead, by the new ballpark.

We can count out-of-state plates on the way.

—Derrick Goold
St. Louis, January 2011

Acknowledgments

One of the things about having the opportunity to cover the Cardinals in baseball-mad St. Louis is the appreciation you get not only for the city's rich history of baseball but also for the city's rich history of baseball writers. If St. Louis truly has the most knowledgeable fans in baseball, writers like Bob Broeg, Bob Burnes, and Rick Hummel are primary reasons. It is these scribes and many others to whom I owe the most thanks. They wrote the first (and best) drafts of Cardinals history, and without them the club's color would have faded.

Many people helped piece together the 100 most important landmarks, moments, and characters, starting with Mr. Hummel, affectionately known as "the Commish," who offered both guidance, anecdotes, and patience. The writings of Bob Broeg were essential and rewarding to reread. Columnist and friend Bernie Miklasz offered support and needed perspective. The works of Mike Eisenbath and Rob Rains were a wealth of information and each an excellent compass, as was our contemporary coverage, especially that of colleague Joe Strauss. The expertise, memories, research, insight, and, in some cases, libraries of Ron Jacober, Tom Ackerman, Dan McLaughlin, Mike Smith, Steve Pona, and generous neighbor Richard Buthod were invaluable. Will Leitch and Larry Borowsky helped me round out the list with what a ravenous fan would value. Joe Posnanski, Bryan Burwell, and Vahe Gregorian, a cherished mentor, helped me wrap my copy-clogged head around organizing a book, and dear friend Alan Hahn did that with a spoonful of encouragement. My first sports editor at the *Post-Dispatch*, Larry Starks, gave me the green light, and his successor, Reid Laymance, supported my drive to the finish, as did assistant editors Roger Hensley and Cameron Hollway. At

Triumph, Michael Emmerich first approached me about this book and showed patience I didn't earn while I finished it, and Adam Motin rebooted the endeavor with a jolt of energy.

This would be a lot thinner book were it not for Brian Finch, whose enthusiasm was contagious as he took me on a tour of Cardinals history. His curiosity and nose for details is an asset to the Cardinals Hall of Fame and his vigilance sets the bar for preserving Cardinals lore. Joan Thomas took me on a wonderful trip through old-time baseball in St. Louis. Many thanks to others with the Cardinals and around the ballpark: Paula Homan, Jim Anderson, Brian Bartow, Melody Yount, Tony Simokaitis, Ernie Hays, and Tim Falkner. Dan Kimack, at Fleishman-Hillard, dug into Rawlings Gold Glove history on his own to answer my quirky question, and a special thanks to Joe Vanderford who among his many assists helped contact Sharon Slaughter. Dick Zitzmann was essentially helpful with both guidance and his storehouse of stories. Other current and former members of the Cardinals who gave their time for interviews were: Lou Brock, Bob Gibson, Mike Jorgensen, Bob Forsch, Jose Oquendo, Bill DeWitt III, Ken Reitz, Glenn Brummer, Al Hrabosky, John Vuch, Buddy Bates, Jeff Suppan, Jim Edmonds, Scott Rolen, numerous members of the current club, living monument Red Schoendienst, and, of course, the best storyteller of them all, Mike Shannon.

Two gentlemen, who were generous with their time for all of my questions and helped illuminate the load-bearing pillars of how the Cardinals play the game and how they nurture their fans, have died since the interviews for this book. In their own remarkable ways, both the late Marty Hendin and great George Kissell defined the organization and what many believe it means to be a Cardinal.

And finally, family.

My father, Steve, told me all about baseball, and my grandfather, Fran, told me all about Cardinals baseball. Both instilled a reverence for history in the fan that I became. The only baseball book my forever giving mother, Elizabeth Holman-Goold, has ever read was this one, which meant it had to gain Mom's approval first, and that's really the way it should be. The wife, Erika, deserves special thanks for the support, the time, and exerting the right mix of pressure and guilt to get me back at the computer. She even gave me time on our vacation so several sections of the book could be completed. It might be the first time Glenn Brummer's steal of home was described off the coast of Greece, and for that I have the wife to thank. For a lot I have the wife to thank. Skip Bertman called her my "4-for-4 day."

He underestimated her expectations.

Meet Me at Musial

For generations of fans, the crossroads of Cardinals Nation was Walnut Street and Broadway in downtown St. Louis, signified not by the concrete monolith of a stadium in the background but by a 10'-tall statue that stood as their cultural epicenter. The bronzed batter became the traditional meeting point for the devoted. Many trips to Busch Stadium for a baseball game started with the universally understood invitation: "Meet me at the Musial statue."

A statue of Stan Musial has stood sentry outside the Cardinals' home ballpark for parts of six decades. Far more than a totem to the team's best and most-revered player, it is a landmark, the magnetic north of Cardinals Nation by which almost all visits to the ballpark are oriented. Engraved into it are words Cardinals fans can readily recite, like the opening stanza of a beloved nursery rhyme for the red-dressed masses:

> *Here stands baseball's perfect warrior.*
> *Here stands baseball's perfect knight.*

The words are from former baseball commissioner Ford Frick, said when Musial retired from the game. Musial's last day in cleats was the inspiration for the local chapter of the Baseball Writers Association of America to raise money for the gift of a statue to place outside the ballpark. The "Perfect Knight" statue was unveiled in 1968, and even then it was a polarizing depiction of the Hall of Famer. It was abstract, showing a broad-shouldered, narrow-waist, wispy-legged Musial tucked into his trademark

1

batting stance. The face was too angular to be true to Musial's. Fans and media groused. Musial hoped the original plan, which included an autograph-seeking kid, would be used to soften a potentially pretentious tribute. Sculptor Carl Mose favored the interpretive take on the Cardinals great.

While acceptance of the statue's aesthetics differs, its location has long been embraced as a beacon for far-flung fans and locals alike.

And it's the fans who make the monument.

"The fans are what makes St. Louis," longtime Houston Astros star Craig Biggio once said. "The fans are still going to be here. Yankee Stadium is its own entity. Fenway Park is. Wrigley Field is. But St. Louis is known for its fans."

The Cardinals were the first major league team west of the Mississippi River, and for much of the 20th century they were the furthest team south as well. That gave them access to draw from an unprecedented expanse of America. The reach of the club's flagship radio station, clear-channel KMOX/1120 AM, helped amplify the interest, taking Cardinals baseball well beyond their time zone. The Cardinals' roots are so deep in some areas that even decades after rapid expansion and cable television obliterated baseball's geographic boundaries, the club had radio affiliates in nine states. A Harris Poll taken in 2007 revealed the Cardinals as the fourth-most popular team in the country, trailing only popularity powers New York Yankees, Boston Red Sox, and Atlanta Braves. But the Cardinals were easily the most beloved team in the Midwest and the overall favorite of the 18- to 29-year-olds age group.

"They love to see the team win, but they have this history here in St. Louis, they have a way of celebrating baseball," said Scott Rolen, a onetime Cardinals third baseman. "They love coming to the ballpark. It's a family affair still, and they come here to watch baseball. They really have a lot of respect for the game and they believe that this is their team."

The Stan Musial statue was unveiled outside the new Busch Stadium by the legend himself in 2006.

The depth of the franchise's history and the breadth of the franchise's reach made the bronze Musial an obvious and fitting place for an informal town square to develop. It is a destination point for pilgrimages from across Cardinals Nation. No journey to the ballpark is complete without seeing "baseball's perfect knight," because when you come to watch the Cardinals, the same is true now as it was when he played—Musial shows the way.

Red Schoendienst

2B…Inducted into Hall of Fame, 1989…Number retired, 1996

The man who would spend more time in a Cardinals' major league uniform than anyone else, Red Schoendienst, started his Hall of Fame career by answering an ad in the paper. In 1942 Schoendienst, a Germantown, Illinois, native, and a buddy picked up a newspaper that carried an announcement: the National League ballclub in St. Louis—some 55 miles away—was holding open tryouts at Sportsman's Park. Come one. Come all. Bring a glove.

"It's probably the only ad I ever read," Schoendienst grinned more than six decades later while still wearing the Birds on the Bat.

Schoendienst and his pal hitchhiked to St. Louis to take part in the tryout—not necessarily because they thought they had a chance, but because they would get to stick around for the game that followed. Albert Fred Schoendienst, all country-boy thin, red hair, and freckles, thrilled scouts with his agility around the horn and with a bat. He didn't have to hitch home—the Cardinals gave him a ride so that they could sign him. After 19 years, 14½ of which were spent playing for the Cardinals, Schoendienst retired with 2,449 hits, two top-five finishes in MVP voting, and two World Series rings, one with the Cardinals. He went on to be the organization's winningest manager for the latter half of the 20th century.

The Cardinals got much more than they advertised for.

"We played mostly baseball as kids, a lot of ragball, and when we saw that ad, we thought, *Let's try it out,*" Schoendienst said. "I just wanted to see about it, see if I could play. I guess they saw something in me."

It took Schoendienst a couple seasons in the Cardinals' expansive minor league to surface in the majors in 1945, and he did so as the fill-in for Stan Musial, who was serving in the military. That season Schoendienst hit .278, was second on the team with 89 runs, and led the NL with 26 steals. The next summer, with Musial back in the lineup, Schoendienst began his migration around the infield before settling at second, where he would ultimately merit induction into Cooperstown. Schoendienst led his position in fielding percentage seven years, four times as a Cardinal. In 1949 he set records for consecutive games and consecutive chances at second without an error. In 1950 he broke both records. Nine of his 10 All-Star appearances came as a Cardinal, and in 1953 he finished second in the batting-title race with a career-best .342. Never a power hitter, Schoendienst nevertheless had a three-day, extra-base binge for the ages. In June 1948 he ripped eight doubles and one home run to set a league high for doubles and extra-base hits.

"Besides Jackie Robinson, for 10 or 15 years there, Red was the best second baseman in the league," Musial, the man who batted behind Schoendienst and roomed with the redhead, once said.

He did it through injuries and illnesses that would have deterred or derailed others. Schoendienst caught a wire staple in the left eye as a teenager and played with double vision for years. A shoulder injury in the minors slowly sapped his arm strength, and for two years in the 1950s Schoendienst played with tuberculosis.

Red Schoendienst was a 10-time All-Star during his playing days and later managed the Cardinals to back-to-back World Series appearances in the 1960s.

He was with Milwaukee at the time of the diagnosis and had just hit .300 in the '58 World Series for the Braves. He spent more than 100 days in the hospital and had a chunk of his lung removed. He returned to the Cardinals in 1961 as a part-time player and put the finishing touches on a .289 career average.

But not the finishing touches on a career.

Schoendienst's second act with the Cardinals was as successful as his first. Named as manager in 1965, his first season was spent defending a World Series title. Within three years he had won his own. The affable, quick-to-grin Schoendienst had the ideal temperament to pilot one of the highest-priced rosters in the majors. He deftly integrated Yankees great Roger Maris into the lineup, eased Mike Shannon into the infield, and knew never to take Bob Gibson out in the middle of an inning. Schoendienst shepherded the Cardinals to the title in 1967 and the pennant 1968. Including two good-soldier turns as an interim skipper for the club, Schoendienst went 1,041–955 as manager, a total-wins record that stood until Tony La Russa snapped it in 2007. La Russa threatened to vacate the job to avoid breaking Schoendienst's record. The Ol' Redhead just had La Russa promise to share a toast that night after it was broken.

If Musial is the face of the Cardinals, Gibson the fire, and coach George Kissell the sage, then Schoendienst is the soul. For nearly seven consecutive decades, Schoendienst has worn a baseball uniform to work.

"I make sure I don't get in anybody's way," he said one sunny day during batting practice. "I mean, what would you do if they let you be around the big leagues every day? The Cardinals gave me an opportunity to play. I'm trying to give what I can back. Being around this is what keeps your lights burning."

3 Attend Opening Day in St. Louis

Around Major League Baseball each spring, there are 29 Opening Days and one experience. It is a civic spectacle that starts with Clydesdales.

Opening Day at Busch Stadium is unlike any other in baseball. It is a signature event for the Cardinals, one that is designed to sew together the debut of the current team and the rich tapestry of the franchise's past. Longtime Cardinals manager Tony La Russa and several transplanted players have said that a ballplayer has only been to *an* Opening Day until he has been to St. Louis for *the* Opening Day. "What stands out is the execution of everything and the fan reaction to everything," La Russa said. "It becomes this tremendous blend of the year you're playing and the past, all rolling out onto the field at the same time."

The annual concert of Clydesdales, Corvettes, and Cardinals is the brainchild of the late Marty Hendin. In the late 1970s Hendin wanted to reinvigorate a fan base by reviving the successful past. Hendin said he wanted to "find a way to take the tradition, all that energy and success, and the fact that each year may be a different team but the same franchise and bring it all together." He invited players—all sorts of them, from fan favorites to Hall of Famers to just Cardinals—for a homecoming. He organized a parade, with the Anheuser-Busch Clydesdales leading the way each year and pulling the iconic beer wagon, complete with Dalmatian. The right-field gates at the past two Busch Stadiums were specially modified to allow for the Clydesdales to reach the warning track for the annual lap. The cars carrying the current Cardinals and Hall of Famers follow behind. Organist Ernie Hays has to prep his fingers and back for the event because the parade often means playing "Here Comes the King" continuously for 35 to 40 minutes. He hesitates to calculate how often he'll traipse though the 32 bars of the anthem. "I play and I play and I play until my hands feel like they're about to fall off with the next note," he said, "and then I play some more."

On the field is only a slice of the spectacle. Throughout the region, fans who cannot avoid or ditch work for the day wear red, and the color is universal around the city. Those who can get away gravitate downtown, where even those without a ticket mill around the ballpark just to be near the epicenter of the first tremor from a new season. It is a civic event. Hendin said his Opening Day eventually became an organism all its own, spreading out from the ballpark but also expanding from year to year within the ballpark. For the final year of Busch Stadium II, Hendin plotted "the greatest Opening Day we've ever had." He had players from four decades of Cardinals history, and he said he felt chills as he saw the Hall of Famers and the oldest of Cardinals "slapping hands with the newest of Cardinals."

"You don't really know what to expect until you've seen it yourself," said shortstop David Eckstein, whose first Opening Day as a Cardinal was the last Opening Day at Busch II. "The red. The fans. The Clydesdales. It's definitely an experience, an experience every player has to see to understand what Opening Day really can be."

4 Cy Young and the Birth of the Cardinals

Although the St. Louis Cardinals franchise can trace its roots back more than a decade before April 15, 1899, the true history of the modern-day club began that afternoon with a first pitch thrown by the first name in pitching.

With a chilly wind testing the 18,000 fans, Denton True "Cy" Young led a lineup of transplanted professional ballplayers, each decked out in posh new uniforms ornamented by rich red socks and accents, onto League Field. Young, whose name now adorns the award given to the best pitcher in each league, delivered a six-hitter and a victory in what arguably is the genesis of today's St. Louis Cardinals.

Professional baseball had been around for decades in St. Louis, and Young and his teammates actually played the inaugural game at the city's second major league ballpark, the so-called New Sportsman's Park (later Robison Field). In 1882 Chris Von der Ahe gained membership in the American Association and fielded a team, dressed the players in white-and-brown uniforms, and called them the St. Louis Browns. Under the player/manager guidance of Charles Comiskey—who later owned the Chicago White Sox—the Browns won four consecutive American Association championships, from 1885 to 1889. In 1886 the Browns defeated the Chicago White Stockings with Curt Welch's "$15,000 slide," so nicknamed because it won the series and scored the gate receipts for the champion Browns. Newspapers called Von der Ahe "der boss manager of der boss glub," and author Robert Smith later wrote St. Louis "was the Boss City" because of the Browns' success. It was fleeting. During the next few seasons, Von der Ahe imploded his roster out of frustration for losing a championship series; other American Association owners grew weary of the Browns' freewheeling approach to winning; the association itself started to splinter; and the National League improved its foothold. In 1892 Von der Ahe moved his annually successful club into the National League— and then watched as it finished no higher than ninth in seven consecutive seasons.

After a disastrous 1898 season that included a 12th-place finish, a fire that torched the ballpark's grandstand, and the inferno of lawsuits and creditors that followed, Von der Ahe had to sell.

The Robison brothers, Frank and Stanley, bought the bankrupt team and, in cahoots with the National League, orchestrated a unique transfer. Disappointed in the crowds their winning Cleveland Spiders team drew, the Robisons uprooted the Spiders' roster and sowed them into the new St. Louis franchise. Cleveland got the threadbare Browns' lineup. The Robisons changed the name of the ballpark to League Park, changed the look of the club to include the cardinal red that would later become the team's nickname, and ditched the Browns moniker entirely. Future Hall of Famers Young, Bobby Wallace, and Jesse Burkett would take the field on April 15, 1899, for a team briefly called the St. Louis Perfectos.

In a cruel twist of the schedule, the Perfectos debuted against the exiled Cleveland Spiders, winning 10–1. Their manager, Patsy Tebeau, was a St. Louis native, and he had two of the 16 hits the Perfectos rapped in their debut. Three came from catcher Jack O'Connor, another St. Louis native. Young, that strapping right-hander from Ohio, won 26 games that season with a 2.58 ERA. Of his record 511 wins, Young collected 45 while pitching for St. Louis. After the 1900 season—the year the team wearing cardinal became the Cardinals—Young left for Boston and an American League paycheck.

His Opening Day win for St. Louis was the first of seven consecutive victories to start the 1899 season. It was also the first game of a direct lineage with the contemporary Cardinals. The franchise has changed owners and changed homes, but it hasn't changed its league, its look, or uprooted its roster since. Young's pitch may not have been the absolute first in franchise history, but it was the first one delivered by a Cardinal.

The 1899 club gathered wins and fans quickly as they held onto first place until late May. Though they won 84 games, the Perfectos faded to fifth. They remained incredibly popular but only occasionally in contention. The St. Louis club, so stout under Von der Ahe in the American Association, didn't finish higher than third from 1899 until winning its first NL pennant in 1926. By then, Young had been retired for 15 years.

5 King Albert

Back in late 2000 the Cardinals' Triple A affiliate, the Memphis Redbirds, had a comfy lead in their Pacific Coast League division and some time to pad their roster for the postseason. Farm director Mike Jorgensen dialed manager Gaylen Pitts to discuss how best to augment the lineup.

"I'd like a right-handed bat," Pitts said.

"Somebody who can hit lefties," Jorgensen nodded.

"What about this Pujols guy?"

"He's in A ball."

"I'm hearing a lot about him," Pitts insisted. "A lot."

He hadn't heard anything yet.

Pitts' seemingly small request for a bat that would pound left-handed pitchers helped launch Albert Pujols from an unknown Class A infielder to a Triple A playoff MVP and, within a year, history. The next spring he began an incomparable start to a major league career as the best hitter of his generation. He's the only player in history to start his career with 10 consecutive years with a .300 average, 30 homers, and 100 RBIs. He was the fastest ever to 1,000 hits and 200 home runs, and the youngest to reach 250 homers. Pujols won three National League MVPs and finished second in the voting four times in his first 10 seasons.

"There is nobody out there better," his manager Tony La Russa said. "He's the one in a generation. He's in that [Stan] Musial, [Henry] Aaron [class]. He could hit in their league. He's one of the greats. He's the perfect player."

With MVPs in 2005, 2008, and 2009, Pujols matched Stan Musial's three MVPs, a franchise high, but he will fall forever short

Albert Pujols is the only player in baseball history to hit .300, slam 30 home runs, and knock in 100 RBIs in his first 10 big-league seasons.

of Musial's status. Pujols' run at Musial's career records and opportunity to join "The Man" as a civic icon ended suddenly after the 2011 season. The Los Angeles Angels lured Pujols, a free agent for the first time, away from St. Louis with a record-setting 10-year contract worth more than $250 million. Baseball leaders from Reggie Jackson to commissioner Bud Selig all publicly wished for Pujols to embrace his legacy and remain a Cardinal for life. Negotiations faltered in December 2011 and the Cardinals declined to meet Pujols' demands, opening the way for the Angels to swoop in with a stunning offer. "It's hard to quantify iconic value," general manager John Mozeliak said. "We tried."

Pujols left St. Louis after 11 seasons unmatched in club history, and one of his final acts was a fitting parting gift: the best single game by a hitter in World Series history. In Game 3 of the 2011 World Series, Pujols joined Babe Ruth and Jackson as the only players in history with three homers in a single game. Pujols bested them with five hits total, six RBIs, and a record 14 total bases.

La Russa called Pujols' three-homer feat "the greatest in [107] years of the World Series," and it allowed the first baseman to leave the Cardinals as the player he became with them—the best hitter in the game and the face of baseball. Several times in 2011, teammates referred to him as "Babe Ruth over there." Mike Piazza, the all-time leader in homers by a catcher, said, "Next to the definition of what it means to be a great player there is a picture of Pujols so you know what it means." Teammate Lance Berkman bluntly told reporters at the 2011 World Series, "He's a better hitter than Babe Ruth and there's no doubt about it."

Beyond the raw numbers and his relentless metronome of production, Pujols proved capable of making the uncanny commonplace, as he did with his Game 3 performance. His home

A Peerless Performance

Albert Pujols had 11 seasons of unparalleled production for the Cardinals that included the finest decade to start a career in baseball history. How his 11 seasons in St. Louis compare with the first 11 years by four Hall of Famers:

Player	Years	BA/OBP/SLG	HR	RBI	Runs
Albert Pujols	2001-11	.328/.420/.617	445	1,329	1,291
Hank Aaron	1954–64	.320/.376/.567	366	1,216	1,180
Joe DiMaggio	1936–49*	.331/.401/.589	317	1,344	1,204
Stan Musial	1941–52*	.346/.431/.579	227	1,014	1,149
Ted Williams	1939–52*	.347/.484/.634	324	1,264	1,275

* DiMaggio, Musial, and Williams missed several years each to serve in the military. Musial was a September callup in 1941 for 12 games.

run off Brad Lidge in Game 5 of the 2005 National League Championship Series brought the Cardinals back to Busch Stadium for one last night at the condemned ballpark. His 1,000th career RBI came on a grand slam. He once scored a game-winning run from second base on a groundball to the second baseman. For several years, the Cardinals hosted a "Buddy Walk" day in conjunction with the National Down Syndrome Society, and each time Pujols, whose daughter has Down syndrome, fielded the children's requests for a home run. On "Buddy Walk" day in 2006, he hit three.

"The idea for me is you don't ever want to be satisfied with what you do every year," Pujols says. "I know what I can do. It's just being consistent, and then in the long run you can accomplish everything you always dream."

Pujols came from the Dominican Republic to the United States at 15 and eventually settled in Independence, Missouri, where he starred in high school and at junior college. His bat was potent, but his thick frame said "project, not prospect." He went in the 13th round to the Cardinals in 1999; 401 players were drafted ahead of him. A year later, the Cardinals were talking trade with San Diego for a catcher, Carlos Hernandez. The Padres targeted two prospects. They favored fourth-round pick Ben Johnson but were intrigued by Pujols. Knowing a Padres scout was following the Peoria affiliate where Pujols played, Jorgensen promoted him to "get him off the radar, as best I could." Johnson went to San Diego, and a few weeks later Pitts lobbied for Pujols. Had Pujols been a first-round pick, Jorgensen doubts he could have jumped two levels like he did.

Pujols repaid the rapid promotion by batting .367 in the playoffs and hitting a game-winning home run in the 13th inning that cinched the Pacific Coast League championship. At major league camp the next spring, Pujols kept hitting. Mark McGwire stood near La Russa during a spring training game and whispered, "The kid's got to make the team."

Pujols left the Cardinals no choice.

Well, there was one.

When the equipment manager went to select a number for Pujols' jersey, then–general manager Walt Jocketty told them to make it a low number, one of the single digits not yet retired. Let him make it great, was the message. On April 2, 2001, Pujols debuted in left field wearing No. 5. In just his second full professional season, he was the unanimous pick as the NL Rookie the Year. Five years later, he set career highs with 49 home runs and 137 RBIs, won a Gold Glove at first base, and catapulted the Cardinals to their first World Series title since 1982. When he left for California, only three players in Cooperstown had better career BA/OBP/SLG averages than Pujols: Ruth, Ted Williams, and Lou Gehrig.

During one spring training, legendary Green Bay Packers general manager Ron Wolf stood watching Pujols take batting practice. He marveled at the crisp crack of Pujols' bat. "That sound," he said. "That is what it must have been like to hear Ted Williams or Babe Ruth hit."

For 11 years, the Cardinals certainly couldn't tell the difference.

6 Stan "the Man" Musial

OF/1B…Inducted into Hall of Fame, 1969…Number retired, 1963

The man who defined what it meant to be a Cardinal was nearing the end of his fabled career, seemingly rewriting a record with each of his signature swings, when a young ballplayer, a local boy named Mike Shannon, decided to take a peek at the wand that made such magic. Shannon pulled a few of Stan Musial's bats from the rack and marveled at what he saw. The only bruises left by the ball on Musial's bat were clustered around the sweet spot. No blue smudges down near the handle, no chips or scars near the top. The marks on the bat were as remarkably consistent as the batter.

He never failed to make sincere contact with any pitch, just as he never failed to make his contact sincere with any person.

Stanley Frank Musial, the Sir Galahad of baseball, was as genuine on the field as he was off, transitioning gracefully from the greatest Cardinal ever to the club's gentleman ambassador and icon of St. Louis. In 22 years as an outfielder and first baseman for the Cardinals, Musial set franchise records in every major offensive category: hits (3,630), home runs (475), RBIs (1,951), runs (1,949), total bases (6,134), and games played (3,026). When he retired as a three-time MVP and three-time World Series winner, he held 29 National League records, 17 major league records, and nine All-Star Game records. And those numbers pale compared to the others that define him as the Man. Even late into his eighties, Musial carried a dozen of the 8,000-plus autographed pictures he always had ready just in case he ran into fans—a trick he learned from friend John Wayne. There are wives and grandchildren of Hall of Famers around baseball who have rings made out of $1 bills, fashioned for them by Musial, often with a $1 from his own wallet. There are countless fans who have been serenaded by Musial and his trusty harmonica, just because he was there.

"I'm kind of a tough person to ooh and ahh over people, but with Stan...Stan is the Cardinals," said Hall of Fame pitcher Bob Gibson. "It's really tough to think about the Cardinals organization or team without thinking about Stan. It kind of seems like he invented it. He's been here, he's been the best player ever in the organization, he's been there forever. When you think of the Cardinals, you think of Stan Musial."

Born Stanislaw Franciszek Musial in Donora, Pennsylvania, a mill town 28 miles outside of Pittsburgh, the left-handed-throwing teen got his baseball break when a neighborhood friend ran out of pitching on his semipro team. He sent Musial, the bat boy who would later change his given name to a more familiar pronunciation, to the mound. Musial struck out 13. In 1937 the Cardinals signed him to a $65-a-month deal and shipped him to Class D, where he would pitch. Three years later Musial had shown such ability at the plate that his minor league team would play him in the outfield when he was not on the mound. In August of 1940 one career ended and another took off just that way, with a diving catch in center field. Musial landed hard on his left shoulder, jarring it severely. He struggled to pitch and thought his career was over. But by the end of the next season Musial's bat had carried him to the majors.

During a September promotion in the heat of 1941's pennant race, Musial hit .426 and slugged .574 in his first 12 games as a Cardinal.

The next season he was the rookie force behind a World Series winner, and he began his run of 16 consecutive seasons with a .300 average. In 10 of his first 12 seasons he didn't hit less than .330. In 1943, his second full season, Musial won his first MVP, leading the NL in hits (220), doubles (48), and triples (20). And, with a .357 average, he won the first of seven batting titles. He earned his nickname from Brooklyn Dodgers fans who were so weary of their team's inability to get him out that they said, "Here comes that man again." That man became "the Man." There wasn't an offensive column on his baseball card that he couldn't fill with elite numbers. From his first full season to his last in 1963, Musial had 1,372 extra-base hits, nearly 500 more than the next closest total in that span, Ted Williams' 878.

"No man has ever been a perfect ballplayer," Hall of Famer Ty Cobb wrote in 1953. "Stan Musial, however, is the closest thing to perfection in the game today. I've seen great hitters, great runners, and great fielders, but he puts them together like no one else."

In 1948 Musial won his third MVP as he batted .376, drove in 131 runs, and slugged .702, at the time the highest ever by a left-handed hitter in the NL. Musial came one home run shy of a Triple Crown, a feat no NL player has accomplished since the Cardinals' Joe Medwick in 1937.

Stan "the Man" Musial set every major franchise record during his 22-year career with the Cardinals, including most hits, home runs, RBIs, runs, total bases, and games played.

As a boy in Oklahoma, future All-Star and general manager Jerry Walker clipped pictures of Musial at bat so he could mimic his swing. Feet close together. Slightly hunched. Shoulder closed and neck craned just so, as if playing peek-a-boo with the pitcher. It wasn't elegant like Joe DiMaggio or upright like Ted Williams, but when Musial uncoiled from it, he was just as effective. Carl Erskine once described his approach with Musial: "I've had pretty good success...throwing him my best pitch and backing up third." Musial laced his 3,000th hit in 1958, hit a home run on the day he became a grandfather, and in his final at-bat—on September 29, 1963, at home—scorched an RBI single past a diving Pete Rose to set the NL record at 3,630 hits.

That same season Musial became the first Cardinal to have his number retired, and in 1969 he was a first-ballot Hall of Famer. He would go on to serve as the team's general manager for the 1967 World Series champions, but his legacy is also the outreach work he did for baseball and the Cardinals. A restaurateur after retirement and a tireless emissary, Musial served as President Lyndon Johnson's national physical fitness adviser. In 2000 he became the first sports figure inducted into the Hall of Famous Missourians at the state capitol. "He was more than an athlete," then–House Speaker Steve Gaw said, "he was an artist."

While the brilliance of his career doesn't attract the national attention of others from his era—fans failed to vote him onto baseball's All-Century Team, for example—Musial remains a ballplayer's ballplayer. His peers named him the "greatest living hitter," in a 2003 poll of Hall of Famers by the *Rocky Mountain News*. Forty-six years after his last hit only two players in history had more extra-base hits than he did. He was sustained excellence personified as a player, and was even better when he took his cleats off.

"He's the standard that people should go by, on and off the field," Gibson said. "He was one of the best ballplayers ever. He's also one of the nicest people you'll ever meet. If there is somebody you should try to copy just in life, you couldn't go wrong by copying Stan."

7 Yadier Molina and the Night Shea Went Silent

National League Championship Series Game 7—October 19, 2006

One of the most riveting and tense postseason Game 7s in history made Adam Wainwright a star. It made Jeff Suppan an MVP. And it made Scott Rolen weep. But this rain-soaked, captivating October evening at a throbbing Shea Stadium in New York wouldn't have made the St. Louis Cardinals National League champions had it not been for a young catcher vigorously chasing away the numbers from his maddening season.

While Wainwright's curveball, Suppan's clutch, and Rolen's clash with manager Tony La Russa soaked up all of the ink that night, years have provided clarity for the thread that tied up the pennant for the Cardinals. It was as one Cardinal said, summing up that victory against the New York Mets: "It was all about Yadi."

Yadier Molina inherited the starting job at catcher from his mentor, Mike Matheny, at the start of the 2005 season. At the tender age of 22, he'd made a brief postseason name for himself in 2004 by confronting Manny Ramirez at the plate during his first World Series start. Molina sternly told Ramirez that he wouldn't suffer David Ortiz relaying pitch location from the on-deck circle. There was no doubting Molina's poise, his instincts, nor his Gold Glove defense. All were ready for the job. Though in 2006, as he struggled at the plate and hit .216, he began to doubt his bat. October offered an elixir, a chance to drown the gamey taste of that .216. He kept that goal mostly to himself as he cranked out a team-best 19 hits and hit one of the biggest home runs in Cardinals postseason history. "I knew," he said, "how important it was that I do my job."

The night before Game 7 the Mets seized control of the best-of-seven National League Championship Series by upending Cardinals ace Chris Carpenter. The Mets had been the NL's best team all season, and the Cardinals limped into the playoffs with 83 wins. Game 7 at home was only the start of their advantages. The previous 11 home teams in baseball history to force a Game 7 with a Game 6 victory had won that Game 7. The Cardinals, however, countered with a calm, collected, and seasoned battery.

Throwing that night to Molina was Suppan, an understated pitcher with an underrated career. He had been in an NLCS Game 7 before, outdueling Roger Clemens for the pennant in 2004. Before the game Suppan was his usual self, willing to talk about anything but the game. He asked the team photographer if he was nervous about shooting pictures at a Game 7. He asked reporters if they got nervous covering a Game 7. When the questions were reversed, he shrugged. Like his catcher, he kept his body language cool.

The subplot to the entire NLCS had been a growing fissure between La Russa and his sublime third baseman, Rolen. La Russa didn't start Rolen in Game 2 of the series, a slight the third baseman took as nothing short of "a benching." The erosion of their relationship would lead to Rolen being traded after the 2007 season, but at issue this October was Rolen's failing shoulder. Exhausted and weakened by injury, Rolen could not get around on up-and-in fastballs. His power had been sapped. The Mets knew it. La Russa knew it. And Rolen knew it. But standing at his locker in the corner of Shea's cheerlessly compact visitors' clubhouse, Rolen delivered a sermon to a few reporters on what he believed made a ballplayer, injured or not. "I'm 100 percent of what I can be when I go out there," Rolen said. "I believe in the man. I believe in the heart."

For a moment, in Game 7, he believed he had a home run.

With Suppan having shepherded the Cardinals to a 1–1 tie through five innings and Jim Edmonds on first, Rolen finally got hold of a pitch he could handle. Mets starter Oliver Perez winced as Rolen drilled a pitch to deep left field. It would have easily cleared the fence and given the Cardinals a 3–1 lead had it not been for the catch of Endy Chavez's life. The Mets' left fielder, leaping from a full sprint, reached over the wall—his elbow clearing the top of the padding—and pulled Rolen's homer back. Many players called it the best clutch catch they've seen, including Edmonds, who was doubled off first to end the inning.

"That's kind of the way things were going for me," Rolen said.

Chavez received two curtain calls from the Shea faithful for his catch. The ballpark was rocking from an overheated sound system, and its crowd of 56,357 quivered as the Mets seized momentum. With one out and one on in the bottom of that inning, Suppan coaxed a routine grounder from David Wright. Moving to his left, Rolen scooped, glanced to see if there was a play at second, and then fired to first base—wildly. His nightmare inning continued as his throw floated into the stands. Robbed of a chance to win the game with his bat, the man who trusted his heart was now giving the game away with his arm. In the postgame celebration, a weeping Rolen, his arm draped over his friend and rescuer, Suppan, said between squeezes, "That was not a very good inning, emotionally, for me."

Suppan showed no emotion after Rolen's error.

With Molina as his guide, Suppan intentionally walked Shawn Green to load the bases and face Jose Valentin. The Mets' infielder swung over a curve for strike two. After he fouled off a change-up, Molina called for a curve again. The young catcher, all of 24 at the time, was so nimble behind the plate that his pitchers felt comfy planting their curves in the dirt; they knew Molina would stop them. Even with the bases loaded and a pennant on the line, Suppan fired a curve low and inside to Valentin. Molina scampered over to scoop it just as Valentin swung over it for the second out of the inning. With Shea's crowd crackling for potential of poetry, Chavez came to bat with the bases loaded and his catch still echoing around the ballpark. Molina hopped up and quickly chatted with Suppan. The right-hander got over-eager Chavez to pop up the first pitch.

"When you've got a guy like Soup, a smart pitcher, it's easy to get through something like that," Molina said. "I remember that inning. That inning stays with you forever. He did his part. Now it was our turn to help."

The score remained deadlocked, 1–1, into the ninth, when the Cardinals again turned to Molina. Buoyed by his four RBIs and home run already in the NLCS, La Russa played a hunch and batted Molina seventh, one spot higher than he had in any game in the series. With rain parked over the ballpark, Rolen, batting sixth, singled off Aaron Heilman. Molina came up and creamed the first pitch he saw deep over the left-field fence. Not even Chavez could catch it. Shea went silent.

"I think that's the nature of Yadi," Wainwright said. "He's not a guy looking to hear his name called out or having people shower him with that attention, but who better in that situation? Soup got us to that point. Endy kept us there. Yadi, the whole game revolving around him, comes up with a home run that is going to be pretty tough to top. It was the ultimate game. I've never been in one better. And it was his."

But first it was in Wainwright's hand.

As soon as Molina's home run cleared the fence, pitching coach Dave Duncan dialed the bullpen to get Wainwright warmed up. The rookie closer, who took over the role in September, allowed singles to the first two batters he faced in the ninth inning. He got two outs from the next two batters before walking Paul Lo Duca and enticing trouble. With the bases loaded, Carlos Beltran was going to bat. In two NLCS against the Cardinals—one with Houston in 2004 and here in 2006 with the Mets—Beltran had hit .360 with seven home runs and 20 runs scored. A single would tie the game. An extra-base hit would send the Mets to the World Series. Molina raced out to talk with his rookie closer. He suggested a get-ahead fastball. On his trot back to the plate, Molina had a bolt of creativity. He called for a change-up. Beltran took it for strike one. He fouled off a curveball for a 0–2 count. Molina knew what pitch Wainwright trusted. "I got myself into a tough situation here, and my best pitch is my curve," Wainwright said. "I was going to throw the best pitch I'd ever thrown. If he beats me, I will know he did it against my best."

Beltran didn't.

Wainwright's curve froze him.

A called strike three gave the Cardinals the 17th pennant in club history and sent Molina leaping through the rain and out to the mound to celebrate. In the champagne-splashed clubhouse afterward, his teammates chanted, "Yadi! Yadi! Yadi!" even as Suppan accepted the NLCS MVP trophy.

"One of the best moments of my life," Molina said of the game. "Always in my heart, always, for the rest of my life."

Mike Shannon: Native Son and Iconic Voice

As a boy in south St. Louis, Mike Shannon would bounce a tennis ball off the front steps of his house and pretend to be fielding sharp hoppers and playing alongside his Sportsman's Park heroes. But Shannon didn't stop with recreating highlights—he also supplied the soundtrack:

Shannon dives to make the play!
Shannon throws, bang-bang play at first!

Vintage Shannon.

There he was daydreaming about life as a star St. Louis Cardinal, and really he was preparing for both of his careers in baseball. Shannon has spent more than 50 years with the hometown club—first as a rookie sparkplug for a World Series winner, then as a starting third baseman, and finally, for a majority of his life, as the voice of the club, so recognizable that his baritone "heh-heh-heh" laugh and signature tangents are part of the fan base's lexicon. Everyone speaks Moonman.

The gregarious Shannon was one of the most accomplished high school athletes ever in St. Louis, starring in football and basketball. He had a scholarship to play quarterback for the University of Missouri, only to leave school before his sophomore year to accept a signing bonus from the Cardinals. He debuted in 1962 but seesawed between the minors and majors until arriving in 1964 with 43 RBIs and nine home runs in an 88-game stint that pushed the Cardinals to the pennant. Shannon homered off New York Yankees great Whitey Ford in that October's World Series. He'd make a habit of that. Shannon started every game in the three World Series he played. He homered in each series.

The Last Shall Be First

Only two players in Cardinals history share a remarkable coincidence of power. St. Louis native and hometown hero Mike Shannon hit the last home run at Sportsman's Park (Busch Stadium I) on May 8, 1966. Four days later Shannon hit the first home run at the new downtown ballpark (Busch Stadium II). Forty years later Albert Pujols echoed the feat as the Cardinals again moved addresses. Pujols' home run in Game 2 of the 2005 National League Championship Series was the last homer at Busch II hit by a Cardinal.* The first homer hit by a Cardinal at Busch Stadium III came in the third inning of the ballpark's opener, on April 10, 2006. It was a solo shot by Pujols.

The last regular-season home run at Busch II was hit in the ballpark's regular-season finale by rookie Chris Duncan.

A year removed from a top-10 finish in the league's MVP voting, a routine physical during spring training revealed a life-threatening kidney disorder that dry-docked him in the hospital for a month. Though Shannon tried, the team doctor said he was too weakened by his illness to finish the season. Shannon didn't play again. But he barely missed an inning, sliding at the owner's suggestion from third base to broadcast.

"I never got to where I should have been as a player," Shannon said. "The mental part of the game was the biggest thrill for me, though, so when I went from the field to the booth, it just enhanced it."

With little more than his front steps play-by-play for his experience, Shannon debuted. His intense instinct for the game and his boundless enthusiasm, coupled with a maestro like Jack Buck, rounded Shannon into the cherished and distinct voice of his boyhood team. He once spoke of Whitey Herzog's "photogenic mind" and said from a road game, "If you people in St. Louis could see this moon." When a game develops a plot twist, Shannon remarks, "Ol' Abner's done it again."

In 2007 the Cardinals celebrated Shannon's 50 years with the organization at Busch Stadium III, fêting the man most know as "Irish." He said later that, as the anniversary approached, his place with the organization became more profound to him. As people implored him to stay behind the mic, Shannon appreciated how his role had transcended from job to community covenant.

"It's the link, how they identify with Cardinals baseball is through the broadcasts," Shannon said. "That's how it was for me, too, growing up. All I wanted to do was play and win. It didn't matter how I did it. I've come to realize how important the position is and how lucky I am. I hit a home run off Whitey Ford in my own hometown.

"I'm a dreamer," he said, "but even I can't dream that well."

9 Enos Slaughter

OF…Inducted into the Hall of Fame, 1985…Number retired, 1996

The man who made the legendary mad dash to win the 1946 World Series always felt that no matter where he was headed, or how hard and fast he insisted on getting there, his home would always be with the Cardinals. That's why he described the news of his trade, after 13 seasons in St. Louis, as a stab deep into his chest.

When management told him, he wept.

"Those words shocked me as much as anything that happened to me," Slaughter wrote in his autobiography. "I may have had marriages come and go, but I always thought that I would be able to retire in a Cardinals uniform…. I was no match for the news. Tears gushed from my eyes like water from a broken pipe."

Slaughter's trade on April 15, 1954, was a shock, not just because Slaughter had come to identify himself as a Cardinal but because he captured the identity of the Cardinals. Slaughter was a tenacious, agitating, open-throttle player who slid in spikes high and never met a diving catch he didn't try. He would wade through a viper pit if it stood between him and an extra base. Slaughter, a 10-time All-Star, brought a little of that Gas House Gang grit—and Gas House Gang glee—into the 1940s. He was the left fielder in the greatest of Cardinals outfields, the one that sandwiched captain and top-flight defender Terry Moore between Stan Musial and Slaughter, two Hall of Famers.

The left-handed-hitting North Carolina native, nicknamed "Country," hit better than .300 eight times as a Cardinal. Fifty years after he retired from baseball, Slaughter ranked fourth in games played as a Cardinal, with 1,820, and he played every one with unbridled ferocity. Inducted into the Hall of Fame in 1985, Slaughter's plaque uses words like "hard-nosed," "hustling," "daring," and "clutch." Those were more than adjectives to Slaughter. They were a code of conduct.

Born in Roxboro, North Carolina, Slaughter was raised on a tobacco farm. He built his strong, pinpoint throwing arm hunting rabbits as a boy, knocking them out with stones. Slaughter played second base for a mill team, and that's how he earned a tryout with the Cardinals. How he learned to hustle came two years later.

In 1936 Slaughter struggled for the Cardinals' minor league affiliate in Columbus, Ohio. Weighed down by his .220 average, he shuffled off the field only to find manager Eddie Dyer waiting for him.

"Tired, kid?" Dyer scolded. "I'll get some help for you."

Slaughter never strolled again.

"I realized that here it was, the depths of the Depression, and I was cheating the people paying their quarters, dimes, and nickels to see me play," Slaughter said on the eve of his Hall of Fame induction. "I vowed never to walk on a ballfield again."

Slaughter hit .382 the next season and was in the majors to stay in 1938, running all the way. The outfielder ushered in the era of the St. Louis Swifties with his 1942 season. Slaughter led the league with 188 hits, drove in 98 runs, batted .318, and finished second in the league's MVP voting to a teammate, pitcher Mort Cooper. That October Slaughter appeared in the first of his five World Series, two with the Cardinals and three with the Yankees. He won two with each club. Slaughter missed the seasons between his two World Series with the Cardinals to serve in the military, but returned in '46 to lead the NL with 130 RBIs and hit .320 in the Series.

Years after his retirement, talk of Slaughter's career often came cloaked in the perceived racism by his hard slide into Jackie Robinson, and whether or not he deliberately stomped on

Enos Slaughter spent his first 13 seasons with the Cardinals and was inducted into the National Baseball Hall of Fame in 1985.

Robinson's leg. Slaughter said he would have bulldozed into anyone playing the position—that's just how he played the game. Full speed. That is how he reached Cooperstown, a .300 hitter in his career, the only player since World War II to twice drive in 100 runs with fewer than 15 homers, and with 2,383 hits. He played six more seasons and for three more teams after the Cardinals traded him, but he never stopped being a Cardinal.

Slaughter retired to a 150-acre farm in North Carolina and at 81 still exercised vigorously three times a week. In 2002 illness forced him to miss his first Hall of Fame induction weekend since his own. His absence prompted 47 living Hall of Famers to sign a get-well card. A few weeks later "Country" died at 86. His gravestone bears the Birds-on-the-Bat logo. And, as his daughter confirmed for this book, he was buried in a No. 9 Cardinals jersey. It is the jersey he never wanted to take off.

10 See the Cardinals' Treasures

To confirm they had one of the most important jerseys in Cardinals history, the staff at the team's Hall of Fame had to do some detective work, a little memorabilia forensics. They knew for certain this was pitcher Grover Cleveland Alexander's road jersey from the 1926 season, but they wanted to know if this was the jersey "Old Pete" wore that night in Yankee Stadium when he clinched the first World Series championship in franchise history.

The pinstripes told them it was.

"Pinstripes," said assistant curator Brian Finch, "act as a fingerprint."

The staff used photos of Alexander from that World Series to compare the placement and distance of the buttons on the jersey, the stitching and wear on the jersey, and, yes, the uniqueness of the pinstripes. The subtleties of the thread revealed its identity. It is, club officials believe, the jersey Alexander wore when he came out of the bullpen to strikeout the Yankees' Tony Lazzeri with the bases loaded and launch the Cardinals toward their place among the game's royalty.

This Hall is where they keep the crown jewels.

One of the few dedicated team-specific Halls of Fame, the St. Louis Cardinals Hall of Fame Museum has more than 13,000 artifacts, representing eras from the 1880s to the present. As the official repository for the club, the Hall has the first brick made for Busch Stadium III, a jersey from 1904, scorecards galore, and a baseball signed by the Cardinals' first championship team, the 1926 club. Crammed near Rogers Hornsby's autograph is one notable interloper: Babe Ruth. His familiar loops are the only non-Cardinal on the ball.

Located at the Bowling Hall of Fame in downtown St. Louis from 1997 until 2008, the Hall covered only 5,000 square feet. The team hoped to let the Hall spread its wings with a new location in Ballpark Village, a planned development on Busch Stadium II's footprint that has been delayed indefinitely and left the Hall to limited showings.

The Hall opened in June 1968 as the St. Louis Sports Hall of Fame. But as Busch Stadium II became baseball-specific in the 1990s, so too did the Hall, yielding to the wealth of its newest collection: Stan Musial's.

Musial donated 75 percent of his personal treasures to the Hall. There were bundles of bats, stacks of silver platters, a Silver Slugger award, and keys to many cities. The first ball he hit for a home run is here, brought back from Pittsburgh in September 1941. The first ball he hit for a home run as a grandpa is here, too.

With them is the letter he wrote to National League president Warren C. Giles on October 8, 1963. In it, Musial requests a new designation, "voluntarily retired."

Alongside all the Musial goodies is the Man himself: a wax statue of Musial, purchased from Madame Tussaud's. The statue wears the uniform Musial had on in his last game. His word was all the forensic proof the Hall needed.

11 "The Greatest Comeback Team in the History of Baseball"

2011 World Series: Cardinals defeat Texas Rangers 4–3

At the club's lowest point of the 2011 season, a tar pit 10 games deep and from which few teams ever emerge, Cardinals ace Chris Carpenter approached manager Tony La Russa about holding a players-only meeting. La Russa worried such a thing would appear "phony" or "staged," but trusted his pitcher and asked only that the veteran spread a message of playing with "urgency."

The right-hander had another word in mind.

Carpenter gathered his fellow Cardinals on August 24 and said that they were about to be "embarrassed." Others, like All-Stars Lance Berkman and Matt Holliday, echoed that sentiment, describing how a club that fancied itself a contender was about to be certified underachievers and destined to be forgotten. Two months later, they pulled off the unthinkable and became unforgettable.

On the day of the team meeting, the Los Angeles Dodgers finished a sweep of the Cardinals and prompted La Russa to call the team's performance "as bad as it can get." A web site that runs hundreds of simulations to determine a team's probability of earning a postseason berth pegged the Cardinals' chances at 1.1 percent on August 27. They were three games behind Atlanta with five to play. A shutout from Carpenter on the final day of the regular season—coupled with a Braves loss in extra innings—clinched the National League wild card. The Cardinals won 34 of their final 50 games, rallied twice in the World Series when down to their final strike, and won the franchise's 11th World Series title. While hosting the champions at the White House in January 2012, President Barack Obama introduced them as "the greatest comeback team in the history of baseball."

"People will always want to know how it happened," La Russa said. "How did we come back? Guts. This team had great guts."

In the final six weeks of the regular season, starting the day after Carpenter's meeting, the Cardinals went 23–9 to overtake the capitulating Braves. The deficit the Cardinals erased was the largest in NL history that late in the season. Starters Carpenter, Kyle Lohse, Jaime Garcia, and Edwin Jackson, the jewel of a transformative July trade, went 9–0 combined in that stretch. Jason Motte took over as closer a few days after the meeting and the team went 13–1 in games he appeared in the season's final month. The Cardinals claimed victories in their last at-bat throughout the month: utility infielder Nick Punto won a game on a sacrifice fly; September callup Adron Chambers scored a walk-off run on a wild pitch; and Albert Pujols laced a two-out, two-run single off Braves closer Craig Kimbrel that led to a win on September 9. Kimbrel hadn't allowed a run since June 11. The Cardinals were finally playing like the sum of their parts.

La Russa believed those late-game wins not only pulled the Cardinals out of a crater; it pulled the team together and steeled them for October drama ahead.

On the brink of elimination in the best-of-five NL division series, the Cardinals won twice against the supercharged, 102-win Philadelphia Phillies to advance. Carpenter won the decisive Game 5 with an epic 1–0, complete-game win against his friend and Phillies ace Roy Halladay. The game's only run came in the first inning. The Cardinals then upset rival Milwaukee in the NL Championship Series for the franchise's 18th league pennant.

"Maybe all it took was looking around the room in that meeting and realizing, 'Hey, this is a really talented group of guys…let's finish strong,'" Holliday said. "We didn't want it to end like that. We didn't want it to end at all."

The Texas Rangers awaited the Cardinals in what became the most riveting World Series in a decade. Albert Pujols made history in Game 3 by joining Babe Ruth and Reggie Jackson as the only players with three home runs in a single World Series game. That provided the Cardinals a 2–1 Series lead they would squander by Game 5. Late in that loss, La Russa found himself disconnected from the bullpen despite several phone calls and greeted rookie Lance Lynn on the mound with a simple question: "What are you doing here?" The pitching glitch cost St. Louis the game and put the Rangers on the brink of their first title.

A sloppy start to Game 6 gave way to a genuine classic and minted a new October hero in St. Louis native David Freese. In many ways, the young third baseman came to personify the Cardinals' resilience and redemption. Undone by ankle injuries the previous two seasons, Freese showed a preternatural cool in his first postseason. Freese had hit .545 and three homers against Milwaukee to claim the NLCS MVP. Early in Game 6 of the World Series, a popup bounced off his head and his first thought was "that picture being on the front page of the paper if we lost." That appeared likely as the Cardinals headed into the ninth inning trailing 7–5 before Freese came to the plate with two on and two out.

That was the first of two times in Game 6 that the Cardinals were down to their final strike of the season, and each time La Russa phoned the bullpen to remind the relievers that after a loss they had to report to the dugout and join a salute to the fans. That would have to wait.

In the ninth, Freese tied the game with a two-out, two-strike triple off the right-field wall. In the 10th, Berkman tied the game with a two-out, two-strike single. In the 11th, Freese won the game with a homer that forced Game 7. Like the Cardinals, Freese refused to let his unexpected October opportunity slip away, no matter the odds.

Freese tied Game 7 with a two-run double in his first at-bat to set postseason records with 50 total bases and 21 RBIs. Carpenter then finished what he started back in August. Able to pitch Game 7 on short rest because of a rainout earlier in the series, the ace won his fourth game of the postseason. The only time the Cardinals popped champagne at Busch Stadium in 2011 was that night as they celebrated a title. La Russa called it a "fairy tale."

Only he knew the depth of that description.

The World Series win was the beginning of the end on several fronts. La Russa retired two days after Game 7, leaving the position he held for 16 seasons and walking away as a champion. Pujols hit free agency and followed $250 million to the Los Angeles Angels. A month later, pitching coach Dave Duncan took a leave of absence. Any encore was going to require a different cast. The Cardinals started by hiring Mike Matheny, the club's former catcher, and charting a future hitched to Holliday, Adam Wainwright, and a new perspective on what's possible.

Once concerned about being embarrassed, these comeback Cardinals finished as one of the most charismatic Cardinals clubs ever. As they bent the standings toward their will, the Cardinals gave St. Louis a new mascot (the "rally squirrel" that scampered across home plate during an NLDS game); a true talisman (the necklace rocker Carlos Santana gave La Russa that he never took off); a pet project ("Torty," outfielder Allen Craig's beloved turtle); and a rally cry, "Happy flight!" Coined by shortstop Rafael Furcal, the Cardinals repeated the mantra on getaway days, including three pivotal times in October. T-shirts were inevitable. Although they took an unlikely route, they cemented their place in history in a more traditional way as well—with a championship.

"This is one of the greatest and most pleasurable seasons I've had with a group of guys," Carpenter said. "It [was] a crazy ride. No matter what [happened] this group of guys is very special. They can't take anything that we've done away from us. It's going to be the year I'll never forget."

He has the ring to always remind him.

12 Gold Standard

No club in Major League Baseball has been as decorated defensively as the Cardinals. From 1957 through 2011, Rawlings has awarded 983 Gold Gloves, and no team in the majors can match the Cardinals' 80. They have won at least two at every position, have six positions where at least three Cardinals have won awards, and can even brag about providing a Midas touch, as several players have won Gold Gloves shortly after leaving the Cardinals. Led by shortstop Ozzie Smith's 11 Rawlings Gold Gloves, the Cardinals have 17 more than the second-place Yankees and 19 more than the Orioles.

Rawlings, a St. Louis–based manufacturer of sporting goods, began awarding the Gold Glove awards in 1957, and in 1958 the company honored one player at each position (including three out-fielders, not specific to position) in each league. That year Ken Boyer won the first of his five Gold Gloves. He was the first of four different Cardinals to win the award at third base. Cardinals pitchers have combined to win 14 Gold Gloves. In 2002 three Cardinals infielders—second baseman Fernando Vina, third baseman Scott

Cardinals Who Won a Rawlings Gold Glove Award, Listed by Position

P
Bobby Shantz (1962–1964)
Bob Gibson (1965–1973)
Joaquin Andujar (1984)
Adam Wainwright (2009)

C
Tom Pagnozzi (1991–1992, 1994)
Mike Matheny (2000, 2003–2004)
Yadier Molina (2008–2011)

1B
Bill White (1960–1963, 1965)
Keith Hernandez (1978–1982)
Albert Pujols (2006, 2010)

2B
Fernando Vina (2001–2002)

3B
Ken Boyer (1958–1961, 1963)
Ken Reitz (1975)
Terry Pendleton (1987, 1989)
Scott Rolen (2002–2004, 2006)

SS
Dal Maxvill (1968)
Ozzie Smith (1982–1992)
Edgar Renteria (2002–2003)

OF
Curt Flood (1963–1969)
Willie McGee (1983, 1985–1986)
Jim Edmonds (2000–2005)

Rolen, and shortstop Edgar Renteria—won Gold Gloves. But it's not just quantity, it's consistency. From Boyer's award in 1958 through 1973, the Cardinals had at least one Rawlings Gold Glove winner per season. Another streak started in 2000 with at least one winner in every season since save for 2007. In the field, the Cardinals, as a franchise, are the Gold standard.

Ozzie Smith

SS...Inducted into the Hall of Fame, 2002...Number retired, 1996

Several years after he landed his last crowd-pleasing back flip, Ozzie Smith made a weeklong cameo appearance in a St. Louis–based production of the play *The Wizard of Oz*. He had one line—to be delivered with theatrical gusto—but with a flip of the script, he stole the show every night.

"I am the mighty Wizard of Oz!" the legendary shortstop said to the four famous travelers. "But folks around here just call me Ozzie."

Smith embraced the mythology of the nickname he shared with the Emerald City illusionist and even adopted L. Frank Baum's classic as a metaphor for his own journey. He often described his career as the result of his brain setting a goal, his heart pushing for it, and his courage to pursue it. Never the biggest player, never the best hitter, Smith was always a show-stopper with the glove.

The Cardinals' shortstop won 13 consecutive Gold Gloves (his first two with the San Diego Padres), led the league in fielding percentage eight times, and entered the Hall of Fame as arguably the best defensive shortstop in history. While it evolved to a larger meaning, the original inspiration for his nickname, "the Wizard," stayed true: his gymnastics in the field and uncanny sleight of hand were magic. Smith's defense was a draw. His arrival helped revive the Cardinals from the doldrums of the 1970s.

"Revolutionized defensive play at shortstop with his acrobatic fielding and artistic turning of double plays," reads Smith's plaque in Cooperstown. "His congenial personality, consummate professionalism, and trademark back flip made 'the Wizard' a fan favorite."

Osborne Earl Smith developed his gift for snatching the baseball on the front steps of his family's home in the Watts neighborhood of Los Angeles. With a paper bag rolled up on his hand, Smith would field whatever sharp or quirky bounce he could create by skipping a ball off the front steps. Sometimes he would toss the ball high toward a street light just to purposefully blind himself before he could find and catch the ball. His glove got him where his size and his bat never would—onto a college baseball team and then into the pros, where he spent just 68 games in the minors. "Yes," he said, "my glove has given me much."

From 1978 to 1981, Smith hit .231 as the starting shortstop for San Diego. Frustration with his contract led Smith's agent to publish an ad in the local paper under the headline "Jobs Wanted." "Padres Baseball Player wants part-time employment to supplement income," it began. In St. Louis, the Cardinals had their own shortstop issues. Garry Templeton, an All-Star in 1977 and '79 for the Cardinals, had to be dragged off the field by manager Whitey Herzog in August 1981 after Templeton made an obscene gesture to fans. He torched his relationship with the team.

In December 1981 the Cardinals and the Padres swapped shortstops. Out of two necessary divorces, a love affair bloomed. Smith had instant impact on the Cardinals. They won the World Series in his first season at shortstop and went to two others in his

Known as arguably the greatest defensive shortstop of all time, Ozzie Smith was a 15-time All-Star and won 13 Gold Glove awards.

first six years with the club. Record-setting crowds flocked to see the Wizard perform feats of defense nightly.

Herzog believed that Smith's glove was good enough to take away multiple hits a game, but he also made Smith a bet that his bat could be better. For every groundball or line drive Smith hit in their first season together, Herzog would pay him a $1. For every fly ball or strikeout, Smith owed Herzog a $1. Halfway through the season, Herzog called the bet off—it was too costly. Improving every season, Smith finished his career with 2,460 hits and 580 stolen bases. In 1987 he hit .303 with 104 runs scored, 75 RBIs, 40 doubles, and not one homer. That MVP-caliber season received a Silver Slugger award and pushed the Cardinals to their third pennant since he arrived.

His signature highlight was with a bat—the "Go Crazy!" home run of the 1985 playoffs. But in most of his career Smith was wearing a glove. There's the lunging catch of a liner followed by a somersault. There's the dive deep into the hole and throw from his knees for a ho-hum 6–3. There's the nimble pirouette at second base, and the death-defying catch on August 4, 1986. In the top of the ninth of a 2–2 ballgame, Philadelphia's Von Hayes flared a blooper into shallow left field. Smith and left fielder Curt Ford converged on the fly ball—clearly on a collision course as both left their feet to make the catch. In mid-flight, Smith shifted, avoided Ford, and snared the ball with a shoestring catch. A decade later, Ray Knight told the *New York Times*, "If I had to pick one guy to catch the ball with my life on the line, I'd pick Ozzie."

Smith's defense made him the highest-paid player in the National League before he was a .300 hitter. Smith took his glove to 15 All-Star Games, and he retired as the National League's all-time leader in fan voting. It took him to the end of his own Yellow Brick Road: Cooperstown.

Smith retired after the 1996 season, the same season his No. 1 joined the other numbers of Cardinals greats. His last year was marred by a feud over playing time with manager Tony La Russa, but his last game was vintage. He scored four times and hit a home run. Five years later, he became a first-ballot Hall of Famer.

"Ozzie Smith was not a uniquely talented person," Smith said in his induction speech, brandishing a copy of Baum's novel in his right hand. "Ozzie Smith was a boy who decided to look within. A boy who discovered that absolutely nothing is good enough if it can be made better. A boy who discovered an old-fashioned formula that would take him beyond the rainbow. Beyond even his wildest dreams."

14 Ken Boyer

3B...Number retired, 1984

In the winter of 1957 the Philadelphia Phillies approached new Cardinals general manager Bing Devine about trading for his center fielder, a former All-Star who spent the season playing mostly out of position. Devine rejected the Phillies' offer of pitcher Harvey Haddix and outfielder Richie Ashburn, a future Hall of Famer, and did so knowing he gambled his young reputation on one player.

Devine felt Ken Boyer was the worth that risk. "I'm banking on Boyer becoming a full-fledged star," he said. He became much more than that.

The next season Boyer returned to his natural position, third base, and won the first of five Gold Gloves. He started four consecutive All-Star Games and hit .348 in 10 midsummer classics. The 1964 National League MVP, Boyer was the cornerstone—as a key contributor and steadying presence—of the Cardinals' great teams in the 1960s. His place in Cardinals history is best described by the title everyone knew him by: "the Captain."

A Missouri native who grew up with Cardinals in his blood, Boyer was born in Liberty, Missouri, and became a prep star in Alba, Missouri, a four-and-a-half-hour drive from St. Louis. Sons of marble cutter Vern Boyer, Kenton Lloyd Boyer and brother Clete were two of the seven Boyer boys who signed professional baseball contracts. Inked in 1949, Kenton went into the minors as a pitcher and struck out 75 batters and walked 105 in his first pro season. He also went 15-for-33 at the plate with three home runs. He pitched the next season as well, but during one game the third baseman was injured. Boyer took over at the position, hit .342 with 61 RBIs, and he slugged nine home runs in his 240 at-bats.

Boyer never pitched again.

In 1958, the season after Devine didn't trade him, Boyer had the first of four consecutive seasons with at least a .300 average, the first of seven consecutive seasons with at least 20 home runs and 90 RBIs. Boyer is widely considered one of the finest gloves ever at third base, compared often with contemporaries like Ron Santo and the slickest of them all, Brooks Robinson. In 1964 Boyer won the league MVP award with a .295 average, 100 runs scored, 24 home runs, and a league-best 119 RBIs. He received the honor a few days after the highlight of his career—a World Series win against the New York Yankees, and their third baseman, brother Clete. They would both homer in the decisive Game 7 of that series, and Ken had three hits in that game. In Game 4 Ken hit a grand slam that produced a 4–3 come-from-behind victory. On his way around third, he playfully patted his brother Clete on the posterior.

Traded to the New York Mets after the 1965 season, Boyer returned to the Cardinals as a coach and minor league manager in the 1970s, mentoring such stars as Keith Hernandez, and he took over as big-league manager in April 1978. Nearly 45 years after his final game as a Cardinal, Boyer ranked third in home runs (255), sixth in RBIs (1,001), and seventh in games (1,667). He was diagnosed with lung cancer in the early 1980s and he died at the age of 51 in 1982. Two years later the Cardinals bent their unwritten rule of only retiring the numbers of Hall of Famers to put Boyer's No. 14 up with the others.

The man years later still known as "the Captain" belonged.

"I know of no other player who has the name Captain anymore. It's a weird name, really, for baseball," teammate Tim McCarver told the *St. Louis Post-Dispatch* shortly after Boyer's death. "He filled it better than anybody I've ever seen. That's a point of reverence, to be called 'Captain' years after he played. Kenny Boyer was a pillar of strength in the Cardinals organization."

The Knothole Gang

When school was over, the race to Sportsman's Park was on for thousands of St. Louis youth. Between the two World Wars, few things did as much to cultivate and nurture several generations of Cardinals fans as the major leagues' first Knothole Gang.

It started as a way to draw local investors into a plan to purchase the club, and it became one of the primary reasons Cardinals baseball had such deep roots in the community. In early 1917 James C. Jones, a lawyer for Cardinals owner Helene Britton, organized a group of local buyers to keep Britton from selling to Cincinnati-based brothers. Jones' idea was to offer stock in the team. To draw investors, local insurance man W.E. Bilheimer added to the plan, saying that for every $50 contributed, a free season's pass would be given to a local youth. They eventually put together an armada of investors and bought the team.

Jones and his group touted the Knothole Gang as a way to stem juvenile delinquency. It became a movement.

The Knothole Gang, officially established in 1917, provided underprivileged youths with an official membership card. And that was all they needed to get into Cardinals games. Branch Rickey later expanded the program so that all kids, age 10 to 16, could join the Knothole Gang, get a membership card, and attend games for free. In the late 1920s fan-favorite Jim Bottomley won the National League MVP, and more than 10,000 Knothole Gang members attended the ceremony.

There is evidence of a "Knothole Gang" in New Orleans in the late 1880s, but it's believed the Cardinals first brought the practice to the majors. From St. Louis, Rickey took it to Brooklyn, where the Knothole Gang lent its name to *Happy Felton's Knothole Gang*, a popular television show filmed at Ebbets Field. Other Knothole Gangs continue today around the minors and even still in St. Louis, where a similar, though reduced, program still exists.

The initial membership cards, about the size of credit cards, were distributed by the local YMCA, the Boy Scouts, churches, and schools. When classes would let out, students would dash to Sportsman's Park, sometimes to get there before the start of the second inning. Summer offered the same full access, and full games. Armed with only their Knothole Gang cards, they lined up along Spring Avenue and entered through a kid-sized gate to find a seat in the left-field grandstands. Among the thousands who awaited the arrival of their Knothole Gang membership each year and sprinted to the ballpark to use it were Bob Broeg, who grew up to be the printed voice of the Cardinals and a Hall of Fame baseball writer, and Bing Devine, who grew up to be the Cardinals' general manager and built the pennant-winning teams of the 1960s. Bill Clay, a representative from St. Louis in Congress for 32 years, once said he used his score-card as an alibi for missing school. He caught the Cardinals bug from the Knothole because nothing is as contagious as free baseball.

As Window Closes, the Core Delivers

2006 World Series: Cardinals defeat Detroit Tigers 4–1

Stirred to do something, anything to acknowledge what he felt might be the play that revived a giant, Cardinals center fielder Jim Edmonds improvised a moment that became a defining ritual.

The Cardinals, stumbling and slumping their way into the postseason, had just defeated San Diego in Game 1 of the National League Division Series, doing so only after Ronnie Belliard's bacon-saving, diving stab in the seventh inning freed the Cardinals and their 5–1 lead from a bases-loaded mess. Edmonds didn't want Belliard's play to go unnoticed, lost in the glare of Albert Pujols' home run or ace Chris Carpenter's seven strikeouts. Baseball didn't have a traditional way for Edmonds to acknowledge a subtle yet pivotal play. So Edmonds improvised.

He hopped up onto a sofa in the visitors' clubhouse at Petco Park, pulled a page out of football's playbook, and awarded Belliard a "game ball." There were some bemused looks, maybe a snicker. Then there was an ovation. Throughout their unexpected October odyssey, the game ball was a rite of victory.

"Looking back on it, it probably meant a lot," Edmonds said a few years later. "I just figured it was the one chance to acknowledge something that we were missing. Here's a new guy, still new to our team, and we'd been through a lot already. I remember the moment he made the play, thinking, *He just saved us. He just gave us a chance to be in the next series....* We had rushed through a whole bunch of playoffs in the past, never sort of stopping to look at where we were. I thought this is one opportunity to really stand up and just make

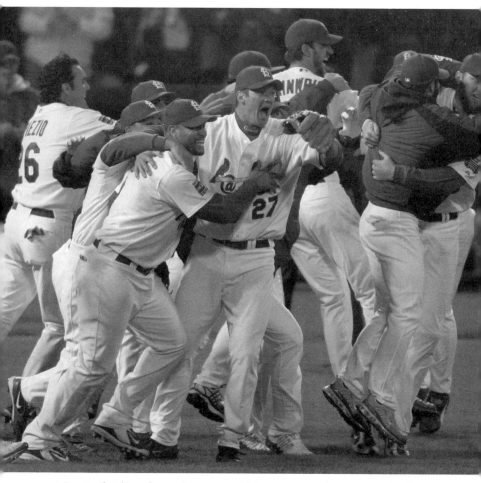

Despite finishing the regular season with just 83 wins, the 2006 Cardinals fought their way to a World Series victory over the Detroit Tigers.

this a little bit of a special moment. It kind of got going from there. Just a snowball effect."

The previous two Octobers the Cardinals entered the postseason as juggernauts, clubs that were built to win and did so more than any other team in the majors. This era of Cardinals, built upon the backs of Edmonds, Pujols, and Scott Rolen, had won 205 games from 2004 to 2005 and never played a series, postseason or otherwise, in which they weren't the favorite. These Cardinals had appeared in two National League Championship Series, won one pennant, but had yet to win a game in the World Series. Entering 2006, it was widely believed that their window of opportunity was closing.

By September, it appeared shut tight.

The 83-win Cardinals reached the 2006 postseason with the second-fewest victories ever for playoff team, and 12 teams in the majors had a better record that summer. The Cardinals became the first team in baseball history to have two eight-game losing streaks and never fall out of first place. On September 20 they had a seven-game lead in the National League Central. They then lost seven consecutive games. A Houston loss on the final day of the season—not a Cardinals win—cinched their playoff invite.

The Cardinals were not the favorite in any series they played that October, and even after outlasting the New York Mets in the National League Championship Series, a national columnist scoffed while making his pick for the World Series: "Detroit in three." But these Cardinals were closer to their 100-win predecessors than anyone expected. One reason: they had their health.

Edmonds had just 15 at-bats in September as he struggled to clear the cobwebs from a concussion. David Eckstein had 23 at-bats in September and didn't return to the lineup until September 22 because of a strained oblique. Rolen kept playing even though fatigue settled into his surgically repaired left shoulder. It all clicked the day Edmonds hopped up on a sofa to salute Belliard for his diving lunge into right field that turned Todd Walker's bases-loaded skipper into a groundout. The '06 Cardinals didn't have the 100 wins, but with their health, they played as well as, if not better than, the previous two October teams.

The Cardinals dispatched San Diego in four games. Through rain and drama, they toppled the favorite Mets in a seven-game NLCS that concluded with an epic Game 7. That night at Shea Stadium, catcher Yadier Molina had the go-ahead home run, and

Jeff Suppan pitched a gem. As champagne popped and sprayed in the clubhouse, the players chanted for Edmonds to give out the game balls. Suppan was late to receive the actual NLCS MVP trophy because he was waiting for Edmonds to hand him a game ball.

Back in the World Series for the second time in three years, some Cardinals had redemption in mind. Rolen went 0-for-15 in the 2004 World Series, prompting him to joke: "I had one opportunity as a player to play for a World Series ring and I went 0-for-everything. I didn't get a hit. Big goose egg." Rolen finished the postseason on a 10-game tear, including an 8-for-19 turn in the World Series. Edmonds, 1-for-15 in 2004, drove in four runs against Detroit in 2006, tying Eckstein for the RBI lead. Eckstein edged Rolen for the MVP with eight hits, including the double that broke a 4–4 tie in the eighth inning of Game 4.

Each day Eckstein would come to the park hours before batting practice to begin the ritual of getting his body ready. Treatment included heating, cooling, and acupuncture. Every afternoon he was mummy-wrapped in Ace bandages, and every evening he was a candidate for Edmonds' game ball. The revitalized and rolling Cardinals made swift work of the awestruck and rusty Tigers, who committed eight errors in the series. Rookie Anthony Reyes got a game ball after he pitched eight superb innings to win Game 1 at Comerica Park. Starter Jeff Weaver, who was 3–10 as a Los Angeles Angel before being heaven-sent for the Cardinals in October, got a couple, too. He won a game in all three series, and was the winner in the clinching Game 5 against Detroit at brand-new Busch Stadium.

"From day one in San Diego, our club had so much life—the clubhouse, the dugout, no matter the score or circumstances," La Russa said. "This group, I'll never forget.... It was really fun to be around this group. They were so determined. As we got into it, I started getting concerned because they wanted it so much. I didn't want them to be disappointed."

Clinching with a K

On opening night 2007 the Cardinals brought back the last three pitchers at the time to close out a World Series for the ceremonial first pitch of the season. Hall of Famers Bob Gibson and Bruce Sutter and 2006 postseason closer Adam Wainwright took the field and tossed pitches to the managers of their World Series–winning teams—Red Schoendienst, Whitey Herzog, and Tony La Russa, respectively. The three pitchers shared something else in common. Not just what they did, but how they did it. They each punctuated their World Series wins— three consecutive World Series wins for the franchise—with a strikeout.

Bob Gibson in 1967

The Cardinals' right-hander and MVP of the series blew a fastball by Boston Red Sox first baseman George Scott to end Game 7. It was Gibson's 10th strikeout of the game, and it ended his third complete game in the Series.

Bruce Sutter in 1982

The Cardinals' closer built his legend on a split-finger fastball, but he won the World Series with a fastball up to Gorman Thomas. With a full count, Milwaukee's center fielder fouled off three consecutive pitches before missing the 10th pitch of the at-bat to end Game 7 of the Series.

Adam Wainwright in 2006

The rookie and first-time closer fired two sliders by Detroit's Brandon Inge to get ahead 0–2. There were two on, two out, and Inge was the go-ahead run in the ninth inning of Game 5. But Wainwright went back to his slider, got Inge flailing at it, and ended the World Series with a strikeout for the first time since 1988.

As the unlikely champions readied for a parade through St. Louis that would draw an estimated 500,000, amateur auteur Suppan recorded the festivities. He conducted guerrilla interviews throughout the day, once asking a member of the media: "Did you ever doubt us?" Doubt them? There was ample reason. They had spent the season playing like tattered remnants of an aging titan, the echoes of a fallen champ. But, starting the day Edmonds handed Belliard a ball, they became something else, something the 100-win teams weren't, something much better. "No one believed in our club," Eckstein said. "We had to believe in ourselves."

Dizzy Dean

RHP...Inducted into Hall of Fame, 1953...Number retired, 1974

After a day in Shawnee, Oklahoma, spent scouting some hotshot pitcher hurtling like a comet toward his major league club, Cardinals general manager Branch Rickey sought a moment's peace with that day's newspaper. No sooner had Rickey found a seat in the hotel lobby and opened the paper than that same young pitcher sidled up next to him and showed an early knack for ruining Rickey's mood.

"Hello, Branch," reports would recall the whippersnapper said. "I'm Dizzy Dean, the fella who's gonna win you a lotta ballgames."

It might be the only understatement Ol' Diz ever made.

Dean, the charismatic right-hander with the talent to back all of his talk, would win 134 games for the Cardinals and finish in the top two in MVP voting for three consecutive years, winning the award in 1934. That was the summer that Dean, the son of a sharecropper, went national as a bona fide phenom. Dean was the engine of the Gas House Gang, the winner of two games for the Cardinals in their '34 World Series win against Detroit, and the magnetic personality for an entire era of Cardinals baseball. He did a lot more than win a lot of ballgames for Rickey. Though he did that, too.

In that magical season of 1934, Dean won 30 games—the first National Leaguer to reach that many victories since 1917 and the last to do it the NL.

Jay Hanna Dean was born in Arkansas and crisscrossed the South with his parents, sharecropping from one farm to another and going wherever work would take them. He enlisted in the

Army in 1926 and quickly developed quite a reputation on the ball-field—and off. Biographers trace his nickname, "Dizzy," to his days in the Army. Not that Dean made it easy to trace. Like any good folk hero, his legends began to cloud his truths. The right-hander changed his name to Jerome when he was young and offered sports-writers various reasons for doing so.

Even with all of his yapping, Dean couldn't outtalk his ability. He was part prodigy, part carnival barker, and the finest pitcher of the era. With a peppy fastball and a sweeping curve to go with fluid, almost balletic mechanics, Dean was dazzling on the mound. He finished in the top four in ERA three times in his career, led the National League in wins twice before his 26th birthday, and topped the NL in strikeouts four consecutive years. Once in his career, Dean walked a batter to face New York Giants feared hitter Bill Terry in the ninth inning. As Terry lifted his bat, Dean apologized and explained how he promised some kids at a hospital visit that day that he'd strike Terry out. Dean then promptly did just that.

Dean called himself "Ol' Diz" and "Great Dean," and he always called Rickey for a raise. He threatened more strikes than he pulled off, but he pulled off enough to frustrate Rickey. Even in that magical season of 1934 he skipped a few games to protest the salary the Cardinals paid his brother, rookie Paul. Still, Dean won the 30 games, sometimes pitching in relief or starting a day or so after his previous start. Four of those wins came in the final week and a half of the season—in the heat of a pennant race.

Dean finished 1934 with a 30–7 record, a 2.66 ERA, and 195 strikeouts to go with a World Series ring. He retired with 26 shutouts and 150 victories, the fewest for any starting pitcher from the 1900s in the Hall of Fame. During his induction speech, he said, "I wanna thank the Lord for givin' me a good right arm, a strong back, and a weak mind."

Dizzy appeared in four consecutive All-Star Games, and it was in the last one that this brilliant bolt through baseball began to dim.

The leader of the famed Gas House Gang in the 1930s, Dizzy Dean is also the last National League pitcher to win 30 games in a single season.

A line drive broke one of his toes and forced an alteration in his mechanics that, coupled with the constant use, ruined his arm with injury. He was traded to the Cubs before the 1938 season and was done pitching after 10 games in 1940. The next season, he debuted his second act in baseball: broadcasting. As famous as he was with the Gas House Gang, Dean broadened his appeal with his broadcasting career. He created a lingo all his own: "slud" for slide, "ricketed" for ricochet, and batters who stood "confidentially" in the on-deck circle. Though his arm left him, his boasts never did, and in 1947 he came out of the press box and threw four innings for the St. Louis Browns.

He didn't give up a run.

"There'll never be another like me," he once asserted.

Make that two understatements.

18 A Double Dose of Dean

With him and his younger brother Paul pitching on almost alternating games during that dazzling pennant drive of 1934, Dizzy Dean started a doubleheader like any other—with a shameless and bold prediction. Yapping with a reporter from St. Louis, Dean announced that the Brooklyn Dodgers would get "one-hit Dean and no-hit Dean today." If only he had pitched better, he would have been right, too.

On September 21, 1934, with the Cardinals surging and the New York Giants folding, the Gas House Gang steamed into Ebbets Field on a four-game winning streak. The Cardinals had gone 12–5 so far in the month, and six of those victories had been with a Dean on the mound for the decision. Brooklyn manager Casey Stengel loved that the Cardinals were chasing down their rival Giants, but he loathed the Deans. Including Dizzy's 5–0 record against the Dodgers that season, the family was 7–0 combined. They were about to make that 9–0. Dizzy, the right-handed ace of the Cardinals, took a no-hitter into the eighth inning. Dean held Brooklyn to three hits, struck out seven, and won his 27th game of the season, breaking a club record set in 1899 by Cy Young.

"Once in a while," Paul said, "I gotta do something to top him." The younger Dean, a rookie with the Cardinals in that '34 season, walked Brooklyn's Len Koenecke in the first inning of his start. He then retired the next 27 batters he faced to author the National League's first no-hitter since 1929, the Cardinals' first no-no in a decade, and the only no-hitter thrown by one of the Dean brothers in their careers. The last out came on a scorched grounder that Leo Durocher scrambled to block, pick up, and throw in time to get the runner by a breath. The Cardinals won 3–0 and moved to three games back of the Giants. After his brother's no-hitter, Dizzy chirped, "If I'da knowed you was gonna throw a no-hitter, I'd throwed one, too." The win was Paul's 18th of the season, making good on two Dizzy boasts in one outing. Paul was the "no-hit Dean" that day, and, combined, the Dean Brothers had 45 wins, just as Dizzy said they would during spring training.

They would finish with 49 regular-season wins between them and four more together in the World Series. The double-Dean sweep of the Dodgers started a pressurized stretch that, including the World Series, featured the Deans collecting 10 of 13 Cardinals victories.

"How would you feel?" Stengel lamented later. "You get three itsy-bitsy hits off the big brother in the first game and then you look around and there's the little brother with biscuits from the same table to throw at you."

The Origin of the Redbird Logo

During a snowy winter of 1921, Allie May Schmidt, a member of Ferguson Presbyterian Church, was asked to decorate the tables for the Men's Fellowship Club's meeting to discuss baseball. Branch

Rickey, the famed general manager of the local Cardinals, came to the St. Louis suburb for the meeting. And to honor their guest, Miss Schmidt arranged red carnations for the table centerpieces, as close to red as she could get for the team that took its nickname, Cardinals, from the rich red on their uniforms.

Alongside the carnations, she scattered on the tables tiny cardboard gifts that would forever change the franchise.

Legend has it, her inspiration came on fluttering wings.

As Miss Schmidt looked out her window at a fresh blanket of snow covering the landscape, two cardinals caught her eye, their brilliant red illuminated by the stark white backdrop. The two cardinals landed on a branch within view, and thus was born one of the most recognizable logos in all of professional sports. On February 16, 1921, Rickey came to Ferguson for a meeting and left with a new meaning for his team's nickname.

Miss Schmidt had stenciled, colored, and cut 82 cardinals, complete with yellow beaks, and placed each one on a brown string to represent a twig. Schmidt's father, Edward H. Schmidt, sat at the same table as Rickey and, intrigued by the birds, they began discussing an emblem for the club. Edward Schmidt happened to head the art department at a local printing company, and shortly after the meeting he presented logos just as Rickey has desired.

The twig had become a bat for a solo bird to perch on.

And, in another design, two cardinals were balanced on the same bat, facing each other in what Rickey called "a fighting pose."

About a year after Miss Schmidt made her cardboard birds the Cardinals' famous Birds-on-the-Bat logo debuted. In a 1922 photo of the new jerseys the text announces that the emblem cost $3.75 each and 75 of them were used to decorate the uniforms of the players. Nearly 20 years later Allie May Keaton (née Schmidt) received a gold pin shaped like a baseball diamond with jewels as its bases. In the middle was a cardinal, her cardinal. The pin was a token of thanks from the Cardinals' ownership.

The logo has undergone many evolutions in the decades since the meeting in Ferguson. The two cardinals' tails have pointed up and pointed down. They have appeared to be bowing more than "fighting," and they have had plumage ranging from regal to absurd. The "Slugger Bird," a muscular-looking cardinal with a wide stance, striped socks, and a bat cocked and ready to swing, debuted in 1956. It also experienced a heyday during the baby-blue uniform era and into the 1990s. The "Mean Pitcher Bird," a cardinal leering over his shoulder as he readies to pitch, remains a retro favorite. In the 2000s the "Primary Logo" had gained more prominence, as its single cardinal on a single yellow bat appear on the team's Sunday caps. There was also the subtle change of the beak.

In 1998 Bill DeWitt III, an executive with the team, wanted to bring consistency and a touch of biological correctness to the logo. During his research, he learned that cardinals have red or orange-red beaks, not the yellow that had been a signature of the Cardinals' cardinals since Miss Schmidt colored them on the cardboard birds. That year, the logos that featured the bird all had red beaks. There are still seats in the Cardinals' clubhouse and at spring training that feature a red-beaked bird.

The red beak didn't last long. There was a practical reason to switch back to yellow: the bat was yellow, and the introduction of a new color to a logo—as the orangish-red beak would be—is a tricky matter for licensees. There was the obvious historic reason. And there was a touch of déjà vu. Some in the Cardinals' office tell a story that Bill DeWitt III, wrestling with the beak decision, looked out his kitchen window one day and saw a cardinal, perched on a branch.

Its beak was yellow.

DeWitt laughed when asked to confirm the story.

He didn't really deny it.

20 Lou Brock

OF…Inducted into Hall of Fame, 1985… Number retired, 1979

Shortly after the most celebrated trade in Cardinals history, out-fielder Lou Brock listened to manager Johnny Keane describe his plan to goose the lineup. The year was 1964, and the rival Los Angeles Dodgers boasted a speed demon who was on his way to leading the league in stolen bases for the fifth consecutive season. When it came to thieving, Dodgers shortstop Maury Wills lapped the field. Keane believed the best way to keep pace was to speed up. He wanted a Maury Wills.

So he held a team meeting and asked for a volunteer.

Slow-footed and quick-witted catcher Bob Uecker piped up, much to Keane's chagrin. The rest of the clubhouse remained quiet.

"Brock," Keane said, pointing at his newly acquired outfielder. "Brock, you're it."

Brock was hesitant. He didn't like being pigeonholed as one type of player. He felt that's what the Chicago Cubs did to him as a minor leaguer, and he felt that was motivation for the trade.

"Would you like to play regularly on this team?" Keane asked.

"Well, yes," Brock replied.

"Then you will steal bases."

Steal he did. Steal his way to history.

After '64, Brock didn't steal fewer than 50 bases for the dozen years after the meeting. In 1966 Wills finished behind Brock in the National League, and Brock led the NL in steals for four consecutive years and eight of the next nine. When Brock retired after the

1979 season, he held the single-season steal record with 118 in 1974 and the career mark of 938, 46 more than Ty Cobb. At the time of his first-ballot induction into the National Baseball Hall of Fame in 1985, Brock was still the career leader. To think, he was slow to embrace his calling.

"The whole thrust, the whole idea of being a perfect ballplayer was to be a well-rounded player or a complete player and cover all the five areas—hit, run, throw, catch, and field, and hit with power," Brock said four decades after that transformative conversation with Keane. "I had them all covered. So what's a base-stealer? Right away, a base-stealer is not a complete player. He can't gap the ball. He's not going to hit home runs. He's not going to hit .300. He's asking me to take on that role. That was hard. That was not my mindset. But that was the prerequisite: steal bases, be on the team."

Buck O'Neil, the famed ambassador of the Negro Leagues, scouted Brock and signed him for the Cubs. In 1962 Brock was a regular before his 23rd birthday. He struggled through two seasons with the Cubs, usually being reminded what he wasn't and rarely told what he could be. On June 15, 1964—a watershed date for the Cardinals—they traded 20-game winner Ernie Broglio and two others to the rival Cubs for a package of three players that included Brock. It's now seen as one of the most lopsided deals in club history, and it sparked the Cardinals' sweeping success of the 1960s.

The left-handed-hitting Brock batted .348 for the Cardinals after the trade, and .300 with a home run in the '64 World Series. As he provided the foot power for three pennant winners and two World Series titles, Brock became a devout student of the steal. Brock knew it was 13 strides to second base for an average runner and "11 strides and a slide" for him. He decoded pitchers and knew by their balance when it was time to run.

While he made his name as a man of steal, Brock's fear of being tagged a "one-dimensional player" was never realized. He was the first

Lou Brock broke Ty Cobb's all-time record for most stolen bases in 1977 and still holds the National League record with 938.

player to hit 20 home runs and steal 50 bases in the same season. He hit better than .300 eight times in his career, including a .304 average in his final season. At 40, he pushed back the criticism that the game had passed him up and stole 21 bases, scored 56 runs, and blistered his 3,000[th] hit. He was at his best in October, hitting .391 with 34 base hits—13 of which went for extra bases—in 21 World Series games. He also stole a record 14 bases in three World Series.

Though Rickey Henderson zoomed by him for the all-time lead, Brock's career steals still lead the National League, and his name adorns the trophy that goes to the league's stolen-base leader. For years he coached base running for various clubs and has been a fixture at Cardinals spring training since 1995. He still preaches the gospel of a "power jump."

For a while Brock said his "biggest battle" was embracing "the stolen base, because the stolen base was an animal that implied you are a one-dimensional player." Swiping bags may have been how he got around the bases, but it's not the only path he took toward immortality. Keane's demand gave him direction. Brock took the role and ran with it—all the way to Cooperstown.

21 The Pioneer Who Covered Center

Dal Maxvill, the shortstop who played in front of center fielder Curt Flood for so many years, was surprised to find his teammate sitting across from him on a flight to San Juan, Puerto Rico, in 1969. They had the same destination—a players' union winter meeting on the island. Maxvill was going to represent the Cardinals.

Flood was going to forever change baseball.

Early in the morning on October 7, 1969, Flood woke to a phone call and the news he had been traded to the Philadelphia Phillies. He refused to go and never played an inning for the Phillies. He had been a Cardinals stalwart for a dozen years, Bob Gibson's road roommate for a decade, a member of three World Series teams, and, for a time, the finest defensive center fielder in the league. In a letter to baseball commissioner Bowie Kuhn, Flood challenged the notion that a player was a "piece of property" to be bought, sold, and traded without recourse. He rejected the legitimacy of baseball's reserve clause that bound a player to a team and sued for the right to choose his place of employment. Flood, who flew to San Juan to tell the union members of his intentions and gather support, was about to change the way professional sports did business. His refusal to leave the Cardinals became the spark for the brushfire of free agency.

"It was personal at the beginning, a 'They can't do this to me,'" said Allan Zerman, the St. Louis attorney who helped organize and state Flood's case. "Somewhere early on it became clear this was something bigger than he was."

What tends to be lost in Flood's quest for free agency and even the push to preserve his legacy as a trailblazer, is that the wispy, speedy outfielder was a superb player. General manager Bing Devine saw Flood, that target of his first deal, as a possible answer for the Cardinals' opening in center. He became a piston for the Cardinals' sleek teams of the 1960s. For nearly two complete seasons, Flood handled 568 chances in 226 consecutive games without an error. The right-handed hitter learned to use his speed and whip swing to spray singles, hitting for a career average of .293 and better than .300 six times as a Cardinal. In 1968, while his roommate reshaped the rules of pitching with a 1.12 ERA, Flood finished fourth behind Gibson in the MVP balloting. The next year he won his seventh Gold Glove. Contract negotiations were contentious, as Flood sought a $100,000 salary. A few days before the World Series, the Cardinals dealt him to Philly.

The reserve clause put such a clamp on a player's options that Flood, 31 at the time, could report to Philly or retire. In union chief Marvin Miller, Flood found an ally willing to battle for an alternative. In 1970 Flood's suit against baseball eased toward

Center of Attention

For a quarter of a century, from 1982 to 2007 and a span of 3,980 games, center field for the Cardinals was manned by essentially three men. Willie McGee started the era, won an MVP there, and then played right field in the game where Ray Lankford made his 1990 debut in center. Lankford moved to left in 2000 when Jim Edmonds inherited center. Such stability is a bedrock trait of a remarkable position for the Cardinals. Five of the gloves who spent at least 1,000 games in center for the Cardinals:

- Terry Moore, 1935–1942, 1946–1948: Four-time All-Star who captained Swifties
- Curt Flood, 1958–1969: Seven consecutive Gold Gloves and six-time .300 hitter
- Willie McGee, 1982–1990, 1996–1999: Three Gold Gloves, MVP in 1985
- Ray Lankford, 1990–2001, 2004: Franchise-best 123 homers at Busch II
- Jim Edmonds, 2000–2007: Six consecutive Gold Gloves, two 40-HR seasons

court, and Flood was in Europe when his peers reported to spring training. He surfaced in Washington in 1971 for 13 disappointing games and was clearly done playing by 1972, when the case reached the Supreme Court. Soft-spoken and artistic, Flood returned to baseball as a color man and as an American Legion coach, but it took years for him to be the conquering hero. His case stirred momentum for a federal arbiter's decision in 1975 that established free agency. Flood is widely viewed as the index case for the labor movement that led to the galactic-sized salaries of today, with an average salary 120 times what it was in Flood's final full season. In 1998 President Bill Clinton signed an act that eliminated baseball's antitrust exemption for labor matters. It carried Flood's number—21—through Congress and was named the Curt Flood Act.

He lost his case. He lost his career. But he won for others.

In 1995 Flood returned to a union meeting like the one back in 1969. The players had just lost a World Series to a strike and were being lampooned or excoriated in public. Flood walked in, and everyone fell silent until an ovation spread through the crowd. Two years later Flood died on Martin Luther King Jr. Day.

"Because he came our way, we are better," Rev. Jesse Jackson said at Flood's funeral. "Baseball didn't change Curt Flood. Curt Flood changed baseball. Curt opened the floodgates."

Toss a Seat Cushion, Twice

What's been forgotten from the night a blizzard of seat cushions blanketed Busch Stadium was the initial flurry that came at the first whisper of Tom Herr's heroics. The Cardinals trailed the rival New York Mets 5–0 early in that April game at Busch Stadium. Herr singled and scored and walked in a run as the Cardinals rallied to tie the score in the fourth inning. He drove home the tie-breaking run with a double in the sixth. That was when the initial cushions flew. Only a few fluttered in that time. Just snowflakes floating, spinning and solitary in their celebration.

The storm came later.

April 18, 1987, was Seat Cushion Night at the downtown ballpark, and the thousands of fans who had the free giveaways had little reason to use them. The game, against the despised Mets, kept fans on their feet. The teams traded leads four times before the Cardinals rallied in the ninth inning to force extra innings. Helped by a wild pitch, the Mets took a one-run lead in the tenth inning.

Pinch-hitter Tom Pagnozzi, a rookie in '87, tied the game with an RBI single. Three batters later, ageless lefty Jesse Orosco was on the mound, and Herr came to the plate.

For his boyish good looks and a starring role in Whitey Herzog's 1980s charismatic clubs—Herr drove in 110 runs in 1985 despite hitting fewer than 10 homers—the Cardinals' second baseman was quite the crush for many St. Louis girls. In 1987 the fair-haired Herr drove in 83 runs for the pennant-winning team and did so while hitting only two home runs and 31-extra base hits. His first homer inspired a salute of seat cushions.

Orosco delivered. Herr mashed. His first career grand slam, the sixth walk-off grand slam in franchise history, cleared the left-field wall and gave the Cardinals a 12–8 victory. Said Orosco that night: "I was hoping it would hit a bird or something." Before Herr could round the bases, cushions came fluttering from every level of the ballpark. Ushers took up garbage bags and quickly filled them with the fly-away giveaways. Some relievers helped with the cleanup. It took most of the evening to clean and ready the field for the next day's game.

"I guess," Herzog said, "that will be the end of seat cushion day."

Executives echoed that sentiment, with one saying even more than a decade later that Herr's homer wasn't the end of the first Seat Cushion Night, it was the end of any more Seat Cushion nights. And it was...until 2006.

Flirting with the team's longest losing streak in a quarter century, the Cardinals had lost eight consecutive games and entered the ninth inning on June 29, 2006, against Cleveland trailing 4–3. Tens of thousands of seat cushions had been given out before the game, and slowly the boos that ushered the team off the field in the eighth inning gave way to the thunderous clapping of fans crashing seat cushions together like cymbals. The din grew when Indians catcher Kelly Shoppach dropped a popup and So Taguchi reached second on the error. He scored on Aaron Miles' game-tying double. Miles moved to third on a groundout and then raced in for the win when Cleveland shortstop Jhonny Peralta bounced his throw to first base on a potential groundout.

The seat cushions came flying out of the crowd, Frisbee-like, seconds after Miles tapped home as the winning run in a 5–4 victory. The longest losing streak in team history since 1988 was over. While two errors by Cleveland doesn't have that memorable verve of Herr's grand slam, the two nights share more than just posterior promotions. Every season there has been a Seat Cushion Night that ended in a downpour of plastic has also ended with a National League pennant. The morning after the win against Cleveland, the stadium operations staff still had boxes and bags loaded with discarded cushions. Someone suggested there was enough around to hold a Seat Cushion Night a few days later. Nobody laughed.

23 The Voice of the Cardinals

For generations of Cardinals fans, the greatest moments in their team's history aren't just memorable for what happened or for what it meant, but for how it *sounded*. The soundtrack of their memories is distinctive, colorful, and gravelly—all courtesy of Jack Buck.

If Buck didn't call it, it might not have happened.

One of the most beloved sports figures in St. Louis history, Buck called Cardinals games from 1954 to 2001. He was famous for the timbre of his voice, the detail of his calls ("He mops his brow" as Bob Gibson prepares to throw a no-hitter), his vibrant verbal improvisation ("Wake up Babe Ruth!" after Mark McGwire's 60th home run), and his contagious enthusiasm for the moment ("I don't believe what I just saw" as a hobbled Kirk Gibson homers in 1988). The album of Cardinals highlights since the 1950s is packed with hits, from Stan Musial's 3,000th hit to Lou Brock's 105th stolen base in 1974 to Ozzie Smith's heroics in the 1980s, and Buck provided the vocals.

St. Louis shared their voice with the rest of the sports world as Buck was the radio voice of *Monday Night Football*, called the 1967

Jack Buck's voice was synonymous with Cardinals baseball. For nearly 50 years, Jack and/or his son Joe were part of the St. Louis broadcast team.

Ice Bowl, and was the lead announcer for many World Series. Buck was more than great games and great calls. He was a treasured presence in the city's community. His friends recall a boundlessly generous Buck. Young broadcasters and sportswriters would try to pick up the check after lunch with Buck and never be successful. He was too quick, premeditatedly giving. He became one of the most desired emcees in St. Louis—joking in his autobiography that he spoke to both the optimists and the pessimists—and he knew the magnetic pull his presence would have for a charity.

"The people of St. Louis know that he's not a phony," his wife, Carol Buck, once told the *Post-Dispatch*. "Sometimes you find out your heroes are not who they seem and you're disappointed. No one will ever be disappointed by Jack."

A winner of the Purple Heart for his military service, Buck came to St. Louis after the war and joined the Cardinals' broadcast in 1954, adding to a packed booth that already included Harry Caray and Milo Hamilton. Buck shared the booth with Caray during the pennant runs of 1964, '67, and '68. From 1972 to 2001, he was the lead voice of Cardinals games, sharing the microphone with friend Mike Shannon. The Cardinals commissioned a bust of Buck at the microphone in 1998, and in 2002 they retired his "number"—a banner shouting his signature phrase, "That's a winner!" Buck died in June 2002, and more than 10,000 people attended his memorial at Busch Stadium. Less than a year earlier, his ability to unite a community went national, as his poem "For America" welcomed baseball back for the first game after the terrorist attacks of September 11. From a podium on the infield at Busch Stadium on September 17, 2001, Buck, challenged by his Parkinson's and riddled by lung cancer, was still able to articulate a shared grief with singular grace. "The question has already been answered," announced Buck from a podium on the field. "Should we be here? Yes!"

Other Voices

Other prominent play-by-play and color men from the colorful history of Cardinals broadcasters (in alphabetical order): Joe Buck 1991–2007...Harry Caray 1945–1969...Bob Carpenter 1984, 1995–2001, 2004–2005...Dizzy Dean 1941–1946...Joe Garagiola 1955–1962....Wayne Hagin 2003–2006... Milo Hamilton 1954...Rick Horton 2004–present...Dan Kelly 1980–1984 .... Dan McLaughlin 1999–present...Jay Randolph 1975–1986, 2007–2010... John Rooney 2006–present...Mike Shannon 1972–present...Ozzie Smith 1997–1999...Gabby Street 1945–1950.

Great Calls from the Greatest

"Sutter from the belt. To the plate. A swing and a miss! That's a winner! That's a winner! That's a World Series winner!" —*when the Cardinals clinched the 1982 World Series*

"Swing and a long one into left field. Adios! Good-bye! And maybe that's a winner!... They may go to the World Series on that one, folks." —*for Jack Clark's three-run home run in Game 6 of 1985 NLCS*

"Gibson swings and a fly ball to deep right field. This is going to be a home run. Unbelievable! A home run for Gibson.... I don't believe what I just saw. I don't believe what I just saw!" —*on Kirk Gibson's pinch-hit home run in Game 1 of 1988 World Series*

"He takes off his cap. He mops his brow. He looks in and gets the sign. He starts the windup. Here's the pitch and it's—a called strike! A no-hitter for Gibson! Simmons roars to the mound, embraces Gibson, who is engulfed by teammates." —*calling the end of Bob Gibson's no-hitter in 1971*

"Well, open up the history book, folks. We've got an entry for you." —*after describing the ball bouncing through Boston Red Sox first baseman Bill Buckner's legs and allowing the New York Mets to win Game 6 of the 1986 World Series*

"Swing and there it goes. This is it. It's a home run. Wake up, Babe Ruth. There's company coming, and it's Mark McGwire with home run number 60." —*calling McGwire's 60th home run in 1998*

"Mike Morgan is the pitcher. Here it comes to McGwire. Swing! Lookit there. Lookit there! Lookit there! Number 61! McGwire's Flight 61 headed for a Planet Maris. History! Bedlam! What a moment. Pardon me while I stand up and applaud." —*describing Mark McGwire's 61st home run in 1998*

Buck is a broadcast member of both the National Baseball Hall of Fame (inducted 1987) and the Pro Football Hall of Fame (inducted 1996). His legacy also includes Citizen of the Year awards and a spot in the Radio Hall of Fame. During his induction in 1995, he thanked the ballplayers whose feats he described. "I am grateful for the bat of Stan Musial, the arm of Bob Gibson, the legs of Lou Brock," he said, "and the glove of Ozzie Smith." Not one of which would have been the same without the voice of Jack Buck.

"Go Crazy, Folks!"

It took a home run that defied description to inspire the call that made them both legendary.

In the 1985 National League Championship Series that featured a runaway tarp that devoured Vince Coleman and two clutch home runs to clinch the pennant, one improvised exalt by broadcaster Jack Buck is the lingering echo. It was the only way to describe what Ozzie Smith just did.

Crazy.

The 101-win Cardinals had fallen behind in the best-of-seven series against Los Angeles by losing the first two games at Dodger Stadium. Gutsy pitching performances by Danny Cox and John Tudor as the series shifted back to Busch Stadium leveled the series for Game 5. On October 14, 1985, the hosting Cardinals dinged Los Angeles Dodgers starter Fernando Valenzuela for a couple runs in the first inning. The Dodgers answered with Bill Madlock's two-run homer in the fourth. And the game sped toward its improbable conclusion.

The Cardinals had stranded 10 men on base, and Valenzuela had pitched valiantly to the ninth inning. Reliever Tom Niedenfuer replaced the lefty starter to face switch-hitters Willie McGee and Smith. McGee popped up, and Smith stepped into the batter's box. Smith had not hit a home run in 3,009 major league at-bats from the left side of the plate. In his career, only five of his 1,661 hits from the left side would be homers. He fouled off two Niedenfuer pitches, took a ball to setup Niedenfuer's 1–2 pitch, and then swung. That's where Buck took over with a call generations of Cardinals fans can recite.

"Smith corks one into right, down the line. It may go!" Buck said. "Go crazy, folks! Go crazy! It's a home run, and the Cardinals have won the game by the score of 3–2 on a home run by the Wizard!"

Buck did more than call the home and state the vitals; Buck coined an anthem. Quicker than Smith's homer ricocheted off a pillar behind the right-field wall and his teammates mobbed him at home plate, "Go crazy, folks!" became an enduring battle cry for Cardinals Nation.

Rogers Hornsby

2B…Inducted into the Hall of Fame, 1942… Number retired, 1997

A feisty, abrasive fireplug who whipped the Cardinals to their first World Series championship, Rogers Hornsby didn't smoke, didn't drink, carefully watched his diet, and valued his sleep. He didn't care to read books and absolutely refused to go see a movie. Hornsby avoided anything that he feared would put a strain on his precious eyesight. Hornsby fine-tuned his life for one pursuit: hitting.

It's hard to argue with the results.

In a dozen seasons with the Cardinals, several of which were spent as a player/manager, "Rajah" transcended the league and became the best all-around hitter of his era and arguably the greatest right-handed batter in baseball history. Hornsby's .358 career average trails only Ty Cobb's .367. His .424 average in 1924 is the highest batting average of the 1900s. He and Cobb are the only two players in baseball history to hit .400 three times in their careers, and he and Ted Williams are the only two players to win multiple Triple Crowns, as Hornsby did in 1922 and again in 1925.

The Decade Triple Crown

In the 1920s no player in the National League hit as many home runs, drove in as many runs, or had a better batting average than Rogers Hornsby, giving him what researchers have nicknamed the "Decade" Triple Crown. Eight decades later another Cardinal accomplished the same rare feat. Albert Pujols even spotted the league a year and still led in all three categories (National League rank is in parentheses):

Cardinal	Decade	BA (rank)	HR (rank)	RBI (rank)
Rogers Hornsby	1920–1929	.382 (1st)	250 (1st)	1,153 (1st)
Albert Pujols	2000–2009*	.334 (1st)	364 (1st)	1,098 (1st)

Pujols did not make his major league debut until 2001.

Hornsby's devotion to hitting was singular, and his reason transparent. "Baseball is my life," he said. "It's the only thing I know and care about."

Hornsby was born in a small Texas town, the youngest son of a cattle rancher. He honed his game by playing against men in the area baseball leagues. In 1915 a Cardinals scout caught sight of the teenager and sent him to St. Louis. That same summer he debuted in the majors at 19. Weighing all of 135 pounds, Hornsby was told that he was too small for the big leagues and would have to be "farmed out." He responded to the criticism literally and worked the winter on his uncle's farm, packing muscle onto that slight frame and reporting in 1916 ready to be a regular.

After flirting with .400 for a few seasons, he hit .401 in 1922 and won his first Triple Crown with 42 home runs and 152 RBIs. That season Hornsby led the NL in 10 offensive categories, many by a great distance. His .401 batting average was 47 points better than the second-best. He had 16 more home runs than anyone in the league, and he collected 136 more total bases than anyone in the league.

Hornsby began his swing with an unimposing stance, his feet close together, and wedged deep into the back corner of the box.

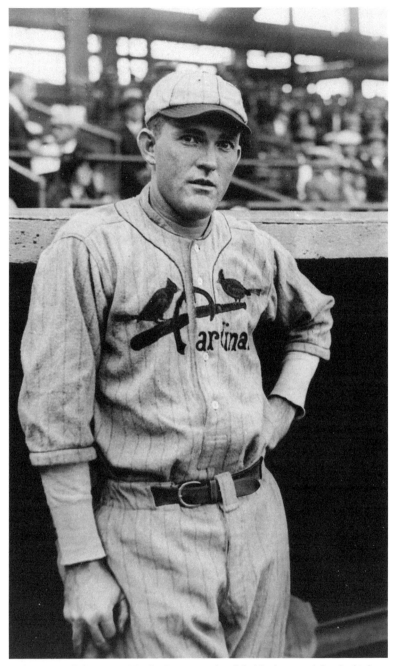

Rogers Hornsby won two Triple Crowns and still holds the record for the highest career batting average in National League history (.358).

But he quickly uncoiled from that stance to drive pitches to all fields. He said hitters who stand flatfooted are called "golfers," and that he had no interest in being a golfer because he preferred to hit balls for someone else to chase.

"Every time I stepped up to the plate with a bat in my hands, I couldn't help but feel sorry for the pitcher," Hornsby once said.

In 1925 Hornsby seized his second Triple Crown, leading the league with a .403 average, 39 home runs, and 143 RBIs. He won the first of his two MVPs—his only one with the Cardinals—and he set an NL record for slugging percentage with .756 that stood until 2001. That season concluded his run of six consecutive batting titles and a five-year span when he hit .402 overall. He remains the only player ever to hit better than .400 in a five-year span. The '25 season was also the year he took over as manager. The next season he steered the Cardinals to their first World Series championship. Hornsby, fittingly, applied the tag on the final out of the Game 7 clincher.

His outspokenness and prickly, often arrogant demeanor caught up with him that winter. Even the afterglow of a championship couldn't keep him a Cardinal. After years of rejecting the New York Giants' overtures for the second baseman, the Cardinals agreed to trade him for Frankie Frisch. Hornsby passed through three clubhouses and won an MVP in '29 before his return to the Cardinals in 1933. By the end of the year he had been let go again—this time to manage and play for the St. Louis Browns. Hornsby, a seven-time batting champ and the first National Leaguer to hit 300 home runs, received induction into the Hall of Fame five years after he retired. Five decades later the Cardinals retired an interlocking "STL" for the player/manager who didn't wear a number as a Cardinal but put up some of the franchise's greatest numbers. He remains the franchise's leader in batting average, at .359.

Also in the 1990s Williams, whom Hornsby once mentored in the minors, opened a Hitters Hall of Fame and named Hornsby the fourth-best hitter in history. His gruffness and intensity was honored in celluloid. Tom Hanks' classic rant in *A League of Their Own* includes how his character didn't tear-up when Hornsby ridiculed him, because: "There's no crying in baseball." Wrote the *Sporting News* in Hornsby's obituary in 1963, Hornsby held "baseball in such high esteem that he could not tolerate those who did not."

Old Pete and the "Final Crisis"

1926 World Series: Cardinals defeat New York Yankees 4–3

Grover Cleveland Alexander already had more than 300 wins and a reputation as one of the game's greatest pitchers when greatness beckoned him into the seventh inning of the seventh game of the 1926 World Series. It became the moment immortalized on his Hall of Fame plaque. But first he had to wake up.

Alexander, "Old Pete" to his chums, had thrown nine innings for the Cardinals against Babe Ruth and the New York Yankees the day before and, legend has it, looked like he had gone nine rounds (at least) with his celebrating pals later that same night. The right-hander's complete-game victory in Game 6 at Yankee Stadium forced this Game 7, played on a day so chilly and drizzly that a rainout was feared. Alexander spent most of the game dozing in the bullpen as his teammates played for the championship. He was "tight asleep in the bullpen, sleeping off the night before, when trouble comes," catcher and '26 National League MVP Bob O'Farrell recalled in the oral history *The Glory of Their Times*.

Trouble was the bases loaded, a 3–2 lead, the Cardinals' knuckle-baller Jesse Haines unable to continue, and Yankees second baseman Tony Lazzeri coming to bat. Cardinals manager Rogers Hornsby signaled to the bullpen for Alexander. Hornsby marched from the mound to the outfield to meet Alexander on his way in. The right-hander knocked loose the cobwebs as he trudged to the mound.

"Can you do it?" Hornsby asked him.

"I can try."

The midseason acquisition of Alexander was one of two masterstroke moves by Hornsby and roster architect Branch Rickey to catapult the Cardinals to their first National League pennant. At spring training, Hornsby, who also played second base, gathered the team for a meeting in the clubhouse and told them, "We are going to win this year's pennant." By June, the Cardinals were jousting with Cincinnati for the league lead. Eight days after the deal for Billy Southworth, who hit .317 in 99 games, Rickey plucked Alexander off waivers at the insistence of Hornsby. Alexander had been with the Chicago Cubs the previous eight seasons. But he returned from serving in the war with epilepsy and was struggling in '26. In his autobiography, Hornsby wrote that Alexander was seen as "dissipated, drank too much, and was finished as a major league pitcher."

He went 9–7 for the Cardinals with his best ERA since 1920.

A pennant within reach, the Cardinals finished the season on a 24-game road trip, a month away from home on a rigorous jaunt that included a series in every other city in the league. Despite the cruel schedule, they clinched on September 24 and finished two games ahead of the Reds. Awaiting the Cardinals in the World Series: the Murderers' Row Yankees. Alexander pitched the Cardinals to victory in Game 2, and Haines tossed a five-hit shutout in Game 3 to give the Cardinals a 2–1 lead in the best-of-seven series with two more games at Sportsman's Park. Ruth forced the series back to Yankee Stadium with one of the single greatest games in World Series history—hitting the first pitch he saw for a home run, homering in his second at-bat of the game, and driving a ball some 500′ in the sixth inning for his third home run of the game. He set eight World Series records in a 10–5 victory. The next day, Lazzeri's tenth-inning sacrifice fly was the difference, and the series shifted to New York with the Yankees on the verge of taking the championship.

Alexander held Ruth hitless and the Yankees to two runs in Game 6. Southworth, who hit .345 in the Series, scored three runs in a 10–2 win.

In Game 7 the Cardinals got all their runs in the fourth inning off Waite Hoyt, two coming on Tommy Thevenow's single. Haines guarded a one-run lead two outs into the seventh when he loaded the bases and brought up Lazzeri, a rookie starting his Hall of Fame career. Hornsby visited Haines to see that a blister on the pitcher's finger had busted and begun to bleed.

Out went the wakeup call to Alexander.

"I wanted to find out if he could see," Hornsby told Hall of Fame reporter J. Roy Stockton about why he met the right-hander in the outfield. "He recognized me all right, which was encouraging.… So I told him we were ahead, but that the bases were filled, two out in the seventh, with Lazzeri at bat. I had told him he was our best bet." One legend holds that Alexander listened to Hornsby, nodded, and replied, "I reckon I'd better strike him out."

Alexander didn't take many warm-up tosses—five or three, depending on the report—and struck out Lazzeri. Ol' Pete worked two more spotless innings, tempting the Yankees in the ninth when he walked Ruth. The Cardinals were one out from a championship when Ruth—the tying run—broke unexpectedly for second. O'Farrell's throw to Hornsby at second caught Ruth easy. The Babe got up and shook Hornsby's hand.

A celebration greeted the Cardinals' first championship club at Union Station when their train arrived. Alexander's strikeout was the stuff of lore and the inspiration for the inscription on his plaque at Cooperstown: "Won 1926 world championship for Cardinals by striking out Lazzeri with bases full in final crisis at Yankee Stadium."

27 Visit Sportsman's Park

Hall of Famer Red Schoendienst recalls riding the streetcar, elbow to elbow with Cardinals fans, from his home and up Grand Boulevard to the grassy cathedral at the heart of St. Louis' passion for baseball—Sportsman's Park. At the corner of Grand and Dodier, as famous an address in these parts as 1600 Pennsylvania Avenue, rose a square ballpark, built into the city grid and boasting an unrivaled history. Ten World Series and three All-Star Games were played there. It was the last ballpark—and probably always will be the last ballpark—to host every game of a World Series, as it did in the Streetcar Series of 1944.

The ballpark, like that streetcar line on Grand, is long gone now. But traces of its history still remain.

Drive west from downtown St. Louis, where major league baseball has been played since 1966, and head north from the Saint Louis University campus on Grand. Rising up on the left will be the sign marking the former home of baseball in St. Louis: "Site of Sportsman's Park 1881–1966." The sign goes on to brag that 30 Hall of Famers and "former greats" played there. It was here that Stan Musial played every home game of his career, and where Satchel Paige once set up a rocking chair in the bullpen. It was here that outfielder Curt Welch hid beer behind an advertisement on the outfield wall, where Enos Slaughter made his famous dash, and where 3'7" Eddie Gaedel, wearing No. ⅛, famously took an at-bat for the St. Louis Browns. A batter has cranked three home runs in one World Series game three times in history. Twice Babe Ruth did it, and both times it was at this little corner of St. Louis.

Baseball was played at the corner of Grand and Dodier as early as the 1860s, and when a National Association franchise started in St. Louis, it called the Grand Avenue Grounds home. In the 1880s the ballpark was renamed Sportsman's Park, and it hosted four American Association champions. In the early 1900s Sportsman's was the home of SLU football, and therefore the crucible for the invention of the forward pass. When the Cardinals returned to Sportsman's in 1920, they took up office space on the Dodier side of the ballpark; the Browns kept their offices on Grand. After a 1922 season that featured George Sisler hitting .420 for the Browns and Rogers Hornsby hitting .401 for the Cardinals, Sportsman's owners expanded the grandstand from 18,000 to 32,000. That still wasn't enough nearly 10 years later when more than 45,700 attended a game between the Cardinals and the Chicago Cubs. The crowd tipped capacity, and the overspill put thousands in the field of play. Accounts of the game say more than 100 baseballs were lost in the thicket of fans that surrounded the diamond.

Sportsman's charm was like the other neighborhood ballparks of its era—Wrigley Field and Fenway Park, the most enduring. One of the club's first owners, Chris Von der Ahe, had a pub nearby, and hotels, like the Fairgrounds, became famous for housing ballplayers. The streetcar ran by the ballpark, and Schoendienst said it was common for him to sign autographs for passengers as he made his way each day to the game. The dimensions of the field changed over time, from 460′ to dead center to 422 to center and 309½′ to right field during Musial's career. A 12′ wall in left was opposite a 36′-high, 156′-long screen in right that made pavilion seats less than desirable. There was a flagpole in play until 1953, when renovations at the ballpark moved it as well as installed the Anheuser-Busch scoreboard that became a hallmark. It featured a swirl of neon and other lights that could flash a Redbird swinging a bat or the A-B eagle flying.

Those were not the only renovations initiated when the brewery took ownership of the ballpark. The ballpark got a new name, Busch Stadium. And after a 12-year run that included Musial's final base hit and the 1964 World Series, the Cardinals decided to leave their aging home. At 3:15 PM on May 8, 1966, a double play ended the final game at Sportsman's Park. Orlando Cepeda, playing for the San Francisco Giants, caught the ball at first base. That evening, as home plate was transported from Grand and Dodier to downtown, Cepeda was traded from the Giants to the Cardinals, just in time to start the first game at their new home four days later.

There isn't much left of Sportsman's Park at its former address. There is the sign. There is a plaque. There is the famous address. And there, on the same ground the Man starred and the Gas House Gang roared, now stands the Herbert Hoover Boys Club, another landmark. The Cardinals left, and their field is gone, but on the same corner professional baseball lived for a century, the games go on.

28 Visit Robison Field

Located about a mile walk from the celebrated address of Sportsman's Park is where the main entrance used to be for Robison Park, but the actual distance between the Cardinals' first home and their next home was much less. Robison was enormous, and the two ballparks were so jammed onto the same cluster of blocks that their outfields nearly touched. It's possible to imagine a well-struck shot from home plate skipping to within a few feet of Sportsman's center-field wall.

From 1893 to 1920, the franchise that would become the St. Louis Cardinals called Robison home, at the corner of Natural Bridge Road and Vandeventer Avenue. While Robison is the most familiar name of the former ballpark, it was known by many different names throughout its years. When it first opened, wooed to the location by a streetcar circle, the ballpark was known as New Sportsman's Park. Later it became League Park, then Robison Park, and much later, just before the team left, Cardinal Field. The actual team went through almost as many name changes. When they moved into New Sportsman's, the ballclub was known as the Browns. The Robisons purchased the team in 1899, switched the colors to a rich red, and renamed them the Perfectos. That lasted until a female fan raved about the team's cardinal red embroidery, and it was while calling Robison Field home that the team became the Cardinals.

The day it opened, copies of that day's newspapers were buried underneath home plate, and there they probably stayed well beyond the final game—June 6, 1920. Robison was known for its vast outfield and its carnival air. The dimensions of the field when it first opened were 470′ down the left-field line and 520′ (or more without the fence) to the deepest point of center field. The ballpark held horse races on its outfield track, and it had a water slide out past the left-field wall. The slide "Shoot the Chutes" caused just one of the openings in the wall that would allow balls to pass through for homers. At least two fires swept through Robison and turned the wooden grandstand nearly to ash, including one fire during a game. Players reportedly had to leap into the rescue effort. Robison was a raucous place even as it was long considered one of baseball's finest. It hosted the advent of the Knothole Gang in 1917 and the careers of Hall of Famers like Rogers Hornsby, Roger Bresnahan, and even Cy Young. It closed as the last wooden ballpark. It left a legacy.

Sam Breadon sold the land to the Board of Education, and in its spot rose Beaumont High in 1926. There is a plaque on school

Other Pro Baseball Ballparks to Visit in St. Louis

Red Stockings Park, Compton Avenue & Gratiot Street

Due to a rainout that washed away the first scheduled professional game in the city, on May 4, 1875, Red Stockings Park hosted the first completely professional baseball game played in St. Louis. The footprint of the ballpark has been usurped by Bi-State Development Agency's repair facility. The Red Stockings lost 15–9 and lasted just 19 games total. Later in 1875 a barnstorming group of women, Blondes & Brunettes, played an exhibition game, and in 1867 the field hosted the city amateur championship. It is one of the earliest known ballfields in St. Louis.

Stars Park, Market Street & Compton Avenue

A short walk from Red Stockings Park, nestled next to Harris-Stowe State University's active baseball field, is where a ballpark was constructed for St. Louis' Negro League ballclub, the Stars. Built in 1922, Stars Park was the "first professional baseball field in the United States...owned exclusively by African Americans," the plaque placed there says. The ballpark was home to championship teams in 1928 and 1930. Three Hall of Famers played there: Cool Papa Bell, George "Mule" Suttles, and Willie Wells. Suttles, according to legend, used to launch home runs into the streetcar barn beyond the outfield wall.

Handlan Park, Laclede Avenue & Grand Boulevard

Located in the shadow of Saint Louis University's Marchetti Towers is a plaque marking the former home of Federal League Park, or Handlan Park. The park was built for the Terriers, one of three big-league clubs playing in St. Louis in 1914 and 1915. Hall of Fame pitcher Mordecai "Three Finger" Brown played and managed for the Terriers. In 1915 lefty Eddie Plank won 21 games, including his 300th victory, at this ballpark.

Union Association Park, Cass Avenue & Jefferson Avenue

At this otherwise nondescript corner of central St. Louis, the juggernaut St. Louis Maroons debuted in 1884 on their way to a 94–19 record in the Union Association. The Maroons continued to play here even after hopping to the National League. According to local ballpark historian Joan Thomas, Maroons owner Henry Lucas' ballpark was referred to in national publications as the "Palace Park of America." The grandstand was painted white, bluegrass made up the infield, rows of opera chairs extended to the outfield, and there was clover framing the outfield.

grounds, facing Natural Bridge Road, marking Robison's entrance. The ballpark is gone, but baseball must remain in the soil. In Robison's footprint, big leaguers have bloomed. No high school in the St. Louis area has produced as many major leaguers as Beaumont, from Hall of Fame manager Earl Weaver to former Philadelphia Phillies general manager Lee Thomas to All-Star Roy Sievers and at least 14 others who managed or played in the majors. Could be all those ashes fertilizing the dirt.

29 The Architect of the Cardinals

When a new civic-based ownership group took control of the St. Louis Cardinals, the head of its leadership gathered a handful of sportswriters and editors to ask their opinion on who should lead the club. Each scribe scribbled out a name on a piece of paper, and later, when the ballots were unfolded and read, each one had the same name on it: Branch Rickey. His hiring was unanimous.

Baseball would never be the same.

Rickey would later make his name as one of the most significant cultural revolutionaries of the century. It was Rickey who spotted, nurtured, and signed Jackie Robinson to the Brooklyn Dodgers, thus integrating baseball and giving an athletic booster shot to the Civil Rights Movement. But before he was breaking down barriers, Rickey was renovating and innovating almost every nook of baseball and its business. He started with the Cardinals.

Rickey had been a field manager and executive with the St. Louis Browns when offered the job leading the Cardinals. He leaped at the chance to escape a feud with the Browns' owner, and felt that the Cardinals would give him the latitude he needed to begin taking his designs from theory into policy. Rickey was an Ohio native, a Michigan law school graduate, a tuberculosis survivor, and a former semipro football player whose career as a major league ballplayer didn't last beyond an arm injury. He had a fiercely brilliant and nimble mind, and he became so respected as an orator that he was said to have once fancied a debate against Clarence Darrow, the renowned lawyer. His verbal skills paled to his keen eye for talent.

He signed Hall of Famer George Sisler for the Browns and filled his pet project, the farm system, with scads of future stars for the Cardinals, from Chick Hafey to Dizzy Dean, Enos Slaughter to Stan Musial.

The real genius of "Mr. Rickey" would manifest in the front office as he turned a franchise that had just four winning seasons from 1900 to 1920 into the most successful National League club of the 20th century. He kept costs low, frustrated players with his penny-pinching, and yet was able to build a successful, even dominant, roster year after year. The cigar-smoking Rickey brought St. Louis its first championship in 1926 and constructed a culture that would win a total of nine pennants and six World Series championships in the next 21 years. Including his stint in Brooklyn, from 1943 to 1950, and a turn in Pittsburgh, a Rickey-built club won 15 pennants.

In 1967 Rickey was inducted in the National Baseball Hall of Fame, and his plaque is a chronicle of his enduring effects on the game. It cites specifically his invention of the farm system and his role in integration. He also was among the originators of the pitching machine, encouraged the use of the batting tee, and invented the sliding pit. His detailed notes and statistics on his players and others were the forefathers of today's statistic-heavy analysis of splits and tendencies. Such an attention to detail was the backbone of his ability to identify latent talent and also tinker with the game's framework. His brainstorms knew no bounds. Once in Denver, he stitched lines on his team's jerseys to duplicate the strike zone—for practices only.

Late in his 60 years at the frontier of baseball, Rickey became president of a rival league that, though it never played, is credited with forcing the major leagues into the era of expansion.

Rickey died in Columbia, Missouri, in 1965. Bob Broeg, the sports editor of the *Post-Dispatch*, wrote: "Branch Rickey was responsible for every St. Louis-developed star since Rogers Hornsby and before Ken Boyer. Every standout player…was bought, signed, scouted, or approved by the game's foremost visionary. Rickey and revolution have been synonymous in baseball. He wasn't a dealer in superficial revisions."

"Luck," Rickey famously said, "is the residue of design."

The Cardinals continued success is the residue of Rickey's design.

30 Rickey's Farm System: The Seeds of Championships

When Branch Rickey assumed the leadership of a rudderless Cardinals franchise, he had to conjure a bit of baseball alchemy—a formula to spin a small-market, cash-strapped club from a two-team Midwest town into a bona fide pennant contender. He didn't want a one-year wonder or a cyclical challenger. He wanted a dynasty. Rickey's epiphany came when he realized the only way to achieve such major aspirations was to start minor.

Long before Rickey began constructing an elaborate and inno-vative farm system—his "chain store" of ballclubs—the minor leagues had prospered and proved a fertile ground for major league teams to harvest talent. But it was on their terms. Minor league clubs would sell to the highest bidder, and that made things tricky for Rickey, who was already known for his nose for talent. If he came calling for a player, the club spread the word to drive up the price. No, Rickey wanted exclusive rights, and from that spawned the idea to create a baseball academy of sorts, a vast flow chart of talent that the Cardinals owned, directed, and, as important, nurtured. "Rickey visualized a chain of minor league teams of various classifications—a kindergarten, grade school, preparatory school, and a university of baseball—which eventually would graduate shining Phi Beta Kappa students of the game," wrote Hall of Fame baseball writer J. Roy Stockton in his book on the Gas House Gang. Rickey wanted complete control. First, he needed capital.

The sale of the land that housed Robison Field provided the first seed money for Rickey. Early in the 1920s owner Sam Breadon gave Rickey's plan his blessing by bankrolling the purchasing completely or seizing a majority stake in minor league teams as far flung as Syracuse, New York; Houston; Sioux City, Iowa; and Fort Smith, Arkansas. The ability to sign and plant players in these minor leagues allowed for the Cardinals to cultivate and keep their own talent at their price. It is Rickey's inventive twist on the farm system that became the foundation of the Cardinals' World Series teams of the 1920s, '30s, and '40s. Fourteen of the players on the 1926 World Series–winning roster had spent their entire career in the Cardinals' organization. In 1942 the St. Louis Swifties won 106 games and the World Series with a roster that featured only two active players from outside of the farm system—both reserve pitchers. Fourteen Hall of Famers spent the majority of their careers with the Cardinals, and eight of them were products of Rickey's farm system, including Stan Musial, Dizzy Dean, Red Schoendienst, and Jim Bottomley. Rickey dispatched and coordinated a nationwide web of scouts to find and sign players, sometimes scooping up dozens at a time in workouts. By 1936 the Cardinals' farm system included 26 minor league teams. That number would swell beyond 30 in the 1940s, and nearly half of them were owned by the

Cardinals. The farm kept the big-league team nourished with talent even as it produced players to sell to other clubs for needed coin.

Rickey wanted a dynasty. He created an empire.

Commissioner Kenesaw Mountain Landis attempted several times to dismantle Rickey's "chain-store baseball," and he accused the architect of exploiting and undermining the history of independent baseball. Rickey's concept spread, rapidly becoming the norm instead of the exception. Though nowhere near as expansive, minor league baseball today reflects Rickey's blueprint. The Cardinals themselves are even rediscovering their farm-system roots, following a familiar recipe. Faced with the bloated costs of free agents and a mid-sized market, the Cardinals soaked money into replenishing and augmenting their minor league system. They took ownership of several affiliates, like Double A Springfield, High-A Palm Beach, and developmental academies in the Caribbean. It was nothing short of Rickey revisited.

A Dash of Pepper

1931 World Series: Cardinals defeat Philadelphia Athletics 4–3

The Cardinals had two of the top three batters in the league and Frankie Frisch, the league MVP, to combat Lefty Grove and the juggernaut Philadelphia Athletics in a rematch of the 1930 World Series. But it took the spice of a frustrated and frustrating center fielder to halt the A's bid for a third consecutive title.

John Leonard Roosevelt "Pepper" Martin, as anonymous a ballplayer entering the series as his name was long, blitzed into the national headlines by wreaking havoc through the first five games of the '31 World Series. As the Cardinals won the best-of-seven series 4–3, Martin led the team with a .500 average, five stolen bases, five runs scored, five RBIs, and five games where he drove Connie Mack's mighty A's batty. Martin's 12 hits came in his first 18 at-bats of the series.

Mack asked pitcher George Earnshaw why the Athletics could not get the fireplug out. The right-hander who won 21 games in '31 told reporters what pitches Martin was able to hit: "Everything we throw."

While Martin stole bases and stole the show in the World Series, it was a far more balanced and relentless lineup that won the Cardinals their fourth National League pennant in six seasons. Second baseman Frisch did not lead the team in any offensive category except steals—with a league-leading 28—but he seized the MVP award with a .311 average and 82 RBIs. Chick Hafey won the batting title with a .3489 average, and Jim Bottomley finished third with a .3482 average. Sandwiched between the Cardinals was the New York Giants' Bill Terry, whose .3486 average completed the tightest batting race in league history.

Frisch called the '31 team the best he ever played on, describing it in his autobiography as "happily efficient." The club was the first 100-game winner in Cardinals history at 101–53, and it took the pennant by 13 games. Frisch, Hafey, and Bottomley—all eventual Hall of Famers—came to be known as the "the Three Musketeers." But another trio, a younger trio, grew into complements for the veteran swordsmen. Rookie Ripper Collins contributed 59 RBIs and a .301 average in spot duty. Right-hander Paul Derringer, also promoted from the minor leagues during the season, went 18–8 with a 3.36 ERA to augment a staff anchored by Bill Hallahan (19–9, 3.29) and "spitball" maestro Burleigh Grimes (17–9). And then there was Pepper.

Tired of running circles in the minors, Martin started the year by demanding a trade if the Cardinals weren't going to play him and finished it as a national icon. Martin had a total of 14 big-league at-bats before joining the Cardinals' lineup in June 1931.

Entering the World Series, all eyes were on the A's. Mack's team won 107 games and was angling for its third consecutive World Series win. Grove won 31 games, including 16 in a row. Al Simmons hit .390. Jimmie Foxx had 30 home runs. The Cardinals were more than underdogs; they were afterthoughts. Grove and George Earnshaw pitched 50 of the 61 innings in the series. Earnshaw allowed 12 hits over 24 innings and struck out 20 to go with a 1.88 ERA. Yet, he lost two games.

Blame Martin.

Backing Hallahan's three-hit shutout in Game 2, Martin singled twice and stole two bases to create both of the Cardinals' runs in a 2–0 victory. In Game 5 Martin had three hits and drove in four of the Cardinals' five runs, including two on his home run. That win snapped a 2–2 tie in the series. Philadelphia rallied to force a Game 7 and then rallied in Game 7, scoring two runs in the top of the ninth.

George Watkins' two-run home run gave Grimes, a spitball-slinger grandfathered into the 11-year-old rule forbidding the soggy pitch, a four-run lead in Game 7. But the Cardinals' veteran right-hander teetered after the A's scored two runs and put the tying runner on base in the ninth. "Wild Bill" Hallahan came in to face the A's Max Bishop. The Philadelphia infielder laced a shot to the left-center gap. Martin, hitless in the final two games of the series, put a punctuation on his series by stealing a hit from Bishop, snagging the fly ball for the championship.

In Murray Polner's autobiography of Branch Rickey, Martin explained it was Rickey, the same GM he approached that spring to request a trade, that stoked Pepper in a pre-series talk:

> "His theme was: The greatest attribute of a winning ballplayer is a desire to win that dominates!" Martin said. "I have never forgotten those words. He brought every single Cardinal off his seat with an address that beat anything I ever heard. He reminded us…we had schemed

and scratched and fought and gone hungry to get here, and here we were, and what in heaven's name were we going to do about it? I actually prayed to God to help me have the desire to win that dominates."

Visit Trinket City

It started, like metropolises often do, with only a few residents, a shared interest, and a dream of expansion. In the late 1970s, Cardinals vice president Marty Hendin got his own office, complete with wood paneling that just begged to be hidden. He started by taping up pictures of the celebrities who visited the ballpark to watch the Cardinals.

He continued wallpapering the place with pins.

Then the army of bobbleheads advanced.

Soon his collection spread like memorabilia kudzu from the wall and the bookshelves to usurping large tracts of his desk and invading all nooks and swallowing every cranny in the room. A wave of curio destiny overwhelmed his office. Knickknacks bumped bobbleheads with bric-a-bracs. Collectible cars. Figures. Christmas ornaments. Signed baseballs. All over the place. Cereal boxes. Signed CD covers. And, somewhere in there, somewhere among the Cardinals souvenir wilderness, somewhere—yes, yes over there—a bundle of mini-bats, including one stained to look like it had been gooped-up by pine tar. That's the one signed by George Brett.

With Cardinals history told in plastic, pennants, die-cast, and a Stan Musial–signed harmonica spread out before him, Hendin nicknamed his empire "Trinket City."

"I've never done stuff we give away at the ballpark," said Hendin, the club's vice president of community relations until his sudden death in January 2008. "I don't put that in there. I take it home. The stuff [in Trinket City] is unique stuff. I always look for the unique."

Hendin has boxes stuffed with unique.

When the Cardinals moved from Busch Stadium II to the current ballpark, Busch Stadium III, one of the trickier chores was relocating Trinket City. It became a town with three addresses. His most treasured residents, two baseballs that had the autographs of every living Hall of Famer, and handfuls of other favorites went to the new ballpark. A total of 45 boxes at Hendin's home—"Trinket City West," he once called it—stored some of the original collection. Most of the Trinket City diaspora found a public home.

Hendin was a University City, Missouri, native and a University of Missouri–St. Louis alum who sat on the school's board. The school offered to display Trinket City at its posh new Millennium Student Center. Up went one of Hendin's signs— "Welcome to Trinket City"—and out came the collection into shiny new glass display cases. Included in the Trinket City UMSL precinct are Hall of Fame induction pins; pins from All-Star Games, including one from 2002 in Seattle that has a compass built into it; and World Series press pins through the 1980s, regardless of the team. Other sites to see at the City:

- A framed front page from the *St. Louis Post-Dispatch*'s Everyday section that celebrated the 100th Anniversary of the Cardinals with portraits of the living Hall of Famers. Hendin had it framed after getting each of the players, including Enos Slaughter shortly before his death, to sign his photo.
- A glove made and branded for former owner Gussie Busch.
- A Rick Ankiel action figure throwing a pitch and sporting No. 66, a number the lefty ditched as his talent began to betray him before it changed him to an outfielder.

- A photo reproduction of a 1968 *Sports Illustrated* cover that is signed by several of the Cardinals in a picture that captures a tremendous clubhouse: Bob Gibson, Lou Brock, Roger Maris, Mike Shannon, Tim McCarver, and Curt Flood.
- A harmonica signed by Musial.

UMSL students stroll by Trinket City mostly unaware of how these little knickknacks were nearly refugees of progress, or how they are now the living reminder of the man known as the public personality of the Cardinals. Hendin kept his battle with cancer private and quiet, still acting as the buoyant and irrepressibly Cardinals ambassador.

"If you were a Cardinals fan over the past 35 years, there was a good chance that you either met Marty or heard his name," Cardinals chairman Bill DeWitt Jr. said shortly after Hendin's death. "He was friends with everyone from Hall of Famers to the casual fan. If you were a Cardinals fan, you were a friend of Marty."

Even in Hendin's absence, Trinket City endures…and thrives. Back at the ballpark, Hendin's collection had run amok in his new office, testing its boundaries. After his death, the Cardinals created a display on the service level of Busch III, right on the walk to the visitors' clubhouse and across the hall from the home of Hendin's beloved invention, the mascot Fredbird. This is Trinket City II, complete with a city welcome sign and pictures of Hendin with celebrities. There are two pebbles marked as authentic concrete from Busch II. There is a blue miniature "All-Time Greats" locker for the only Cardinals with 3,000 hits or strikeouts—Bob Gibson, Stan Musial, and Lou Brock. There's a National Baseball Hall of Fame entry ticket from Ozzie Smith's induction in 2002, and it's autographed by Musial. Sitting close by is an Enos Slaughter nesting doll.

The newest Trinket City looks like a showcase for all the things collected by Hendin, but truly it is a memorial for Hendin, who collected all sorts of Cardinals things and was treasured for being all things to the Cardinals.

Finding the Trinket Cities: One is located on the first floor of the Millennium Student Center on campus at UMSL, 8001 Natural Bridge Road, St. Louis, Missouri. The second is located on the service level of Busch Stadium III, immediately outside the Marty Hendin First Pitch room and near the umpires' dressing room.

The Gas House Gang

Long before anyone had a colorful nickname to describe them, the 1934 Cardinals had the gritty style and rough-and-tumble reputation that needed a tailor-made name like "the Gas House Gang." Led on the field by player/manager Frankie Frisch and fueled in spirit by cocksure ace Dizzy Dean, the '34 club was an ornery, daring, and feisty mishmash of flamboyant personalities and elbow-grease talents. The gang captivated baseball with its late charge to the pennant and scene-stealing appearance in the World Series. At the end of spring training, Frisch gathered his charges in the clubhouse and rallied them under one rule, as related by author Robert E. Hood: "Don't let anybody push you around.… If you'd rather go back to the mines and dig coal [than] ride around the country in Pullmans and live in the best hotels at the expense of the club, speak right up. We haven't any room for softies; no holds are barred. That's the way we are."

His team embodied Frisch's words.

They fought opponents, they fought umpires, they fought the commissioner, they fought their owner, they fought their way back into the pennant race, and they even fought each other. Teammates Joe Medwick and Tex Carleton came to fisticuffs during a batting practice. There were scuffles over card games in those Pullmans. Dean threatened at least two strikes and pulled off one as he protested the salary of his brother, rookie Paul Dean. His eventual suspension had to be adjudicated by commissioner Judge Kenesaw Mountain Landis himself before he returned to win a record 30 games for the Cardinals. The club featured a center fielder who moonlighted as a double for a Hollywood star; an infielder who raced midget cars; a future manager in Leo Durocher, who got married in the thick of the pennant race; and a manager who couldn't shake the college-boy label early in his career. There were hillbillies and highbrows. There was a Phi Betta Kappa on the bench in Burgess Whitehead and an ace on the mound in Dean who couldn't keep his story straight on just what grade in elementary school was his last. The ringleader of the gang, Dean once performed a rain dance in the dugout—complete with a mini bonfire—and even delivered a black cat to the New York Giants' dugout during a game just as the Cardinals chased them down in the National League.

Adjectives strained to capture these Cardinals. Many tried. *Colorful* fell short. *Tempestuous* was too one-sided. *Wild, aggressive, eccentric,* and *swashbuckling* worked well in concert. But like their grimy and scuffed-up uniforms, no label fit perfectly. Only after they chewed up a seven-game deficit with 23 games to play could they really be called anything: pennant-winners. Wrote John Drebinger in the *New York Times,* the Cardinals "spent three-quarters of the year fighting among themselves before they finally struck upon the happy idea of uniting their energies in a common cause."

At any one time Branch Rickey's '34 Cardinals featured a roster with names like Ripper, Dizzy, Dazzy, Ducky, Chick, Pepper, Tex, Wild Bill, Lip, Spud, Pop, Kayo, and Showboat. They had nicknames galore, but the name they would carry together was actually bestowed on them retroactively. The precise origin of the moniker "Gas House Gang" has been lost to legends, but it's clear that '34 team played very few games under its banner. And it just didn't fit the 1935 club. The Gas House Gang became a popular

Other Cardinals Nicknames

Not too long removed from the decade that spawned the New York Yankees' "Murderers' Row" and Notre Dame's "the Four Horseman," "the Gas House Gang" didn't have the menacing overtone of other nicknames from the era, but it didn't lack for longevity. Cardinals' clubs by their nicknames:

The St. Louis Swifties: Hardly named for their fleet feet on the base paths (only two players had more than 10 steals), the '42 team got the speedy nickname for their ebullient style of play. They had a bounce in their step all the way to the title.

El Birdos: Coined by first baseman Orlando Cepeda during his MVP season of 1967, "El Birdos" gained popularity through Cepeda's postgame victory celebrations and actually became a pet name for the team that lasted long after they won the World Series that year.

Whiteyball: As much a philosophy as it was shorthand for a team, the clubs of the 1980s, under the guidance of manager Whitey Herzog, exploited a speed-first, slug-rarely brand of smallball that catapulted them to three pennants and a World Series. It remains a colloquialism for the style today.

sobriquet and eventually synonymous with the team years after the gusto was gone and Gas House had run dry. Robert Gregory, in his biography of Dizzy Dean, says it was a writer for New York's *World-Telegram* who coined the phrase, stating: "The Cardinals have got me worried. They looked like a bunch of boys from the gas house district who had crossed the railroad tracks for a game of ball with the nice kids." Durocher claimed in his autobiography that a cartoon depicting the Cardinals as a couple roughnecks from the wrong side of the tracks had the cutline, "The Gashouse Gang." J. Roy Stockton, writing for Frisch, recalled a story where a Chicago writer taunted the Cubs for nestling into their bunks early at the start of a road trip: "Are you boys afraid that Pepper Martin is on the train? You all better stay on your side of the tracks, or the Gashouse Gang will get you." Martin would sometimes arrive at the ballpark with his face and hands smeared with grease from working on his midget racecar, and the Cardinals were notorious for their ill-fitting, baggy, and stained uniforms—be it from tobacco wiped across their flanks or the dirt ground into the fabric. "We could have thrown [our jerseys] in the corner and they'd have stood up by themselves," Durocher wrote for *Sports Illustrated*. "We looked horrible, we knew it, and we gloried in it." The genesis of the "Gas House Gang" name clearly comes from that Cardinals look, but also what was described often as their "fierce" or "aggressive" style of play.

A spittin', cussin', brawlin', scrappin' band of motley ball players who, as Drebinger wrote, played "like a heard of steer into a children's playground." No holds barred, as Frisch commanded. Where the nickname came from and what it was supposed to mean is academic. The '34 Cardinals weren't defined by their Gas House Gang nickname. They defined it.

Deans Ignite Gas House Gang

1934 World Series: Cardinals defeat Detroit 4–3

Cardinals pitcher Dizzy Dean couldn't make it from the team train to a waiting taxi without pronouncing the 1934 World Series over. If he saw an ear turned his way, he was shouting a promise into it. The Cardinals had just arrived in Detroit, just finished a pennant race for the ages, and already Dean, the brash right-handed ace with the arm to back his boasts, was declaring a victory in the World Series that would launch the Gas House Gang.

Dean was even telling anyone listening how it would happen—he and brother Paul Dean would combine to win four games. Done deal.

"Pitching is duck soup for me, an' I'll knock 'em off easy," Dean said in an article in the *St. Louis Post-Dispatch* that ran before the World Series. "That won't sound like braggin', will it? The way I sees it, braggin' is where you do a lot of poppin' off and ain't got nothin' to back it up. But I ain't braggin'. I know me an' Paul is gonna win four games in this here Series."

It would have been easier for Detroit to dismiss Dean's crowing if the right-hander had not been right with so many other boasts during the 1934 season. He started the year by saying he and rookie Paul would win 45 games combined. They won 49. Thirty of those were Dean's, as he set a franchise record, and four of his wins came in the season's final 10 days. Dizzy and Paul powered the Cardinals to a historic rally, coming from five and a half games back with 17 games to play to win the pennant.

Winning four games against the Tigers would be nuttin'.

"Who won the pennant? Me an' Paul," Dean told writer J. Roy Stockton. "Who's goin' win the World Series? Me an' Paul."

The Cardinals had the characters. Detroit had the better record (101 wins), the budding slugger in Hank Greenberg, and the bona fide ace in Schoolboy Rowe (24–8). At 23 and just starting a Hall of Fame career, Greenberg hit .339, clouted 26 home runs, and drove in 139 runs. In Game 1 of the World Series, Greenberg hit his first postseason home run—but it came late in Dizzy Dean's defanging of the Tigers for an 8–3 win.

Shifted to make his first series start on a day without a Dean, Rowe pitched Detroit to a win in Game 2, and Paul Dean followed his brother's lead with a complete-game gem in Game 3. The younger Dean stranded 13 runners as the Cardinals took a 2–1 series lead.

Even with the Series at home, Cardinals owner Sam Breadon took precautions to protect his outspoken star. Police took turns standing sentry outside Dizzy Dean's hotel room because Breadon was wary of kidnapping attempts. He could not, however, shield Dean from a shot to the noggin in Game 4. Pinch running in the fourth inning, Dean was stuck between bases and took a throw flush off his head. Dizzy was considered well enough to make his start the next day, he just didn't pitch well enough. Detroit's Tommy Bridges held the Cardinals to one run while the Tigers tagged Dean for three runs.

Headed back to Detroit for Game 6, the Cardinals trailed in the World Series by a game, and the championship rested where Dizzy said it would.

On him an' Paul.

Paul Dean dueled Rowe in Game 6, allowing three runs (only one earned) to Rowe's four runs. Cardinals shortstop Leo Durocher laced three hits and scored two runs. With the score tied 3–3 in the seventh, Dean drove in Durocher with a single for the game-winning run, thus setting his braggadocious brother up for a Game 7 start. In the decisive game, the Cardinals' seven-run third inning—two off Rowe—robbed the game of any drama on the scoreboard, but Joe "Ducky" Medwick provided plenty on the base paths. In the sixth inning Medwick, who hit .379 with five RBIs in the series, struck a shot to the bleachers in right-center field. Medwick peeled around second and slid into third base, knocking Detroit third baseman Marv Owen over. Owen stepped on Medwick's shin as he fell, and Medwick retaliated by kicking Owen in the chest. The two hastened to their feet but were separated before exchanging any shoves or punches.

When Medwick returned to his position, left field, for the bottom of the inning, Tigers fans showered him with all sorts of litter—programs, beer, apple cores, banana peels, lemons, and cigar stubs. Commissioner Kenesaw Landis ruled that Medwick had to be removed from the game for his own safety. The delay lasted nearly 20 minutes, with the Cardinals leading 9–0. When Medwick and the debris had been removed, Dizzy Dean resumed filleting Detroit. He retired player/manager Mickey Cochrane, Charlie Gehringer, and Goose Goslin, in order, on three pitches. Three pitches, three outs from three Tigers who would become three Hall of Famers.

Dean struck out five, walked none, and allowed six hits in his complete-game shutout to clinch the world championship. His two wins in the Series fit with Paul's two wins for four, just as he promised. Combined, they threw 44 of the Cardinals' 65⅓ innings in the Series and had a 1.43 ERA. "The Dean boys came through in storybook fashion in the final two games," Frankie Frisch recalled in his autobiography. A Tiger had a different take. Said Rowe: "I'm glad the Deans aren't triplets."

35 Pepper Martin: The Wild Horse of the Osage

Either fervently delighted to be a ballplayer or eager to do whatever necessary to stay a ballplayer—or most likely, a pinch of both— Pepper Martin did a little of everything for his minor league team in Greenville, Texas. Late in the 1925 season, he had 18 home runs and 38 stolen bases. He'd played some outfield, struggled mightily at second base, and even hurled 53 innings as a pitcher. And that was just on the field. He also became a one-man traveling advertisement for the club, driving a wagon around that announced the time of the game that afternoon. He did that each day until it was time to start his duties as assistant groundskeeper.

Anything to stay in the game.

It was during one of these frenetic days of multitasking that the owner pulled Martin into his office for some news. His rights, the owner explained, had been sold to the Cardinals. "Folks," Martin would say later, "that was the nearest I ever came to fainting."

John Leonard Roosevelt Martin burst onto the big-league scene with his pyrotechnic performance in the 1931 World Series, but the man known as Pepper and nicknamed "the Wild Horse of the Osage" had a personality too big for one October. If Dizzy Dean was the leader of the Gas House Gang, Martin was its personification. This broad-chested, big-grinnin', hawk-nosed Oklahoman was an unbridled mustang on the ballfield. Baseball writer Lee Allen described him as a "berserk locomotive" who "slept in the raw and swore at pitchers in his sleep." Martin never saw an extra base he couldn't take, a diving play he couldn't attempt, or a rattlesnake he couldn't catch. "I want a hustling ballclub, a team that will play 'Pepper Martin baseball,' that will take the extra base the way Pepper does," Gas House Gang manager Frankie Frisch told baseball writer Bob Broeg. "You know, a club that will slide and play as hard as Pepper does."

Martin started his baseball career as a teen selling peanuts and soda at a ballpark in Oklahoma City. He advanced to pitching batting practice, then batboy, then shagging flies in batting practice, and finally shagging flies in games. He was a live wire in the field, had chronic difficulty making controlled throws to first, and happily fielded grounders with his chest. But he could run. Boy, could he run. Martin was said to be so fast he could race rabbits. He used to hunt rattlesnakes with a stick and a burlap sack and donate his coiled spoils to the St. Louis Zoo. In order to save the money the Cardinals gave him one season, he train-hopped like a hobo to get to Florida for spring training. At 27, he'd yet to stick in the majors and was fed up. He told Branch Rickey: "If you can't play me…trade me."

The Cardinals played him—played him right to a World Series title. In his first extended stay in the majors, Martin hit .300 with 16 steals and 32 doubles in 413 at-bats in 1931. He then hit .500 with five stolen bases and five RBIs in the '31 Series. In the '31 and '34 Series combined, Martin would go 23-for-55 (.418) with seven doubles, nine RBIs, 13 runs, and seven steals. His untamed style of play gained fame, and his country-boy charm even got him a deal as a vaudeville performer. But by 1937 the Wild Horse had started to slow. The third baseman/outfielder led the league in steals three times, the last being 1936 when he complemented his 23 steals with 121 runs and career highs of 76 RBIs and 11 home runs. He didn't have a 100-game season or more than 340 at-bats in any season after that. He spent his entire career as a Cardinal, playing 1,189 games in the uniform, and doing as much with his personality and verve as his production. Martin energized a country, sure, but he also was the inspiration and untamed forefather for what today is known as the Cardinal Way to play.

An ode in the *New York World-Telegram* after Martin's death in 1965 read: "To a whole generation, John Leonard Martin was the red blood of baseball, the spirit of the game."

# The Mississippi Mudcats

Cardinals outfielder and chief instigator Pepper Martin didn't know many songs on that trusty "git-tar," but his itch to perform was contagious enough that he struck up the major leagues' first jam band. The Mudcats—or, more formally, the Marvelous Musical Mississippi Mudcats—were a rotating cast of Cardinals in the late 1930s that would break into song whenever inspired. Before games. In the dugout. On the train. They even had scheduled appearances, were featured in cartoons, and designed their own outfits.

Pictures of the Mudcats show them wearing baseball pants, cowboy boots, red neckerchiefs, and jerseys inspired by the Cardinals' Birds-on-the-Bat logo. The band's jersey had "Mud" on one side of the zipper, "Cats" on the other, and two birds resting on a bat lodged between the "M" and "C." The copy with a news wire photo from 1938 explained the getup: "Pepper Martin's Mudcats, also known as the Gashouse Gang, but officially titled the St. Louis Cardinals, give a musicale at their New York hotel. The cowboy

Pepper Martin (far right) and the Mississippi Mudcats started as a clubhouse country music band but eventually performed on national radio broadcasts.

uniforms are to lend a wide open spaces atmosphere to lone prairie cadenzas."

The usual Mudcat lineup included:

Max Lanier, P	harmonica	Cardinal, 1938–1951
Bob Weiland, P	jug	Cardinal, 1937–1940
Bill McGee, P	fiddle	Cardinal, 1935–1941
Lon Warneke, P	banjo	Cardinal, 1937–1942
Frenchy Bordagaray, OF	washboard	Cardinal, 1937–1938
Pepper Martin, OF	guitar, etc.	Cardinal, 1928–1944

Martin got the guitar from his wife as a gift, and he came to spring training able to strum one song, "In Birmingham Jail." McGee, who gained the nickname "Fiddler" for his main part in the band, was the most musical of the group, according to the *Post-Dispatch*'s Hall of Fame baseball writer J. Roy Stockton. In 1937 Stockton wrote that for trickier tunes Martin would hand the guitar over and "turn to the harmonica, playing it lustily, while he glances enviously but grinning at Bill McGee." Bordagaray would play his washboard with thimbles, and it had two different-sized horns attached to it. They'd play "Possum Up a Gum Stump" and "They Cut Down the Old Pine Tree." Martin's beloved hillbilly music was the usual refrain, but the Mudcats didn't limit their Marvelous Music to Mississippi.

"We playing everything. We play anything," Martin said in Robert Gregory's biography of Dizzy Dean. "Whether we know it or not."

37 Joe "Ducky" Medwick

OF…Inducted into Hall of Fame, 1968

Joe Medwick was going to swing hard, no matter what the feisty, combative Cardinals outfielder was swinging at—a change-up, a fastball out of the zone, or a teammate's jaw. The hard-hitting, quick-to-brawl muscle of the Gas House Gang earned a reputation for being as hard on his teammates as he was on opposing pitchers. "That Medwick was mean," Leo Durocher wrote years later. "He came to play."

Medwick hit .319 with 106 RBIs and 110 runs in 1934 with the Gas House Gang. The next season, he began a three-year run that defined him as a hitter—three consecutive top-five finishes in

Joe Medwick won the National League's last Triple Crown in 1937, batting .374 with 31 home runs and 154 RBIs.

the MVP, three seasons of at least 220 hits and 110 runs, two seasons of leading the National League in RBIs, and a .359 cumulative average. Medwick punctuated the run with a Triple Crown in 1937—leading the league with a .374 average, 31 home runs, and 154 RBIs—and an MVP award. More than 70 years later he remains the last National Leaguer to win the Triple Crown. "I'll stack my 1937 year with anybody," Medwick once said. And he'd likely slug anybody who challenged it.

The ornery Medwick was a four-sport star at his New Jersey high school, and in order to keep alive the possibility of a football

The Cardinals MVPs

No team in the National League and only the New York Yankees in the American League has produced more Most Valuable Players than the Cardinals. The club has won 20 MVPs, two fewer than the heralded Yankees. The trophy case:

Player	Pos.	Year	Credentials
Albert Pujols	1B	2009	Flirted with Triple Crown as he claimed first home-run crown; hit 47 with .327 average, 135 RBIs
Albert Pujols	1B	2008	Became first Dominican-born player to win two MVPs; hit .357, 37 homers, 116 RBIs
Albert Pujols	1B	2005	After runner-up finishes in two of previous three years, he wins with .330 average, 41 homers
Willie McGee	OF	1985	Gold Glove play in center, the first of his batting titles with .353 average, 82 RBIs, 114 runs
Keith Hernandez*	1B	1979	Rewarded for the only 100-RBI season of his career and a career-high .344 average
Joe Torre	3B	1971	Won batting title with .363 average, topped league with 352 total bases, 230 hits, and 137 RBIs
Bob Gibson	P	1968	Coupled with the Cy Young Award as the spoils of his historic 1.12-ERA turn
Orlando Cepeda	1B	1967	In first full season with Cardinals, El Birdo Grande hit .325, drove in 111, launched 25 homers
Ken Boyer	3B	1964	Captain led NL with career-high 119 RBIs; .295 average, fourth consecutive year with exactly 24 homers
Stan Musial	OF	1948	Led NL in every major offensive category, save finishing one HR shy of Triple Crown
Stan Musial	1B	1946	Received 22 of 24 first-place votes after .365 average, 16 homers, NL-best 124 runs
Marty Marion	SS	1944	Edged Bill Nicholson by one point in vote. Hit .267, but merited MVP with rep as leader
Stan Musial	OF	1943	The Man wins first MVP with his first batting title, hitting .357, slugging .562

Player	Pos.	Year	Credentials
Mort Cooper	P	*1942	Starts three-year Cardinals reign with 22–7 record, 1.78 ERA, and 10 shutouts
Joe Medwick	OF	1937	Last National Leaguer to win Triple Crown with .374 average, 31 homers, 154 RBIs
Dizzy Dean	P	1934	Last National Leaguer to win 30 games; league-high 195 strikeouts and seven shutouts
Frankie Frisch	2B	1931**	Viewed as leader of world champs, Flash hit .311 with 82 RBIs, 96 runs, and four homers
Jim Bottomley	1B	1928	Led NL in triples (20), home runs (31), and RBIs (136), while hitting .325
Bob O'Farrell	C	1926	Boosted 'Birds to first pennant in club history with .293 average, 68 RBIs
Rogers Hornsby	2B	1925	After finishing second in 1924 with a .424 average, won MVP in 1925 with Triple Crown (.403 average, 39 homers, 143 RBIs)

Shared MVP with Pittsburgh's Willie Stargell
** *Considered the first of the modern-day MVP awards, as voted on by members of the Baseball Writers Association of America*

scholarship to Notre Dame, he played minor league baseball under an assumed name, Mickey King. While Medwick was in the Cardinals' minor leagues and playing for Houston, a letter to the local paper from a female fan swooned about the player and said his gait reminded her of a duck. That prompted the nickname "Ducky Wucky," shortened often to just "Ducky." Though the nickname appears on his plaque in Cooperstown, he didn't care for it. He preferred "Muscles," and teammates knew it.

Medwick made his major league debut with a .349 average in 26 games in 1932, and he reported to spring training in 1933 as the youngest player in camp—by two years. At the plate he fought his way to a top-five total in six major offensive categories his rookie year, including runs, RBIs, and homers. On the base paths, he made impressions with his hard slides, the same kind of slide that led to a brawl and his removal—for his safety, said commissioner Kenesaw Mountain Landis—during the 1934 World Series. Medwick once brandished a bat at Dizzy and Paul Dean, threatening to "break up" the brother act. Pitcher Ed Heusser once accused Medwick of lagging on a fly ball during a game, and Medwick responded by knocking him out cold with one punch.

"Durndest man I ever seen," Dizzy Dean said. "Before you even get to do enough talking…Joe whops you and the fight's over."

Medwick had five consecutive seasons of at least 100 runs and six with at least 100 RBIs for the Cardinals before a trade to Brooklyn in 1940. He would return to the Cardinals in 1947 before retiring after 19 at-bats in the '48 season. It took 20 years before Medwick, a career .324 hitter with 1,383 career RBIs and a prickly relationship with the writers, gained election to the National Baseball Hall of Fame. "I felt like I was in a 20-year slump," he joked on the day of his election. Medwick was said to mellow through those decades and even returned to the Cardinals in the late 1960s as a minor league hitting instructor. He was out on the field working with hitters during spring training in 1975 when he died of a heart attack.

38 The "Kidnapping" of Flint Rhem

The stench of stale whiskey that coated him should have been enough to sink Flint Rhem's wild explanation for his absence, except he was just sober enough to make it part of the tale.

In the thick of the 1930 pennant chase, Gabby Street's St. Louis Cardinals seized on the struggles of Brooklyn, Chicago, and the New York Giants to leapfrog from 12 games back into the race. The

Cardinals would win 39 of their final 49 games, and it was in mid-September that they arrived in Brooklyn for a key series against the surging Robins. Brooklyn had won 11 consecutive games and was atop the National League by one game over the Cardinals. Street scheduled Rhem to start the first game of the series, on September 16. But Rhem vanished, going, by some reports, 48 hours without being seen. He returned to the ballpark, soaked in whiskey, and spinning a fantastic yarn about his kidnapping by gunmen.

Rhem, 29 at the time, had always been a confounding talent for the Cardinals. He won 20 games for the franchise's first pennant-winner in 1926, but never more than 12 in any season after that with the Cardinals. He refused to pitch on a Sunday in the 1928 World Series and was suspended a few times for his drinking. Rhem, who came from a South Carolina town named for his family, claimed he got his nickname Shad "because of the fish stories I always told." It was true enough that it may have been a story, too.

Cardinals management, however, could not disprove his outlandish claim in 1930. He said he was outside the team hotel when three gunmen pulled up, spirited him away to New Jersey, and forced him to consume "cups of raw whiskey." "Bandits. Guns. Kidnapping," Rhem said, recounted years later in the *Boston Herald*. "They had revolvers." Police investigated, but came up as empty as those cups of whiskey. They found no hint of the supposed gamblers' plot to tilt the series to Brooklyn. The Cardinals swept the Robins. Rhem won twice in the next week, both at Philadelphia, and he started Game 2 of the World Series two and a half weeks after the alleged kidnapping. He lost, just as the Cardinals did. Years later, at a 25th reunion of the 1926 team, Rhem came clean and said what everyone already knew. The kidnapping was fiction, nothing more than an elaborate cover. Bob Broeg wrote decades later that Rhem "could have been one of the Cardinals' best pitchers if not the thirstiest."

Bruce Sutter

RHP...Inducted into Hall of Fame, 2006...Number retired, 2006

The pitch that made Bruce Sutter a World Series champion and forever a Cardinals icon was not the pitch that put him in the Hall of Fame. It was the pitch that nearly put him out of baseball.

With nobody on base and one out between him and a world championship, Sutter concluded a 10-pitch at-bat with a fastball. There was nothing split about it. Sutter's full-count, garden-variety fastball stunned Gorman Thomas and the Milwaukee center fielder struck out to end the Cardinals' 6–3 victory in Game 7. It was almost a full decade earlier that Sutter's career was flagging because his fastball was lacking. That was when Fred Martin, a pitching coach in the Chicago Cubs' minor league system turned Sutter into a Hall of Famer with a simple shift of the fingers. The new pitch had a simple, fitting name: the split-finger fastball. Sutter popularized the pitch, but few perfected it the way the right-handed reliever did.

"There were players throwing forkballs at the time, and a few guys were using it for a change-up, but nobody was throwing what he called the split-finger," Sutter said in his induction speech. "It was a pitch that didn't change how the game was played but developed a new way to get hitters out."

Sutter came to the Cardinals as part of Whitey Herzog's whirlwind restructuring of the roster in 1980. Herzog dealt Leon Durham, Ken Reitz, and a minor leaguer to rival Chicago for Sutter. The closer was a year removed from winning the 1979 Cy Young Award, with 37 saves and 110 strikeouts in 101⅓ innings. In three of his four seasons with the Cardinals, Sutter led the National League in saves.

Bruce Sutter perfected the split-finger fastball and won the NL Cy Young Award in 1979.

His high was in 1982, when he had 36 saves in the regular season and three more in the only October of his career. The affable Sutter spent more time with other teams in his career, but didn't leave as big an impression as he did with the Cardinals. He left with the franchise record for saves—a mark of 127, since surpassed—and as the first National League closer to reach 200 saves and the league's all-time save leader, all before the age of 30. It all came from one pitch.

111

With long, strong fingers, Sutter had a hand built to grip a baseball with his index and middle finger split along the seams. He could fire it to different levels of the strike zone, and without fail it appeared like a fastball before diving. "Whitey used to say I was the only pitcher who never threw a strike who didn't walk anybody," Sutter told baseball writer Rick Hummel. He didn't need to. In the heat of a pennant race in '82, it was the split-finger he fed Philadelphia third baseman Mike Schmidt for a deciding double play with the bases loaded and the Phillies about to lose to fall a half game back in the division. Sutter finished in the top 10 in MVP voting and top three in Cy Young voting in three of his four years with the Cardinals. He was the most dominant closer in the league and had the game's most bedeviling pitch. In 1984 Sutter signed a record-setting deal with Atlanta that would pay him an estimated $44 million coming off recording a career-high 45 saves his final season in St. Louis. By 1988, a series of shoulder surgeries led to his retirement with exactly 300 saves. He always said he didn't get to leave the game on his terms, and it took 13 tries for Sutter to receive enough votes for induction into the Hall of Fame and the ending he coveted.

The Hall of Fame "brought closure to a baseball career that did not end how and when I had always hoped it would," said Sutter, whose No. 42 was retired by the Cardinals a few months after his induction. "The call answered a question that had been ongoing for 13 years, a question quite frankly I would ask myself every year: Do you belong?" Does a split-finger plunge?

40 The Little General

From 1923 to 1953, the New York Yankees' dynasty claimed 16 World Series titles and lost just twice in the World Series to the

National League pennant winner. Both times the loss was to the Cardinals. Both times Billy Southworth was a reason. Southworth hit .345 as a player to help dispatch the Yankees in the 1926 World Series, and then Southworth managed the Cardinals when they upset the Yankees in the 1942 World Series. Other Cardinals managers are more well known or more beloved for their personalities, but none have been as successful as the skipper nicknamed "Little General."

Southworth first came to the Cardinals as an outfielder, acquired in a trade because his pluck could steady a franchise starting to get its legs as a contender. An ankle injury forced him out of the lineup and into a new career. Offered the post as manager of the Cardinals' minor league team in Rochester, New York, Southworth took the job and won four consecutive American Association championships. Other than a cameo appearance as Cardinals manager in 1929, he didn't return to the majors as a manager until 1940. That is when he began building the St. Louis Swifties. Southworth planted a former pitcher in left field and filled the youngster with confidence. Stan Musial repaid him with an MVP in 1943, the second of three consecutive MVPs for a Southworth charge. Southworth's Swifties won 106 games in '42, rallied to filch the pennant, and then won the World Series. From 1942 to '44, Southworth and the Cardinals won three consecutive pennants and two championships. With his 620–346 record, Southworth's .642 career winning percentage as Cardinals manager easily tops the franchise, and in his five full seasons as Cardinals manager, the club averaged 102 wins. He never had a losing season in any of his full seasons as a manager, and his .597 career percentage is fifth-best in baseball history. "Humbleness," he often said, "is greatness."

Southworth's son, Billy Jr., flew a B-17 bomber in World War II, always wearing his father's '42 World Series Cardinals cap for luck. Shortly before the start of the 1945 season, Billy Jr. died when his plane crashed during a training mission off Long Island.

Southworth spent most of the season mourning and left to helm the Boston Braves that next off-season. He turned them into winners, too, before leaving in the middle of the '51 season. Southworth's teams were famous for being speedy, fierce, and fundamentally sound and young. He had an eye for blossoming talent. His life after managing was spent scouting, where he again flashed that keen eye: signing a remarkable outfielder for the Braves by the name of Hank Aaron. In 2008 Southworth was inducted into the Hall of Fame posthumously. The adjectives on his Cooperstown plaque are big enough to fit the Little General: "sharp, serious, and successful manager with a relentless desire for victory."

41 The Train Rescue of 1911

Before the *Federal Express* train chugged out of Washington, future Hall of Famer Roger Bresnahan made the best call of his managerial tenure with the Cardinals. He said his players needed sleep on the way to Boston, and they couldn't get it with the Pullmans so close to the engine. He asked for the Cardinals' sleepers to be moved toward the back of the train. He likely saved his players' lives.

The Cardinals dealt their best pitcher, Bugs Raymond, and two other players to land Bresnahan as catcher/manager for the 1909 season. Bresnahan was the first to use shin guards and a chest protector and the first catcher inducted into the Hall of Fame, but his playing time was limited by his managerial duties with the Cardinals. After consecutive seventh-place finishes in his first two seasons with the Cardinals, Bresnahan had a competitive bunch in 1911. The Cardinals reached the midpoint of the season three games out of the lead. They ended May of that season rallying from an 0–8 deficit for a 15–8 victory, and they ended June with an umpire reportedly slugging Bresnahan for arguing a few calls.

On July 11 the Cardinals, in contention but beginning to fade, left Washington for Boston. Bresnahan had the team's Pullman relocated for more peaceful travel, and off the train rattled. Outside of Bridgeport, Connecticut, the train derailed and tumbled down an 18' embankment. Fourteen people were killed and 47 injured. None of them were players. The Cardinals, once free of their car, helped pull the injured and eventually the dead from the wreckage, working deep into night. During the rescue, Bresnahan saw that the car that replaced his team's Pullman near the front of the train was crushed and mangled by the crash. Many who died were in that coach.

The Cardinals continued on to Boston and won the first game of a doubleheader 13–6. The players were paid $25 for their rescue efforts and lost belongings.

42 The Daring, Underdog Debut of the Swifties

1942 World Series: Cardinals defeat New York Yankees 4–1

While the Kid Cardinals needed an uncanny run—43 victories in their final 51 games—to reach the World Series, the high-and-haughty New York Yankees sauntered to another 100-win season, another pennant, and another October as the favorite to win a sixth championship in seven seasons. The imposing pinstripes had not lost a World Series in eight consecutive visits, not since the Cardinals toppled them in 1926. The Cardinals' burgeoning young star, Stanley Frank Musial, was all of five years old the last time the Yankees lost in the World Series. There was little reason to think

Whitey Kurowski, Enos Slaughter, and Johnny Beazley celebrate after winning the 1942 World Series against the New York Yankees.

they would start now. Wrote Musial years later, "We were young enough not to worry."

Musial, 21 and in his first full season in the majors, was the youngest of the regulars on the youngest team in the big leagues. The St. Louis Swifties, as they were dubbed that season, featured one regular, center fielder Terry Moore, who was 30 years old. Five starting position players were 25 or younger, and three of the pitchers to make 15 starts that summer were 26 or younger. The innocence of youth may have been why in August, trailing the Brooklyn Dodgers by nine and a half games, the Cardinals weren't seasoned enough to know when to relent. Not even when general manager Rickey once bemoaned: "We don't have a chance."

The Cardinals reached a 22-game home stand in mid-August with an eight and a half-game deficit. The Swifties went 19–3 to close the gap to four and a half games, loose and laughing the whole way. Doc Weaver, at one point, hooked up a toy train's stoplight in the dugout, having it flash green when the Cardinals were batting and red when the opponent was up. The Cardinals even adopted a theme song, Spike Jones' "Pass the Biscuits, Mirandy." "In case you guys didn't notice, St. Louis is winning steadily," Boston Braves manager Casey Stengel told the East Coast media as the Cardinals rocketed up the standings. "Those jackrabbits from St. Louis are coming. Why, I've never seen anything like 'em. Every sonofagun can run like a striped-tailed ape."

By the time the Cardinals overtook Brooklyn and clinched the pennant on the last day of the season, they had set a franchise record for wins that still stands. Their 106 wins were the most by a NL pennant-winner since the 1909 Pittsburgh Pirates, and it was not eclipsed until Cincinnati's 108 wins in 1975. The team was more the sum of its standouts than hitched to one star. Enos Slaughter, all of 26, led the Cardinals in every major offensive category with 13 home runs, 100 runs scored, 98 RBIs, and a .318 average. He led the NL in total bases. Musial, still years away from being the Man, hit .315, third in the NL, and he drove in 72 runs.

Pitching was similar. The Cardinals' 2.55 staff ERA was the lowest in the majors since 1919. Mort Cooper led the NL with 22 wins, swapping jerseys and catering to superstitions all summer. Representative of the Cardinals' easy nature—what Rickey called his "imaginative, daring young club"—was Cooper's constantly rotating jersey numbers. Cooper stalled at 13 wins a couple times and decided, to dislodge his record, he would change his number. He wore No. 14 and won. He borrowed his brother Walker Cooper's No. 15 and won. He pulled on Ken O'Dea's No. 16 and won. This continued late into September, when the 210-pound Cooper stuffed and tucked his way into 157-pound Murry Dickson's No. 22. His outing was equally constricting as he held Cincinnati to two singles in a complete-game shutout.

Six days later, the Swifties welcomed the regal Yankees to Sportsman's Park and, with Cooper pitching, lost. New York had won 33 of its past 37 World Series games going into Game 2, a span that stretched back to their last World Series loss—that 1926 series against the Cardinals. The center fielder on that team, Billy Southworth, had aged into the manager of the '42 Cardinals and saw a similarity between the two teams. "We weren't over-awed," he told reporters.

Johnny Beazley, a right-hander, would go on to win only nine more games in his major league career after 1942. He missed three seasons serving in the Army Air Corps and returned with arm trouble that kept him from ever echoing his 21–6 rookie season. But he won both of his starts against the Yankees—Game 2 to level the Series and Game 5 to finish the Series. The Cardinals swept the Yankees at Yankee Stadium, in front of no less than 69,000 fans at each game, a crowd twice the size of the largest at Sportsman's Park. In Game 5 a 2–2 tie went into the ninth before rookie Whitey Kurowski batted. Third baseman Kurowski, 24, had nine career home runs when he connected on a pitch from Red Ruffing for a two-run, game-winning home run into the left-field stands. The Cardinals' stunning 4–1 series victory let the Yankees know the 1940s were not going to be their private October playground that the 1930s had been.

"That club had what I call the Cardinal spirit," Musial told *Post-Dispatch* baseball writer Rick Hummel more than six decades later. "We thought nobody could beat us."

43 Roomies and Rivals at Lindell Towers

Every time the Cardinals were returning home from a road trip, Ms. Edna Sewell would tidy up her family's apartment, pack any necessities, scoop up her two teenage daughters, Suzanne and Lois, and train home to Akron, Ohio. That was the deal. When the Cardinals were in town, her family wasn't. It worked wonderfully the entire 1944 season until the baseball team her husband managed shocked baseball with an unexpected World Series between the two St. Louis major league baseball teams. The Sewells—Edna, the girls, and father Luke, manager of the St. Louis Browns—suddenly had to consider unlikely housemates: Cardinals manager Billy Southworth and his family.

The shadow of World War II loomed over the 1944 season and the World Series, from the bomber cruising over Sportsman's Park and tilting for a better view of a championship game to the players missing from each team because of military service. Travel restrictions meant that tickets were sold only to people in the St. Louis metropolitan area, and the baseball town was aglow and agog for its Streetcar Series, the first World Series held entirely west of the Mississippi River. For the third—and likely the last—time the World Series was held in one ballpark, as both the American League–champion Browns and National League–champion Cardinals shared Sportsman's Park.

Like their teams, their managers also shared a home.

The war had created a housing shortage, and to find a place for their families in St. Louis, Southworth and Sewell struck an arrangement. With one of their teams always on the road, they would share an apartment at 3745 Lindell Boulevard, the Lindell Towers.

Mrs. Sewell would leave the apartment every time the Browns headed on the road and return to find it clean and empty after Mabel Southworth and daughter Carol had followed the Cardinals out of town. Though their husbands' clothes shared a closet, the two wives reportedly never met during the season. When the Browns won the pennant on the last day of the season—with a victory against the Yankees at Sportsman's Park—the managers realized both families could not fit in the apartment. So they flipped a coin for it.

The Sewells won the apartment.

Southworth moved out and set about winning the series.

The Streetcar Series

1944 World Series: Cardinals Defeat the St. Louis Browns 4–2

The Cardinals made quick work of the National League pennant, storming to a 36–16 start and taking a 19½-game lead in the standings by the end of August. They became the first NL team to win 100 games in three consecutive seasons, and they did so because, while so many teams lost their stars to military service, the Cardinals, for various reasons, were able to retain theirs. Marty Marion won the NL MVP that season, despite six players on his team hitting more home runs and six players on his team having a better batting average. He won the MVP with a .267 average and 63 RBIs, but as the Cardinals' shortstop, he anchored one of the best defensive teams ever. The team set a league record with a .982 fielding percentage while committing just 112 errors and turning 162 double plays.

Marion was able to play for the Cardinals because a back injury moved him lower on the draft list. Third baseman Whitey Kurowski had osteomyelitis. Left-handed pitcher Harry Brecheen went 16–5 during the regular season and threw a complete-game victory in his only World Series start. He was ineligible for the draft due to a spinal malformation. Stan Musial, who finished second in the NL with a .347 batting average, was 23 and robust, but he also had a child just born and was supporting his ill father.

With so many of Southworth's Swifties still in place, the Cardinals were the overwhelming favorites to topple their crosstown cousins. The Browns had finished sixth in 1943, and the '44 pennant was the only one the franchise would win in 52 seasons in St. Louis. Yet these underdogs, in the city and in the standings, had been embraced. For the first time since 1925—the season before the Cardinals' first World Series championship—the Browns outdrew the Cardinals.

Although they were the road team for the first two games, the Browns struck for a 2–1 lead in the World Series, winning Game 1 with George McQuinn's two-run home run as their only offense. Cardinals reliever Sylvester Urban Donnelly—known as Blix to his teammates—rescued the favorites in Game 2, pitching four innings in relief during an 11-inning win. The sidearmer bedeviled the Browns with his curve and struck out seven of the 15 Browns he faced. In the eleventh, McQuinn doubled to right. But on the next batter's attempted sacrifice, Blix pounced and threw McQuinn out at third base to squelch the rally and propel the Cardinals to victory. In Game 3 the Browns battled behind McQuinn's three hits and two RBIs for a 6–2 victory in their first "home" game of the series.

Not that Mrs. Emil Verban saw much of that pivotal game.

The Cardinals' meek-hitting second baseman learned after his team's loss that the Browns management—being at home for Game 3—had given his wife a ticket for an obstructed-view seat behind a post. Furious, Verban found Browns president Don Barnes and barked at him for the disrespect. "You ought to be sitting behind a post," Barnes allegedly scoffed to the infielder. Verban was a glove-first rookie, having hit all of .257 in the regular season—lowest of any Cardinals regular—and starting a career that would consist of 2,911 regular-season at-bats and one regular-season home run. In the first three games of the Streetcar Series, he was lifted for a late-inning pinch-hitter, including in Game 2 when Ken O'Dea delivered the eleventh-inning, game-winning single for Donnelly.

But after he learned about his wife's view of the game, Verban didn't yield to a pinch-hitter—or anyone else for that matter. He had a hit in each of the final three games of the series and punctuated the Cardinals' rally with three hits in Game 6. Verban's run-scoring single in the fourth inning of Game 6 broke a 1–1 tie and brought in the title-clinching run. He hit .412 in the series as the Cardinals became the first NL franchise with five World Series wins. The Streetcar Series decided, Verban bee-lined for Barnes' box. He found the Browns owner and fired: "Now you go sit behind the pole."

Bob Gibson

RHP...Inducted into Hall of Fame, 1981...Number retired, 1975

Several hours before a game, Pittsburgh Pirates All-Star catcher Manny Sanguillen walked in on his teammate, future Hall of Famer Roberto Clemente, to see him standing in front of a mirror wearing only a T-shirt, his socks, and underwear. Clemente struck his batting stance in front of the mirror, but instead of pantomiming his swing, he would glare into the reflection, cock up his hands, and then quickly jerk his head back. He did this repeatedly, each time snapping his head as if trying to avoid a wasp. Sanguillen watched, amused at first, and then confused.

"What are you doing?" Sanguillen asked.

Flamethrower Bob Gibson won 251 games and two Cy Young Awards during his 17-year career.

Clemente didn't take his eye off the mirror.

"We're facing Gibson today," Clemente explained.

Such was the reputation of the greatest Cardinals pitcher—even peers didn't prepare to face Bob Gibson as much as they prepared not to be cowed by Gibson. He was one mean cuss. "I hated the son of a bitch," said former teammate and now best pal Joe Torre who once hired Gibson to coach "attitude." Torre wasn't alone. Few pitchers in the history of the game intimidated like the Cardinals' right-hander with the fierce slider and fiercer demeanor.

"It was said that I threw, basically, five pitches—fastball, slider, curve, change-up, and knockdown," Gibson wrote in his autobiography. "I don't believe that assessment did me justice, though. I actually used about nine pitches—two different fastballs, two sliders, a curve, a change-up, knockdown, brushback, and hit-batsman."

Gibson, a native of Omaha, Nebraska, fought through asthma and a rheumatic heart as a kid. If everything was a battle when he

The Cardinals' Cy Young Award Winners

Bob Gibson, 1968: In the season that changed baseball, Gibson had a league-low 1.12 ERA, a league-high 268 strikeouts, and 22 victories, 13 of which were shutouts. Gibson also won the MVP.

Bob Gibson, 1970: The only time in his career that he led the National League in wins with 23 merited his second Cy Young. Gibson won every start in August (6–0, 2.31 ERA), while also hitting .303 all season.

Chris Carpenter, 2005: In the same living room where two years earlier he had considered surrendering to his injuries and retiring from baseball, Carpenter took the phone call that validated his decision: he'd won the second-closest voting ever for the Cy Young. Carpenter tied Gibson for the National League's longest stretch of consecutive quality starts with 22. And the right-hander became the only pitcher in 89 years of the live-ball era to go undefeated during a span of 16 consecutive starts while never allowing more than three runs and pitching at least seven innings in each. Carpenter ranked second in wins (21), fifth in ERA (2.83), and first in complete games (seven).

was young, Gibson made everything a battle as he became an athletic star. He freely admits anger was his fuel. He averaged 20.2 points a game in his basketball career at Creighton University, and he played with the Harlem Globetrotters in the off-season before, as he explained years later, the Cardinals "paid me enough to stop." He shut out Cincinnati in his first big-league start, in 1959, but it wasn't until 1961 that Johnny Keane installed him as a starter. Three years later, he was one of most feared pitchers in the game.

Gibson had five 20-win seasons, won 251 games, and pitched 255 complete games in a 17-year career that included two Cy Young Awards, an MVP, and a no-hitter against Pittsburgh in 1971. He redefined dominance in 1968 with a 1.12 ERA, the lowest of the era, and 13 shutouts, the most since Grover Alexander's 16 in 1916. "You only have a year like that once in a lifetime where everything is just right," he said on the 40th anniversary of his MVP and Cy Young season. "There are times when you don't have your best stuff when you still have to win. What are you going to count on then? You have to figure out a way to do it." He won his second Cy Young in 1970 after going 23–7 with a 3.12 ERA. "Hoot" led the National League in strikeouts just once in his career, but in 1972 he became the first to have nine seasons with at least 200 strikeouts, and in 1974 he surpassed 3,000 strikeouts, retiring with 3,117.

Gibson's career numbers were great enough to make him the 11th player elected to the Hall of Fame in the first year of his eligibility. His numbers in October made him a legend. In nine World Series games Gibson won seven, pitched eight complete games, and had a 1.89 ERA.

As striking as Gibson's numbers were, the man was even more compelling, complex, and overwhelming. Gibson knew only one way to compete: mad. He and Tom Seaver beaned each other in an exhibition game. In a 1991 Old-Timers' game, 16 years after he retired, Gibson hit a home run. He famously refused to talk to opponents, once going an entire All-Star Game without speaking to

Torre, his catcher, because after the game they would be back on opposing sides. Gibson felt he gained an edge by being unapproachable. He fostered this intense reputation, but he also earned it. Only his closest friends learned that Gibson could be as devoted and kind off the field as he was determined and ornery on it.

Clemente knew first-hand Gibson was not to be trifled with. In 1967 the Pirates outfielder lined a pitch off Gibson's leg, fracturing it. Gibson pitched to three more hitters before relenting to a broken bone. Three months later he held Boston to three runs in three World Series games.

"He represented winning," Torre said. "That grumpy smirk on his face. He'd basically say, 1 hour, 47 minutes of a game, win, lose, or draw, and nobody was going to get the ball from him."

Nobody wanted to. Nobody dared.

Class of Titans

1946 World Series: Cardinals Defeat Boston Red Sox 4–3

Enos Slaughter's immortalized dash for home was only the final 90′ leg of a sprint to the finish for the Cardinals in 1946. For the first time in franchise history, the Cardinals drew 1 million fans to the ballpark, and for the record crowd—which was nearly 350,000 more than the previous high—they put on a home-stretch show. Trailing Brooklyn by seven and a half games two days before the Fourth of July, the Cardinals won 61 of their final 89 games to catch the Dodgers and force another first—the major league's first pennant playoff.

The record-setting crowds came for the baseball, but also because the boys were back. By the start of the Cardinals' 1946 season, most of the ballplayers who served in World War II had returned to the major leagues. Stan Musial was one of the Cardinals who returned after missing the 1945 season. He found many changes to the Swifties' dynasty. Manager Billy Southworth had left to lead the Boston Braves and, in May, the Mexican League plundered the roster for three stalwarts, including pitcher Max Lanier. Money lured Lanier and the others away from the Cardinals. But not Musial. Despite a lucrative offer, the Man remained.

Playing first base for the first time in his career, Musial would win his second batting title with what was then a career-high .365 batting average. During a three-game, two-day, two-city span in August, Musial had 12 hits in 14 at-bats. In a key midseason series against the Dodgers, Musial went 8-for-12, and the nickname "the Man" was born out of a grumble from the Brooklyn faithful. But he was not a Man alone. Second baseman Red Schoendienst would help replace the offense lost by the defections, scoring 94 runs and batting .281 in his first All-Star season. In Lanier's absence, Howie Pollett emerged with his first 20-win season. The lefty went 21–10 for the 98–58 Cardinals. He also started the first game of the three-game playoff against Brooklyn, a predicament that drew the scorn and sarcasm of sportswriters in St. Louis. Hall of Fame scribe J. Roy Stockton raised a glass to Cardinals owner Sam Breadon and, citing several trades and the three departures, pointed to Breadon as the "man who made this close race possible. All the glorious excitement would have been missed."

The Dodgers won the coin flip for the playoff, but manager Leo Durocher elected to play the first game at Sportsman's Park to get two at Ebbets Field. The flip was all the Dodgers would win. Backed by catcher Joe Garagiola's three hits and two RBIs, Pollett pitched the Cardinals to victory in Game 1. The Cardinals laced 13 hits in Game 2 and Harry "the Cat" Brecheen closed the game with two strikeouts.

The victory in Brooklyn set up a World Series heavyweight bout of the game's elite hitters: the Cardinals' Stan Musial versus Boston's Ted Williams.

Both were just back from war and adding an October punctuation to MVP seasons. Williams was second in the American League in each Triple Crown category; Musial led the National League in six offensive categories. Combined, Musial and Williams ranked as two of the top three batters in the majors in batting average, on-base percentage, slugging, runs, total bases, and extra-base hits. Boston general manager Eddie Collins once said, "Musial couldn't hold Williams' glove." The two hitters would provide ample fodder for writers who often compared who was better—the National League's Musial or the American League's answer, Williams. While the '46 World Series didn't provide clarity, it did refute Collins' assertion. Musial didn't need to carry Williams' glove; his hands were full with a title.

Boston killed time and kept ready while the Cardinals played Brooklyn by playing a team of All-Stars. During a pastime game, knuckleballer Mickey Haefner hit Williams on the right elbow, causing it to swell. The Cardinals shifted their infield defense for Williams, causing him to fume. Only shortstop Marty Marion remained on the left side of the infield when Williams batted. The Cardinals held Williams to a .200 average in his only postseason appearance. All of his five hits were singles. Williams' struggles could have been the elbow or that lefty Brecheen handcuffed the hitter who would win a Triple Crown the next season. If nothing else, the Boudreau Shift—named for its originator, Cleveland manager Lou Boudreau—bedeviled Williams. As the Cardinals tied the series in Game 2, Brecheen tossed a 3–0 shutout. He fooled Williams with a screwball so much that the Splendid Splinter lost his grip on his bat. Even as the Red Sox answered the shutout in Game 3 when the series moved to Fenway Park, Williams burned the shift and shocked Boston with a bunt to the left side that he legged out. A headline the next day shouted: "Ted Bunts!"

Musial's average was only slightly better than Williams'. The Cardinals' MVP hit .222, but he had a hit or RBI in every game of the seven-game series, and of his six hits, five were for extra bases. The heavy lifting was done by catcher Garagiola, who had four hits and three RBIs in Game 4, and Slaughter. The right fielder drove in a run as Brecheen pitched the Cardinals to a decisive Game 7 at Sportsman's Park by allowing one run over a complete-game win in Game 6.

Slaughter wasn't supposed to play in Game 6, let alone risk his career again two days later by playing in the decisive Game 7. That game would end with a run for his life, a sprint that was the final flourish of a 21-season span that saw the Cardinals win nine pennants and six World Series.

47 Country's Mad Dash

Here's the pitch. There goes Slaughter. The ball is swung on. There's a line drive going into left-center field. It's in there for a base hit. Culberson fumbles the ball momentarily, and Slaughter charges around second, heads for third. Pesky goes into short left field to take the relay from Culberson. And here comes Enos Slaughter rounding third. He's going to try for home. —Mel Allen's call of Slaughter's dash during the broadcast of Game 7

During Boston's victory in Game 5 of the 1946 World Series, Slaughter took a fastball off the right elbow and was forced from the game. On the train trip back to St. Louis, team trainer Harrison "Doc" Weaver attempted to calm the injury with hot

Enos Slaughter slides home in Game 7 of the 1946 World Series. His run put the Cardinals ahead of the Red Sox 4–3 in the eighth. St. Louis held the lead to win the game and the Series.

packs. Dr. Robert F. Hyland attempted to convince the outfielder with cold truths. He told him that a blood clot in the arm could endanger more than just a few World Series at-bats and pleaded with the outfielder not to play again in the series. Amputation was a possibility. Slaughter responded: "It's my life, Doc. I'll play."

In Game 6 Slaughter made a tricky catch in right-center field, walked twice, and drove in Musial in the decisive third inning. In Game 7 he sprinted into baseball lore.

With the score tied 3–3 in the eighth inning, Slaughter singled to lead off the inning. Whitey Kurowski attempted to bunt him over to second and failed. Backup catcher Del Rice flied out to left. Two outs and Slaughter had not budged from first. But on a 2–1 pitch to Harry Walker, Slaughter took off for second, intent on stealing it. Walker sliced a line drive to left-center field, what will be remembered as a long single but is recorded in the box score as a double. Slaughter wheeled around second, even as center fielder Leon Culberson lunged, cut off the ball, juggled it briefly, and whipped a throw to the cutoff man, shortstop Johnny Pesky. "You'd have called it a fantastic notion that even the fleet Slaughter could score," penned famed sportswriter Red Smith. Slaughter kept chugging.

His famous dash—the "greatest ride since Paul Revere's," Bob Broeg later wrote—may have covered 270', but its history goes back much further. Culberson wouldn't even have been in the game had it not been for Dom DiMaggio injuring himself on the double that tied the score in the top of the eighth inning. Culberson came in to pinch run for DiMaggio and play center. (DiMaggio claimed to chide Slaughter later, telling the *New York Times* decades later, "I would have thrown you out at third, not home.") Slaughter put second behind him with thoughts of Culberson's arm and dug for third with something else on his mind. In Game 1 of the series Slaughter felt he could have scored the run that would have changed the 3–2, 10-inning loss had he not been held at third by third-base coach Mike Gonzalez. Manager Eddie Dyer told Slaughter if he was in the same situation again in the series to "go ahead." The manager promised to take responsibility.

With a World Series to win, Slaughter went ahead.

Culberson collected and threw.

Pesky paused.

Some say he did so in disbelief of Slaughter not stopping at third; others say the Red Sox shortstop froze. Slaughter long insisted nobody yelled to throw home, and when Pesky did throw, it was loopy and up the line. Shortstop Marty Marion said Gonzalez was yelling, "No, no, no." And Slaughter heard, "Go, go, go." Marion may have had the best sight for the dash. He was on deck and is featured in the iconic photo that has Slaughter skidding safely home, the winning run of the World Series: his right arm planted for balance, that injured right elbow that was supposed to keep him on the bench is instead bracing his famous slide. Musial later began to call it "Slaughter's run heard 'round the world." Slaughter had another name for it: routine.

"To me it was just a routine play...I scored from first," he said. "Routine play as far as I was concerned."

48 A Rain Check on Musial's Crown

After the 1947 season that saw him hit just .312, his lowest average yet as a big-leaguer, Stan Musial was frustrated by the Cardinals' second-place summer and his distant finish in the batting race. He used the off-season to shed some irritations—his tonsils and appendix. "Without them," he wrote in his autobiography, "I felt I could hit .350 again." He did even better than that.

Free of the infections and niggling aches that bothered him, Musial also returned to right field and felt so strong doffing a bat in spring that he shifted his hands down an inch, down flush to the knob of the bat. The result was a career year for Musial and one of the most brilliant offensive seasons of any era. At 27, he won his third MVP and established or challenged highs that had been set a decade or more before and wouldn't be tested again until decades later. Musial's new grip and enhanced strength produced a career-high 39 home runs, one shy of winning a Triple Crown. Except...he hit that 40th home run.

Exact details of the lost home run have grown fuzzy and faint with time, and documented proof of the home run has been elusive or inconclusive. But accepted legend—it has been featured in news reports and numerous books about Musial—holds that Musial drilled a home run in New York, most likely at the Polo Grounds, during a game that was lost to rain. Weather erased the homer that would have tied him with Ralph Kiner and Johnny Mize for the National League lead and given him, by definition, the only Triple Crown of his career. It also would have meant an unmatched sweep of the league's offensive categories. Musial led the NL in hits (230), total bases (429), doubles (46), triples (18), runs scored (135), on-base percentage (.450), and the two other gems of the Triple Crown: RBIs (131) and batting average (.376). Throughout Musial's career, no player in the National League had a higher single-season average than Musial's in 1948. He had five *fewer* strikeouts (34) than he did home runs. With that one rained-out homer, Musial would have been the only player in the century to lead the league in every major hitting statistic. He tied Ty Cobb's record with four five-hit games. His 230 hits were the most since Joe Medwick's 237 11 years earlier, and Musial's .702 slugging percentage—a staggering 138 points better than second-place Mize's—was the largest since Hack Wilson's .723 in 1930. Musial's 103 extra-base hits came four shy of tying the National League record. It was another 47 years before any hitter in the majors reached 100.

Yet the grandeur of Musial's overwhelming dominant '48 season hasn't resonated through history because of a rainstorm. In his autobiography, Musial writes he had a homer "washed out by rain." Pinpointing the date and the pitcher has proven elusive, however. Musial received 18 of 24 first-place votes for the MVP that season and became the first National Leaguer to win a third MVP. With that one rained-out homer he would be remembered as the last National Leaguer to win a Triple Crown, instead of Medwick in 1937. Though, to fixate on the one lost jewel, legit or legend, is to miss the true dazzle of a season that outgrew any crown.

"Of all the years I was credited with having 'carried' the Cardinals," Musial wrote three decades later, "1948 would have to be the season in which that exaggeration came closest to being true."

49 Meet Butch Yatkeman

He didn't swing a bat, didn't fire a pitch, and never dirtied a uniform, and yet few were as efficient at keeping them clean as the Cardinals diminutive equipment manager Butch Yatkeman. The Cardinals didn't win any of their first nine World Series championships without him.

The soft-spoken, always proper Yatkeman began working at Sportsman's Park as a bat boy for the visiting team in 1923. He was the Cardinals' bat boy the next summer, and he's one of the young chaps in the team photo for the 1926 World Series champions. In nearly six decades with the club, Yatkeman was there for 13 pennants and was the only employee of the club present for every one of the first nine championships. "The Cardinals never won a pennant without me," Yatkeman said.

In the early 1920s Yatkeman had odd jobs not just around the ballpark, but around St. Louis. He was paid by a tire company to spot balding tires on parked cars and jot down information so that a letter could be sent suggesting a new set. He was doing that when Cardinals trainer Doc Weaver pushed for Yatkeman to be hired full-time. He became the ballclub's Forrest Gump, the constant presence crossing paths with history and keeping their cleats tidy and bats ready. It was Yatkeman who tossed Stan Musial the jersey with a No. 6 on the back. It was Yatkeman who, during Prohibition, fashioned a false lid in some of the teams' red trunks so that scotch or vodka could be squirreled away for the ballplayers. It was Yatkeman who fashioned his own uniform, complete with the baby-blue pants and "Slugger Bird" logo. No matter the moment, it was Yatkeman. It was always Yatkeman.

He handled the mundane while others made history.

Joe Cunningham once joked that the best way to get cleats cleaned was "to put them in Musial's locker."

Talked into delaying his planned retirement one year, Yatkeman remained the team's equipment manager until the end of the 1982 season, which ended with Yatkeman's ninth title with the team. He died in 2000 at 91. "He wore a suit to work every day. He was the consummate gentleman," said Buddy Bates, Yatkeman's spring training roommate, apprentice, and dear friend. "He was too proud to tell you that he only missed one day of work in 59 years. He was recovering from being mugged. They took his World Series ring."

He was back at work a day later, a bandage wrapped around his head. The Cardinals bought him a replacement ring. After all, for decades they didn't have one without him.

Visit Spring Training

Roger Dean Stadium in Jupiter, Florida

On the back fields of the Cardinals' complex in Jupiter, Florida, outside the reach of Roger Dean Stadium's light standards, is really where a ballclub sprouts every spring. It is on the fan of a half dozen diamonds that spread out from the Cardinals' clubhouse that position battles are decided, fundamentals are honed, pickoff plays are scripted, and pitchers develop an annual spring allergy to PFP, or "Pitchers' Fielding Practice." It is on the backlots, during such seemingly humdrum workouts as live batting practice, that baseball is its most intimate—and its most revealing.

It was spring training where Albert Pujols announced his arrival as a bona fide star and forced the Cardinals, entering the 2001

Spring training in Jupiter, Florida, is a great place to get up close and personal with your favorite Cardinals players.

season, to put him on the roster. It was spring training where Stan Musial would put on displays of power during batting practice even as he tutored young players in the way of preparing for a season and being a Cardinal—young players like Bob Gibson. "He hit a home run over the fence at Al Lang Field…way over the street toward a hotel over there," Gibson recalled. "He came over to me and said, 'You ever seen anybody hit a ball that far? No, no, I don't think I ever have,' he says as he looks out there to where the ball disappeared. 'Now, I really hit that ball.' Then he'd just laugh and laugh."

The Cardinals spent 52 consecutive years holding spring training in St. Petersburg, Florida, and 57 years total in the town that became synonymous with the club. Some of that time was spent at historic Al Lang Field, the ballpark made famous, in part, as the home of the New York Yankees' spring-training camp. In 1998 the Cardinals moved to Jupiter, Florida, just north of West Palm Beach. Enticing them to migrate south was a posh, state-of-the-art facility nestled into a new planned community. The 7,500-seat Roger Dean Stadium is the only ballpark in Florida to host two major league teams' spring trainings, as the Cardinals share the facility with the Florida Marlins. That makes for a packed schedule: usually Roger Dean is dark for only one day during spring training. Roger Dean is also the facility used for the Cardinals' High-A affiliate, the Palm Beach Cardinals, and the rookie-level Gulf Coast League Cardinals. And it is home of the Dean Dog, an Italian sausage drowned in grilled peppers and onions. "We believe that's why," joked one Roger Dean employee, "it's the top dog in the Grapefruit League."

It's proximity to the players that makes spring different than any other time during the season, whether it's a seat on the berm behind the Cardinals' bullpen—less than an arm's reach away from that day's relievers—or on those backlots, within earshot of infield practice. The Cardinals have also historically populated their spring training with stars of the past, including Bob Gibson, Lou Brock, and a cast of visiting coaches that has included Willie McGee and Larry Walker. More than the sights, it's the sounds that are the real rites of spring. "One of the beauties of spring is the fans are close enough that they can see what the players are working on, but it's also close enough, personal enough that you can hear what the coach is saying, too," said former manager Tony La Russa. "Literally, every part of the game—offense, defense—is happening on those fields. This is the start of how a season comes together."

Nowhere and no times are better to land autographs than during or after these workouts. At each spring training, La Russa scheduled time to wade through extended pens and pennants and pictures of autograph hounds. Access to the backlots is free at Roger Dean, and the location is primo to score a scribble. Many players do the same as La Russa did, especially when there's a well-placed "please" or a well-timed "Mr." There was only one thing that kept La Russa from his appointed autograph rounds—a loss. Even in spring.

Address: 4751 Main Street, Jupiter, Florida

Web sites: Roger Dean Stadium, www.rogerdeanstadium.com; Palm Beach Cardinals, www.palmbeachcardinals.com

51 Wonderful Willie

The Cardinals, faced with a numbers crunch of historic and beloved players, have recently adopted an informal but exclusive policy when it comes to retiring a player's jersey. One criterion is the player must first be inducted into Cooperstown before his number can be painted on the Busch Stadium wall. A grassroots movement in Cardinals Nation is pushing for one exemption—a No. 51 exemption.

Willie McGee is the people's retired number.

In the waning days of his career, the soft-spoken outfielder returned to his roots and couldn't amble in the vicinity of home plate without eliciting an ovation. One of the most treasured personalities in Cardinals history, McGee had been a World Series hero and an MVP, festooning his popularity with all sorts of titles during his first tour with the Cardinals. It took an encore engagement at the end of his career to turn a star into an icon. "He looks like he doesn't have a friend in the world," broadcaster Jack Buck told sportswriter Vahe Gregorian in 1998. "Meanwhile, all the world is his friend."

McGee came to the Cardinals as an unknown minor leaguer in an unheralded trade in October 1981. A year later he played a

World Series game that got manager Whitey Herzog wondering if "anybody ever played a World Series game better than he did." In Game 3 against Milwaukee, McGee homered twice and stole two home runs with gravity-defying catches in a 6–2 victory. It punctuated a rookie year for McGee that included his May debut and a .296 average. In 1983, his first full season in the majors, McGee was an All-Star and a Gold Glove winner in center field. In 1985 he was the National League MVP with 56 steals and 114 runs. He was a piston for Herzog's teams that won three pennants and one World Series. McGee was known for his slashing, whippy swing that won two batting titles—including a .353 average in '85, the highest in the NL for a switch-hitter—and his unmistakable gait. A combination of hesitant and wobbly as he came to the plate, McGee was a deer in stride when he played the outfield. Bruce Sutter said his favorite characteristic of Busch II was "414′ to center field with Willie McGee out there."

It was that vulnerability when he came to bat as much as it was his glides in center that drew the devotion of the fan base. His No. 51 became famous, for it was as unusual and unexpected as the player who wore it.

"Wonderful Willie" was a shy, unassuming ballplayer, and remained so despite the deluge of attention an All-Star receives. In 1990 the Cardinals traded him and his .335 average to Oakland, his hometown club. He won the NL batting title while finishing the season with the A's. From there he played for San Francisco and Boston before returning to the Cardinals on a minor league contract in 1996. His return was nothing short of a revival. He hit .432 that September for a playoff-bound team, and that's when the ovations started. Almost every at-bat at home inspired one, and McGee would at times tear up as he dug in.

The populist movement to retire his number began a few years later, after he retired in 1999. McGee's No. 51 is not officially retired, yet the people's wishes have been granted as it remains in reserve, saved and unassigned each spring. He's worn it a few times when he appears as a guest instructor. But he does so quietly, saying he's far more eager to talk baseball with the current players than talk publicly about how he played in the past. "You'll look around for Willie McGee one day," he often said, "and he won't be around."

If the fans have their way, however, his number always will be.

Police Action at Sportsman's

The first St. Louis Browns franchise, the forefather of the Cardinals, was well on its way to a third consecutive American Association title in 1887, boasting a stretch where they had won 29 of 31 games and opened a lead as huge as 19½ by early September. Led by Tip O'Neill, who hit .492 in a season when walks counted as hits in the statistics, the Browns would score 1,131 runs that season and finish 95–40.

On July 10 of that season some 10,000 to 12,000 fans came to Sportsman's Park to see the best baseball draw in town, those dominant Browns. Outside the ballpark 25 mounted police welcomed the throng.

Browns owner Chris Von der Ahe had drawn the ire of teetotalers when he began to sell beer at his ballpark, and the spillover had led to a feud with religious organizations, as well. After years of baseball on Sunday under the banner of "amusement," some sects of St. Louis wanted the game reclassified as a "business" so that it fell under a law from the 1830s. Police warned Von der Ahe that he faced arrest if he allowed the July 10 game to start. Before the second inning, an officer interrupted the game and arrested Von der Ahe. Umpire Bob Ferguson attempted to keep the game going until he, too, was threatened with arrest.

It was proving to be that kind of season for the Browns.

Less than a week later, Charlie Comiskey, the manager and first baseman, halted a runaway gang of horses in the middle of a victory at Sportsman's Park. And a month earlier, Curt Welch, the impetuous center fielder, had been fined in June for stopping an opponent from reaching second base by decking him. On June 16 Welch was arrested in Baltimore at second base after sliding hard and upending an opponent. He was arrested for assault and later paid a fine of $4.50.

Here that same Baltimore club was visiting St. Louis, and police were back on the field, having arrested one member of the Browns organization and willing to arrest more. Ferguson called the game in the second inning, and fans were ushered out into the Sunday afternoon. Five days later Von der Ahe argued his case before a judge—and baseball has been legal on Sundays in St. Louis ever since.

53 The Owners

In March 1996 the boy who lent Eddie Gaedel his jersey for one of the most famous stunts in major league history continued a life in baseball by becoming the businessman who owned his hometown club. Bill DeWitt Jr. and two St. Louis natives and school chums— Fred Hanser and Drew Baur—purchased the Cardinals, Busch Stadium II, and surrounding parking garages for a reported $150 million.

The group, which purchased the team from Anheuser-Busch, was steeped in St. Louis as much as it was in baseball. DeWitt's father had owned the American League St. Louis Browns for a couple years, and as the team's batboy, Bill Jr. had the only jersey that would fit the midget Gaedel so that he could make his photogenic pinch-hit appearance for the Browns in 1951. Hanser has a gold pocket watch from his grandfather, Adolph M. Diez. A former vice president of the team, Diez got the pocket watch, with its engraved Birds-on-the-Bat logo, as a memento from the 1944 Cardinals-Browns World Series. After their own baseball practices as boys, the trio would swing by Sportsman's Park for the big-league game.

With DeWitt as the chairman and Hanser handling the day-to-day operation in the early years of their ownership, the group ushered in one of the most successful epochs in franchise history, on the field and financially. They entrusted the baseball operations to Walt Jocketty and Tony La Russa, who got the team to the playoffs in six of their first 11 years together, including the club's 16th and 17th pennants and their 10th World Series title. The trio, along with president Mark Lamping, also oversaw the organization's first season of 3 million in attendance, the first $100 million payroll, and the construction of a new downtown ballpark. Jocketty's assistant, John Mozeliak, took over in 2007, and he and La Russa teamed up to win the club's 18th pennant and 11th World Series in 2011.

"I've been a lifelong Cardinals fan, and it was a chance to work with two of my very best friends," Hanser told the *Post-Dispatch* shortly before the group closed on the deal for the team. "We heard [the brewery] say they wanted to concentrate on their core business.... That's what we're going to do—concentrate on our core business—baseball."

The other prominent owners in Cardinals history:

Chris Von der Ahe (1882–1898)

The Cardinals' first owner was also their most flamboyant. A teen when he immigrated to the States, Christian Frederick Wilhelm Von der Ahe made his name in the Sportsman's Park area with a grocery that specialized in knockwurst and a bar, the Golden Lion

Saloon, that sold beer to wash the knockwurst down. It was beer that brought him to baseball because he had an idea about bringing baseball to beer. Von der Ahe purchased a controlling interest in the St. Louis Brown Stockings, the club that would become the Cardinals, in 1882 and greased their full professional status and membership in the new American Association. Von der Ahe was too colorful to be bound by convention. He had a bushy moustache, a thick accent, and a booming personality. Writers across the country referred to him as "der boss president." Money troubles capsized his ownership, and a fire that blazed through Sportsman's Park was an insurance fiasco that forced Von der Ahe to sell the team at auction. In 1913 a headline ran with his obituary that proclaimed Von der Ahe was "The Man Who Put St. Louis on the Map."

The Robisons (1899–1910)

Frank and Stanley Robison were the owners of the National League club in Cleveland when they took possession of Von der Ahe's franchise. Interested in the larger and more devoted crowds in St. Louis, the Robisons worked quickly to upgrade the St. Louis club—even at the expense and demise of the Cleveland franchise—and, in so doing, sowed the seeds of the modern Cardinals. The Robisons ditched brown as the team's primary color and replaced it with a deep cardinal red that spawned the nickname "Cardinals."

Helene Britton (1911–1916)

With no heir of his own, Stanley Robison handed the Cardinals to his niece, Frank's daughter, Helene Robison Britton. Though she didn't immediately seize control of the club, when she did, "Lady Bee" became the first female owner of a professional sports team. A photo from one meeting of owners is featured at the National Baseball Hall of Fame with a caption that asserts Britton "braved criticism from the media and others."

Sam Breadon (1920–1947)

What began for Sam Breadon as a financial flirtation spurred by civic curiosity ignited a devoted romance and an era of ownership that established the Cardinals' identity as champions. The Cardinals won their first World Series six years after Breadon took majority control of the team, and under his guidance—from 1920 to the moment he tearfully stepped aside in 1947—the Cardinals won nine National League pennants and six World Series titles and produced a legion of Hall of Famers. Not bad for a businessman who came to St. Louis to work in a garage, made himself a millionaire by selling cars, and fell into baseball at the urging of friends. He once called that first stock purchase a "donation." Breadon bought four shares of the Cardinals for $200 in 1917. Four became a few more and then scores more—by 1919 Breadon was one of the largest stockholders. He was playfully known as "Singing Sam," a barbershop man who would break into song when celebrating a win. If baseball took him by the heart, sometimes he took it by the throat. Though later it was insisted the Cardinals routinely had among the highest payrolls, Breadon was notoriously frugal and sharp-toothed in negotiations. In 1947 he sold the team and, as with any love story, the two parties weren't the same apart. The Cardinals went 17 years before winning their next pennant, and Breadon died in 1949.

Anheuser-Busch (1953–1989)

Each year, he was at the reins of the parade that marked the beginning of the baseball season. Riding on the iconic Clydesdales and waving his red cowboy hat, brewmaster August A. "Gussie" Busch Jr. is the enduring image of Cardinals ownership, beloved as much for his unbridled showmanship as for the decades of prosperity his two businesses meant for St. Louis. "The Cardinals, like [Anheuser-Busch], are a St. Louis institution," Busch said the day he finalized the purchase of the Cardinals from Fred Saigh for $3.75 million.

"We hope to make the Cardinals one of the greatest baseball teams of all time." Gussie helped expand the Cardinals' brand off the field—and get a little bump for his beer, as well. In 1954 Anheuser-Busch regained its crown as King of Beers, and the Cardinals were the only major league club in town. Both of Busch's enterprises ruled. Over the next four decades Busch redefined the relationship between brewers and baseball. He perfected advertising at the ballpark, steeled the link between beer sponsorship and sports, and built a new Busch Stadium that was stage, billboard, and monument. Gussie was a folk hero. At spring training, he'd slip into a uniform and take the field with his ballplayers. Manager Whitey Herzog once told *Post-Dispatch* columnist Bernie Miklasz that Gussie sat on the bench during a spring training game only to get up to leave when the Cardinals had a 9–0 lead. "I got you nine," Gussie said. "You take it from here." Busch swore that come "hell or high water" he was going to bring a championship back to St. Louis. The Cardinals claimed three pennants in the 1960s and three more in the 1980s, winning three World Series while Gussie waved them on with his red cowboy hat. In 1984 the team retired the No. 85 for Gussie Busch to commemorate his 85th birthday and his eternal stamp on the franchise.

54 Tom Alston: The Trailblazer

In January 1954 Gussie Busch rented out a suite at the Beverly Hills Hotel and reportedly stocked it with caviar and Budweiser because the first major announcement of his ownership had to be a major production. The Cardinals were going to integrate.

Seven years after Jackie Robinson joined the Brooklyn Dodgers, the Cardinals signed Tom Alston to be the first African American to play on the major league club. One giant leap for the Cardinals, the southernmost franchise in baseball for much of its first century, was also a milestone for Major League Baseball, as it meant more than half of its teams had raised the racial blocks on their rosters. Busch had advocated and pushed for the move since taking ownership of the team. He scattered scouts across the country with the instruction to find and sign a black ballplayer. He famously remarked, "Hell, we sell beer to everyone."

On January 27, 1954, the Cardinals announced they paid the Pacific Coast League's San Diego franchise $100,000 and sent a total of four players west to secure the rights to Alston. He was a strapping first baseman, 6′5″ and 225 pounds, with a slick glove who had just hit .297 with 207 hits, 23 homers, and 101 RBIs for San Diego. Busch was so thrilled with the deal that he flew to California to complete it himself.

"I have been hoping that it would happen, hoping and waiting," Alston said at the press conference, held four days before his 28th birthday. "And now it's a wonderful feeling to know the dream has come true."

On April 13 of that season, Alston made his debut. His first big-league hit was a home run. He'd hit just three more in his career, all coming in that first season. The Cardinals believed that Alston was not just going to be a trailblazer for their roster but also a fixture at first base. He spent parts of four years with the club, mostly shuttling between the majors and the minors. He never had more than 20 at-bats in a season after the 244 he got in 1954. He dealt with racism, both overt and subtle, and executives would later believe Alston heaped too much pressure on himself. He had mood swings, fits of depression, and a severe exhaustion that crippled his career. He was diagnosed with neurasthenia, a mental disorder that manifests with physical ailments. Whether it was physical or mental, Alston's talent eroded. He played his 91st and final game in the majors in 1957. The Cardinals offered him a chance to stay in

St. Louis and receive treatment, but he returned home to North Carolina, graduated, and spent parts of the next decade seeking help at various institutions.

In 1991, two years before Alston died from cancer, Joe Garagiola, a St. Louis native and big-leaguer whose last year in the majors was Alston's first, spoke at an area college about how Alston should never be forgotten as a pioneer. "I called Tom Alston, [and] he could hardly believe it," Garagiola described. "I challenge one, two, or three of you to remember what he achieved.... Make the guy feel that you care."

Frankie Frisch: The "Pilot Light"

2B/MGR...Inducted into Hall of Fame, 1947

Sitting in his hotel room in St. Louis, Frankie Frisch made the career-altering decision to leave town on the next train out and put in motion a journey that would bring him back to St. Louis as part of baseball's first blockbuster trade. In 1926 Frisch was the star second baseman for the New York Giants, a local boy done good and the protégé of manager John McGraw. His relationship with McGraw started to fray, and one night after a game against the Cardinals that Frisch played with aching legs, he decided to respond to McGraw's slights by leaving town. Frisch packed his stuff, left the St. Louis hotel, and trained back to New York.

He'd be back in St. Louis the next season. Feuds on both sides forced an unthinkable trade.

Fed up with Rogers Hornsby's salary demands, Cardinals owner Sam Breadon dealt the fan favorite and future Hall of Famer to the Giants for Frisch. The move came two months after Hornsby led the Cardinals to the club's first World Series victory. Fans threatened to boycott the team. The Chamber of Commerce denounced Breadon. Everyone was furious. They didn't bother to consider the star they were getting in return. Frisch had hit .314 in 1926 and continued his stellar play at second base. While nowhere near Hornsby's equal at the plate, he was the Rajah's echo in the field and an inspiring leader. The erudite Frisch had been captain of the basketball, football, and baseball team at Fordham. He came straight out of college and into the major leagues, never spending a day in the minors. In 1924 he captained the Giants to their fourth consecutive pennant.

Knowing the vitriol that awaited him in St. Louis simply because he wasn't Hornsby, Frisch retreated to upstate New York for the winter and got "in the best shape I've ever been in," he said later. He skied. He ice skated. He ran daily. He challenged bobsledders. And a few months into the season, he won over the Cardinals faithful. In 1927 Frisch hit .337, scored 112 runs, and drove in 78. The switch-hitter struck out just 10 times in 617 at-bats. In the field the stocky and speedy "Fordham Flash" handled 1,037 chances, scurrying and scooping on both sides of second base. It's a record that still stands for middle infielders. "I'll tell you this," Breadon told sportswriters shortly before he died, "the greatest single-season player I had was Frank Frisch in 1927." That season Frisch finished second in the MVP voting. Hornsby, strong for the Giants, finished third.

Frisch would win the MVP with the Cardinals in 1931, coupling a .311 average with a reputation for leading the world champs. Late in 1933 Breadon made it official. Frisch was a player/manager for the Cardinals from 1933 to 1937, guiding the motley crew of the Gas House Gang to the 1934 title. Hall of Fame sportswriter Bob Broeg called him the "pilot light of the wacky Gas House Gang." Author Robert Gregory referred to him as "the hardest-boiled egg in the Redbird nest." He spent 11 years with the

Cardinals and didn't hit less than .290 until his final two years with the club. He was an October fixture, appearing in eight World Series and winning four, two each with the Giants and Cardinals. After leaving the Cardinals, he managed Pittsburgh and the Chicago Cubs and still never spent a day in the minors.

In 1947 Frisch, revered by his contemporaries, was elected into the National Baseball Hall of Fame. He entered five years after the guy he was traded for did. "He didn't make them forget Hornsby," Broeg once wrote, "but rather, remember Frisch."

56 "Hollywood's" Blockbusters in the Clutch

Jim Edmonds' Big Hit and Bigger Catch Win a Theatric 2004 NLCS

Had Cardinals center fielder Jim Edmonds not made the daring catch in Game 7, his dramatic home run in Game 6 would have been lost to the yellowing snapshots and one-night grandstands of Octobers past.

Less than 24 hours after he forced a final and deciding game in the 2004 National League Championship Series with a twelfth-inning, walk-off home run, Edmonds was furiously sprinting, lunging, leaping, extending for a line drive smoked by Brad Ausmus that threatened to blow open Game 7. As his cleats ripped through the Busch Stadium center field and his legs burned, Edmonds had one thought echoing through his skull: this was the catch that would determine the game, the series…the season.

"I remember the moment. I remember the situation. It was a pivotal point in the game. The only other thing I can remember was what I was thinking," Edmonds said. "I do remember when the ball was in the air, I do remember thinking that *If you don't catch this ball, this is going to be it.* I was running and running, and that was going through my head. *This is probably the game right here if I don't make this play.*"

Though it began as a mismatch—the 105-win Cardinals had won the National League Central with a 13-game gap on Houston—the 2004 NLCS became a classic. Every one of the seven games had at least one lead change. The visiting team scored in the first inning in six of the seven games, yet the home team won every game. The series was a showcase of burgeoning stars, pitting Houston's Carlos Beltran against the eventual series MVP, the Cardinals' Albert Pujols. It started in the first inning of the first game of the series when Beltran cranked a two-run home run for a quick 2–0 lead and, in the bottom of the inning, Pujols answered with a two-run home run to knot the game 2–2. Three of the seven games were decided in the last at-bat of the winning team. All seven were decided by three runs or fewer. When Jeff Kent's ninth-inning, three-run, game-winning home run provided the only runs of Game 5, the series returned to St. Louis with the Astros having scored two more runs total than the Cardinals, 25–23. On October 20, 2004, the Cardinals turned to their stalwart starter, Matt Morris, to pitch them back into series. Houston had to cobble together a start, and when Morris left the game, the Cardinals led 4–3. Four innings later Jeff Bagwell's RBI single in the ninth tied it and gave Houston the chance to win the pennant in extra innings.

As the game grew longer, the innings tenser, and the crowd louder, the atmosphere had a tang of electricity.

It was tailor-made for Edmonds.

The Cardinals landed the dazzling center fielder from the Anaheim Angels in a spring training deal before the 2000 season. The trade became the first flicker of one of the most prosperous eras for the Cardinals. Edmonds drove in 100 runs in three of eight seasons in St. Louis, averaged 30 homers a season, and won six consecutive Gold Gloves. He came to the Cardinals with the

Jim Edmonds hit a twelfth-inning, walk-off home run off the Astros' Dan Miceli in Game 6 of the 2004 NLCS.

"Hollywood" label and a showboat reputation to match. His circus catches were stock footage for any B-roll on defensive gems. And his flair for the dramatic only underscored the nickname he was reluctant to embrace.

Throwing despite his busted hand, Julian Tavarez pitched two scoreless innings in relief that night to carry the game to Edmonds' at-bat in the twelfth. Houston reliever Dan Miceli faced the heart of the Cardinals' order—the "MV3" of Pujols, Scott Rolen, and Edmonds. Pujols walked on four pitches. Rolen popped up to the catcher in foul territory. Edmonds took the stage.

He heard nothing.

"When you're in the moment, things just seem to disappear in your head," Edmonds said. "I can't remember even hearing the crowd. I don't remember the swing of the bat. I've seen the video and the pictures. It seems like that is how I remember it. I figured somebody was going to win the game eventually."

With his signature upper-cut swing, Edmonds launched Miceli's second pitch to him deep and gone into the chilly night for a 6–4 victory. Edmonds clutched his fists and double-pumped as he watched the ball reach the right-field stands. Days before he ended the riveting, almost four-hour game, he had told reporters that "it's the postseason…when people do superhuman things." But the impact of his heroics would have faded if not for his catch the next night.

For Game 7, Houston turned to seven-time Cy Young Award–winner Roger Clemens. Opposite Clemens was Cardinals

The MV3

In 2004 the Cardinals boasted three legitimate Most Valuable Player candidates, often batting in succession in their lineup: No. 3 hitter Albert Pujols, cleanup hitter Scott Rolen, and No. 5 hitter Jim Edmonds. The trio inspired the moniker "MV3," and it lasted even beyond their prime season of 2004. Not one of them won the actual MVP award—Barry Bonds did, again—but in a fitting tribute, the three Cardinals finished third, fourth, and fifth in the voting, as if they were listed in order of where they hit.

Player	MVP Rank	Pts	BA	HR	RBI
Albert Pujols	No. 3	247	.331	46	123
Scott Rolen	No. 4	226	.314	34	124
Jim Edmonds	No. 5	160	.301	42	111

starter Jeff Suppan, dueling Clemens for the fifth time that season. He did not win any of the previous four. The Astros' Craig Biggio led off the game with a home run, and in the second inning Houston threatened to bully Suppan into surrendering the pennant. Kent walked, and Jose Vizcaino singled. With one out and Clemens on deck, catcher Brad Ausmus had a chance to bust the game open. Suppan fell behind and fed Ausmus a fastball that he ripped to the left-center gap.

Cardinals announcer Mike Shannon likes to joke that his teammate Curt Flood had such success in center because he played it starting with his back against the wall. Edmonds, Shannon kids, plays center by starting at second base. Ausmus' scorched liner seemed destined to land in left-center and skip to the wall, clearing the bases for a 3–0 lead. From shallow center, Edmonds didn't appear to have a chance.

But he had a great jump.

He had even better closing speed.

His dive had instinctual timing.

And he snared the ball.

Outfitted with a microphone for the game, Houston coach John Tamargo said as Ausmus returned to the dugout: "How in the world did he make that play?" From shallow center, Edmonds had to break quickly to his right and back into the gap after Ausmus made contact. Edmonds made the catch running and lunging with his back to home plate. He had all of three and a half seconds from contact to catch.

"It pretty much changed the game," Ausmus said.

In the sixth inning Pujols tied the game with a double off Clemens, and one pitch later Rolen delivered the pennant with a two-run home run off Clemens. Those hits provided the deciding runs, but it was Edmonds' dramatics, two nights running, that delivered the first pennant in 17 years.

"It could have been anybody," he said. "I'm glad it was me."

57 The Tragedies

On the inside of his left wrist, a private locale usually only he sees, Jim Edmonds has a couple tributes etched into his skin. Both are in black. Both are in simple print. One reads "DK 57" and the other "JH 32." "For teammates," he once explained.

Fallen teammates.

Forever teammates.

Edmonds' memorial tattoos are for Cardinals pitchers Darryl Kile, who wore No. 57, and Josh Hancock, who wore No. 32, both of whom are among the few players to have died during a season in which they played. Kile died on June 22, 2002, when a heart attack kept him from waking up in a Chicago hotel room the morning of a game against the Cubs. Five years later, on April 29, 2007, Hancock was killed in a traffic accident less than a two-minute drive from the ballpark. Since 1975, six major league players have died during the regular season. Two were Cardinals. "This is brutal to go through if it happens in your family," said Tony La Russa, the manager in both seasons. "We know it all too well."

A few days before his death, Hancock arrived late at the ballpark, putting a scare into all of his teammates who had been Cardinals in 2002 when Kile didn't show up at Wrigley Field. Hancock had been a late addition to the 2006 club, earning a spot in the Cardinals' bullpen a few weeks after being released by Cincinnati. It didn't take that long for the other relievers to warm to their social director. He served an inglorious but crucial role in 77 innings that season on the way to a World Series title, often absorbing innings in blowouts. But he did it well enough that the next spring, when numbers threatened to nudge him from the majors, pitching coach Dave Duncan said "what he did was so important. What he did goes a long way."

The night before his death, Hancock did what the Cardinals always asked of him—he pitched three innings in an ugly 8–1 loss to the Cubs. Early the next morning, Hancock's SUV collided with a parked tow truck, killing him instantly. He was 29. Police said he was legally drunk at the time of the accident, and Hancock's death inspired changes to alcohol policies across baseball. More than half of the big-league teams rewrote their rules concerning the availability of alcohol in the clubhouse and on team charters in the weeks after.

A year later, a black circle with Hancock's initials and number hung above the doorway the players pass under each night after a game.

That is, after they walk past a portrait of Kile. Two other club-houses in the majors have a similar portrait of the left-hander—in Houston and in Colorado. Kile called all three clubhouses home in his 133-win, 12-year big-league career. He twice finished in the top five in voting for the Cy Young, including when he went 20–9 with a 3.91 ERA in 2000, his first year with the Cardinals. They acquired him in a trade with Colorado, and they got much more than a durable starter with the league's best knee-buckling curveball. They

The Darryl Kile Award

In 2003 the St. Louis Chapter of the Baseball Writers Association of America began awarding one player with an award named for Kile. The award is chosen by Cardinals and given to a player who displayed leadership and compassion throughout the season. The winners:

2003	Mike Matheny
2004	Woody Williams
2005	Cal Eldred
2006	Chris Carpenter
2007	Russ Springer
2008	Adam Wainwright
2009	Skip Schumaker
2010	Matt Holliday
2011	Lance Berkman

got a leader. They got a mentor. Kile tutored young pitchers Matt Morris and Rick Ankiel. He inspired teammates like catcher Mike Matheny. His on-field tenacity was contagious. His off-field kindness was unmatched. He was the team's most generous tipper.

On June 18, 2002, Kile was the winning pitcher for the Cardinals after throwing 7⅔ innings and holding Anaheim to one run. Kile's victory put the Cardinals in first place, and its final pitch came an hour before Jack Buck, the radio voice for generations of Cardinals Nation, died. Less than a week later the Cardinals found themselves mourning again, as Kile died in his sleep. He was 33.

As they did years later for Hancock, when the Cardinals returned to the field, Kile's jersey hung in their dugout. Morris took a No. 57 jersey to that year's All-Star Game and hung it prominently. A year later an award was established in Kile's name and given annually to the player who best shares Kile's inspiration and leadership. "That award means more to me than anyone could ever know," teammate Russ Springer said. Told of a winner whose approach on the mound mirrored Kile's, a Cardinal said: "Darryl would approve." The Cardinals plan to keep his No. 57 unofficially retired. They never did relinquish the first place Kile got them in 2002, taking the NL Central and reaching the NLCS before losing to San Francisco. On the day Kile didn't join them at the ballpark, the Cardinals were 40–31. Of their next 91 games that season, they won 57.

58 Play a Game of Catch at Stan Musial Field

Built especially for kids but meant for everyone, the Cardinals have dotted the St. Louis region with neighborhood ballparks that are mostly open to the public. On any given weekend, there could be several men's hardball league games at Jack Buck Field while a tripleheader of youth games is going on at Red Schoendienst Field. A grade-schooler can make a tumbling catch at Jim Edmonds Field. A high schooler can mash a homer at Mark McGwire Ballpark.

At the dedication for Lou Brock Field in the Murphy Park neighborhood of St. Louis in August 2007, St. Louis mayor Francis Slay called the youth ballpark "an anchor in a neighborhood that has been revitalized." Brock called it the "centerpiece of a neighborhood" and hoped that it would be the "spark" for the children in the community and a "bridge to help [them] cross the road into the world, into opportunities beyond your world."

The Cardinals' charitable arm, Cardinals Care, has distributed more than $14 million to children's program in the St. Louis area since the program began in 1997. A sizeable portion of that has gone to running the Redbird Rookies program. The Cardinals, with cooperation from local businesses, provide bats, balls, gloves, and other equipment to children ages five to 13 in leagues around the area. In 2007 a total of 22 neighborhoods had teams in several age groups, and approximately 2,000 kids participated. In 2000 the program began refurbishing—or in some cases just building from dust—fields for some of the leagues. Brock's was the 13th field constructed. One of Hall of Famer Ozzie Smith was the 19th, christened in 2009.

In 2001 outfielder Jim Edmonds donated to help construct the second ballpark revitalization by the Cardinals. He said he wasn't quite sure what to expect when he arrived at the dedication of the field "and then you see all the kids and what it means to them and their neighborhood to have a place to go and play," he said. Mark McGwire was a surprise attendee at the dedication for the ballpark that bears his name. The dedication was followed by a high school baseball tournament, and McGwire promised an autographed baseball to the player who hit the first home run at the field.

Dedicated in Their Fields

A selection of Cardinals Care fields dedicated in the St. Louis metro area:

- Hamilton Heights. Located at Clara and Wells Avenues in North St. Louis. Founded September 2000.
- Jim Edmonds Field. Forest Park southeast neighborhood. Founded June 2001.
- Police Athletic League Memorial Park. Located in Fox Park, the field was funded in part by Cardinals pitcher Darryl Kile for St. Louis city police officers who were killed in the line of duty. Founded September 2001.
- Spirit Field. Spanish Lake County Park. Built specifically so that children in wheelchairs could use the park to play baseball. Founded 2002.
- Edgar Renteria Field. At the Jackie Joyner-Kersee Center in East St. Louis, Illinois. Founded July 2002.
- Whitey Herzog Field. A regulation-sized ballfield located in Belleville, Illinois, at Citizen's Park. Founded June 2003.
- Heine Meine Field. Cardinals Care paid for an upgrade in the lighting system and other improvements for the Lemay, Missouri, park. Founded July 2003.
- Jack Buck Field. Located at Midland Boulevard and Purdue Avenue at Heman Park in University City, Missouri. Founded August 2003.
- Mark McGwire Ballpark at Aviation Field. Renovated with the assistance of St. Louis University High, the field is in Forest Park. Founded April 2004.
- Woody Williams Field. In Northwoods, Missouri, a suburb northwest of St. Louis and located just off Interstate 70. Founded August 2004.
- Stan Musial Field. Part of Koeneman Park in Jennings, Missouri. It is located at Robley Drive and Lucas-Hunt Road. Founded June 2005.
- Red Schoendienst Field. Located in Normandy, Missouri. Founded July 2006.
- Lou Brock Field. Built into the center of the Murphy Park neighborhood in central St. Louis. Founded August 2007.
- Bob Gibson Field. Located in the Sherman Park neighborhood, north of Forest Park and in the 1500 block of Kingshighway. Founded August 2009.
- Ozzie Smith Field. Adjacent to Vashon High School, a St. Louis city public school located midtown, on Cass Avenue. Founded October 2009.
- Yadier Molina Field. In Welston, Missouri. Founded April 2011.

While they are built to be used by Redbird Rookies teams, most of the fields can be rented from the various cities or used casually for a game of catch. They have fences, but only to keep cars out, not players. Lou Brock Field had a lock for one of its gates, but when asked about whether it would be open to anyone who wanted to play, a neighborhood member said, "That's what it is here for. For everyone who wants to play."

59 "Sunny Jim" Bottomley's Brightest Day

His hat always tilted comfortably and his grin always beaming engagingly, Jim Bottomley became Branch Rickey's prototype player—one of the first superstars homegrown and harvested from a minor league farm system.

The son and brother of coal miners in Nokomis, Illinois, Bottomley signed with the Cardinals after Rickey's scouts saw him lace three triples in a semipro game. Bottomley was a gifted fielder at first base and had a left-handed swing that would become one of the most potent in the league. The Cardinals cultivated him from area teen to baseball's first MVP plucked from a team's farm system. "We tied him up, shoes and all," Rickey said about signing him.

Bottomley's disposition earned him the nickname "Sunny Jim," and he rapidly became a favorite of the Knothole Gang and his teammates. The power that came with forearms marbled with muscles from his youth as a blacksmith apprentice didn't hurt. Signed in 1919, Bottomley had his first full season in the majors in 1923. He hit .371, drove in 94 runs, and had 194 hits. In a decade with the Cardinals, Bottomley propelled the franchise into its first age as a champion. He led the league in RBIs twice and won the 1928 MVP with 42 doubles, 20 triples, and 31 home runs while becoming only the second player to have at least 20 of each extra-base hit.

Bottomley died in 1959 of a heart attack and was posthumously inducted into the Hall of Fame in 1974. Fifty seasons after his death, one of his major league records still stood. On September 16, 1924, at Ebbets Field, a 24-year-old Bottomley went 6-for-6 with a record 12 RBIs. His record came only four years after the RBI became an official statistic, so the St. Louis papers struggled to define Bottomley's big day, some describing it as if he conjured a previously unforeseen feat. The *St. Louis Globe-Democrat* announced: "First Sacker Creates Major League Record for Runs Driven Over." The *Post-Dispatch* screamed in all capital letters: "BOTTOMLEY SMASHES BATTING RECORD."

Bottomley collected the 12 RBIs on three singles, a double, and two home runs. He got six hits off five different Brooklyn Robins pitchers, including the two homers off Art Decatur. Robins manager Wilbert Robinson watched from the opposite dugout as Bottomley snapped a record he set in 1892 with 11 runs driven in. Robinson actually did more than watch. He abetted. In the fourth inning Robinson called for an intentional walk of Rogers Hornsby to load the bases for Bottomley. The 6′ first baseman then whipped Decatur's pitch out of Ebbets for his fourth, fifth, sixth, and seventh RBI. In the seventh inning Bottomley tied Robinson's record with a two-run single off Tex Wilson. He broke it with an RBI single off

Bottomley's Record RBI Day

Inning	Opposing Pitcher	HIT	RBIs
1	Rube Ehrhardt, RHP	S	2
2	Bonnie Hollingsworth, RHP	D	1
4	Art Decatur, RHP	HR	4
6	Art Decatur, RHP	HR	2
7	Tex Wilson, LHP	S	2
9	Jim Roberts, RHP	S	1

Jim Roberts in the ninth to cap a 17–3 victory. Bottomley finished the year with 111 RBIs, the first of six consecutive 100-RBI years, an accomplishment listed alongside the 12 RBIs on his plaque in Cooperstown.

It was 20 years before another National Leaguer would drive in 10 runs in a game. Bottomley's record, yet to be surpassed, wasn't equaled until late one night in 1993. It took another Cardinal to do it.

60 The Keeper of the Cardinal Way

It could have been any spring training and it could have been any drill, but this was his 65th spring training, and this was bunting, his specialty in those days. Nothing to George Kissell at that moment was more important than proper bunting. Two catchers, one a rising star and the other a veteran whose star long ago dimmed, had just left the cage, when Kissell, 84 at the time, turned to a visitor and said, "I like to see progress."

For seven decades, Kissell was the curator of that progress, the keeper of the Cardinal Way.

Kissell became a Cardinals farmhand on July 5, 1940, became a coach six years later, and spent the next 60 years developing and teaching how a Cardinal plays baseball. The organization claims there isn't a player who came through their system who doesn't have Kissell's fingerprints on his career. Kissell taught Ken Boyer and Joe Torre how to play third base, Terry Pendleton how to play the infield, and Andy Van Slyke how to play the outfield. The team still uses cutoff routes and bunt defenses he devised or advocated. In New Orleans one season Kissell told a young ballplayer named Anthony "Tony" La Russa that he should give up the bat and take up a fungo. He'd make a better manager, Kissell told the man who'd become the winningest manager in Cardinals history.

In 1989 *Sports Illustrated* wrote about Kissell's influence on the club in an article titled "The College of Cardinals." Kissell was its dean, its chief "fundamentalist," as his pupils called him. A substitute teacher in the off-season and a Socrates of the dugout during it, he cloaked lessons in questions and quips. He chided players that his "wife could bunt better" or that spring training was really "spring cleaning—a time to knock the dust out of you." He did more than teach the courses at the College of Cardinals, he authored the textbooks. Sparky Anderson, a protégé, once called Kissell the "smartest man in baseball."

The Cardinals have a rainout, of sorts, to thank.

In 1940 Kissell received an invitation to a tryout in Rochester, New York. His father told him he couldn't go because there was hay to cut and bail. When rain came, hay couldn't be cut, couldn't be bailed, so his father drove him to the tryout. Kissell wore No. 385, but said he left the field that day as one of two players with a contract. Branch Rickey gave his father $20 to cover gas, saying the remainder was Kissell's signing bonus.

As a player, Kissell got as high as Class A. As a coach, he inspired an entire organization. "He is the organization," Torre told the *St. Louis Post-Dispatch* shortly after he became manager in 1990.

Kissell served the Cardinals as a player/coach, a player/manager, a manager, a scout, a special scout, an instructor, a traveling instructor, a special instructor, and, through his 65th spring training, a "senior field coordinator for player development." That's a mouthful for his true title: guru. Surrounded by big-leaguers and wannabe big-leaguers, Kissell was quite like a baseball Yoda, the wizened expert molding the gifted, giving the talented purpose. Or, in some cases, re-purpose.

Boyer was a pitcher who became an MVP at third after working with Kissell. The coach planted Torre in front of a wall, facing it, and then would whip balls off the wall to hone Torre's reaction time

George Kissell spent 69 years with the Cardinals organization as a player, coach, manager, scout, and all-around guru.

with the ricochets. When John Mabry wanted to learn third base, Kissell took away his glove and told him to kneel at the position, fielding grounders with his bare hands. "Basically he took me out there and beat me to death with a fungo," Mabry said. "By the time you know it, you've fielded 500 groundballs."

In 1993 Kissell received minor league baseball's "King of Baseball" award, given for service to the game. He received an eight-minute standing ovation. Another came in 2003, when *Baseball America* gave him the Roland Hemond award for lifetime commitment to the game. Five years later, Kissell died from injuries sustained in a car accident, and at his memorial, which was held at Tampa's historic Al Lang Field, Jim Riggleman, a Kissell protégé and big-league manager, called his mentor "maybe the greatest person who ever wore the Cardinals uniform." True, and also among the most influential.

In 2005 Kissell walked out of the team's spring training clubhouse to find players gathered around the door, waiting for him to step out into the middle of their circle. A day after he told those two catchers that the bat "does what you tell it to," the Cardinals revealed a plaque that commemorated Kissell and renamed the clubhouse in his honor. The fundamentalist wept a bit as a team official read the inscription that ended: "George taught several generations of Redbirds how to play baseball." Which is to say he taught an entire organization how to play.

"I've always been known as a hard-nosed guy, but today you really touched me to the heart," Kissell told the gathered players. "I'll never take the birds off my chest. When I take them off, that's my last day in baseball."

61 Attend a Stan Musial Society Meeting

As one of the Democratic party's most ubiquitous and influential pacesetters, a political legend in many circles, Frank Mankiewicz knows his way around Washington, D.C. Instinctively, it didn't take him long to find the high ground. Mankiewicz would drive up Wisconsin Avenue as often as he could during the summer, park his car near the National Cathedral, and tune in his passion on the radio.

At Washington's highest point, KMOX came in loud and clear, live from St. Louis. Every night, the Cardinals came to perch…even as far away from their home as Wisconsin Avenue.

Mankiewicz has served as the campaign director for George McGovern, a press secretary to Robert F. Kennedy, a head of one of Washington's largest public relations firms, and president of National Public Radio. But his summer days spent listening to KMOX near the National Cathedral gave him a brainstorm that put another line on his ample résumé—cofounder of the Stan Musial Society.

Up on Wisconsin, Mankiewicz started noticing the same cars parking near him. Their drivers were searching for the same familiar tune on their radios, slowing near the apex of the road, sidling into an open parking spot, and just sitting, like him. He saw one car enough that he decided to introduce himself one night, Cardinals fan to Cardinals fan. That is how he met the *New York Times* writer Robert B. Semple Jr. in the early 1960s, who later recalled the anecdote in an editorial for the paper. He believes it was up there—where Semple wrote they all sat "silently in our cars at midnight in a tight pennant year"—that inspiration struck Mankiewicz and another fan, Vic Gold. The Stan Musial Society was born in 1989.

"Word got around," Mankiewicz said before the Society's 2007 meeting, "and we had 100 calls from interested members within a couple days.… Now we probably have three times that many members."

Baseball bridges many gulfs, and it's no different for the cocreators of the Stan Musial Society. Mankiewicz was an instrumental and dedicated member of the Democratic party. Gold was the press secretary for Vice President Spiro Agnew and a press assistant in Barry Goldwater's presidential campaign. They are in many ways each other's political mirror, reflecting each other from across the aisle. Their common bond was the Cardinals, and it forged a deep friendship. Mankiewicz is a California native who fell for the westernmost team in the majors. Gold is a New Orleanian who cheered for the southernmost team in the majors.

"Obviously we had very little in common politically, to say the least," Gold told the *Washington Times*. "The rule of the club is that politics stops at the door, for obvious reasons."

Formal organization of the club took a few years, but its catalyst wasn't much of a surprise—the Cubs. There had been rumblings of a Cubs fan club for years. One was founded in 1975 and would go on to boast such bipartisan members as Dick Cheney, George Will, Hillary Clinton, and Donald Rumsfeld. The Cubs club named itself the Emil Verban Society, a tongue-in-cheek reference to a light-hitting infielder. (A fitting twist: Verban was first a Cardinal who didn't hit so light with a .412 average in the 1944 World Series.) Gold and Mankiewicz decided to allude to their rivals—and needle them in the same swift christening—by choosing Stan Musial as the player to adopt for the "society."

"Unlike the Cubs' fans," Mankiewicz said, "we didn't want any of that irony."

They also didn't want many rules. There is no newsletter. There are no fees, no room for networking at meetings, no "nominations" for membership. There is nothing Beltway about it. Everybody gets the same invitations to the semi-annual luncheons and everybody pays the same fee for a plate. Membership is fluid. So too is the schedule of meetings. McGovern was described in the *American Conservative* as "a member in good standing of the Stan Musial Society." Musial himself has attended a few times—entertaining the crowd with his harmonica and stories from his playing days. Mankiewicz said the goal is to have the only thing D.C. about the Stan Musial Society be its location.

"Frank and I have said that out of all the things we've done in politics," Gold said in 2000, "the thing we'll probably be remembered for the most is starting the Stan Musial Society."

62 The Great Rivalry and Its Greatest Game

In 1908 the St. Louis Cardinals stumbled and scuffled to a 49–105 record, finishing 50 games out of first place, scoring a record-low 371 runs, and drawing the eighth-most fans in an eight-team National League. The Chicago Cubs won the World Series.

Things haven't been the same since.

In the 100 years that followed the Cubs' final championship of the 20th century, the definitive Midwest rivalry drew boundaries in the region because sometimes it was more contentious in the stands, in the front office, and over the airwaves than it often was on the field. The Cardinals-Cubs is the longest-running professional sports rivalry between two teams that have known only one address. It can trace its origins back to the 1870s, when, in a March 1875 article, the *New York Times* reported: "The new St. Louis Club, judging from the players engaged by the managers and the amount of capital invested, is going to make a good fight for the supremacy with its rival.... The St. Louis Club was not organized for the purpose of contending for the pennant so much as for becoming a permanent and formidable rival of the Chicago Club." With that clear mission statement, they feuded from the beginning.

Yet, the Cubs-Cardinals cannot avoid the double-helix nature of their shared histories. It binds and enriches both clubs. While the Cardinals have won 10 World Series and been to 17 in the century since the Cubs' last title and there have been few true pennant races between them, so many of their pivotal moments and players are intertwined. Rogers Hornsby was an MVP and manager for both. The Lou Brock–Ernie Broglio trade in 1964 goosed the Cardinals toward a pennant with the speedy Brock and is remembered on one side as the greatest trade in club history. The other just considers it the worst in club history. Harry Caray called Cardinals games for two decades before he became the bespectacled face of the Cubs, and both mega-channels, WGN and KMOX, wrestled on the radio dial for baseball fans throughout the time zone. Dizzy Dean burned bright as a Cardinal, and burned out as a Cub. When the Cubs won the pennant in 1945, they couldn't win against the Cardinals, going 6–16 that year against their rival, who played the year with Stan Musial serving in the military. Bruce Sutter won his Cy Young Award as a Cub and his World Series as a Cardinal. The Cubs were hosting the Cardinals on the day Sutter went into the Hall of Fame. Though the Cubs won the game, Sutter wears a Cardinals hat on his plaque.

"We weren't always playing for first place," Sutter said during his induction weekend, "but we were always playing for bragging rights."

63 The 50,000-Watt Blowtorch

From the bayous of Louisiana to the big woods of Wisconsin and, as broadcaster Mike Shannon put it, "from mountain range to mountain range and almost everywhere else in there," the megaphone that built and united Cardinals Nation was KMOX/1120 AM. The 50,000-watt clear-channel station, known worldwide as "the Voice of St. Louis," debuted on Christmas Eve 1925, and less than a year later the station carried the Cardinals' first World Series against the New York Yankees.

For the next two decades, KMOX was one of several stations to broadcast Cardinals game, but its signal helped take the western-most and southernmost major league club to an enormous swath of the country. That partnership between the station and the ballclub became exclusive in the early 1950s, creating one of the most successful marriages in sports, a symbiotic identity that lasted 52 consecutive seasons. The Cardinals helped strengthen KMOX locally, and KMOX extended the Cardinals' wingspan nationally.

The bond was forged largely by the charismatic Bob Hyland Jr. shortly after he became general manager of the station in 1952. Convinced baseball was the way to the market's heart, Hyland sold the executives at CBS Radio on the idea of being the home of the Cardinals. Within 10 years, the Cardinals network had grown to 110 stations in 10 states, and within 20 years, they had 115 stations as the nation's largest sports network. It earned the nickname "America's Sports Voice."

Grand Walk-Offs

Since 1930, Roger Freed and nine other Cardinals have hit grand slams to win games in the team's final at-bat, according to the team's research. Freed was down to his final strike as a pinch-hitter in the 11th when he hit his way onto this list:

Player	Date	Opponent	Final Score
Pepper Martin	July 14, 1936	Dodgers	11–7
Joe Cunningham	July 30, 1957	Giants	7–3
Carl Taylor	August 11, 1970	Padres	11–10
Joe Hague	Sept. 24, 1971	Expos	10–6
Roger Freed	May 1, 1979	Astros	7–6
Darrell Porter	July 18, 1984	Giants	8–4
Tom Herr	April 18, 1987	Mets	12–8
David Eckstein	August 7, 2005	Braves	5–3
Gary Bennett	August 27, 2006	Cubs	10–6
Aaron Miles	July 20, 2008	Padres	9–5

The Cardinals became the tentpole for KMOX's big top.

The ringleaders were a parade of gifted play-by-play men who would become the voices of baseball for generations. Headlined by Jack Buck, Harry Caray, and Shannon, KMOX also propelled the careers of Bob Costas, France Laux, Joe Garagiola, Skip Caray, Joe Buck, and John Rooney.

KMOX's umbrella was once estimated at more than 40 states and at least six Canadian provinces. Places as different as Denver and Washington, D.C., shared the same summer phenomenon— fans would seek out the highest point in town and tune in their Cardinals. A young boy in Arkansas listened to Cardinals games on KMOX as he did his homework, and he recalled those delightful days with a reporter years later when visiting Shea Stadium. The Secret Service stood nearby as President Bill Clinton reminisced about KMOX. At his Hall of Fame induction, Lou Brock said he learned to love baseball by listening to Caray and Buck call games on KMOX, which he could get crystal clear in Collinston, Louisiana.

Before the 2006 season, the Cardinals left KMOX for a brief dalliance at another station. The gravitational pull of history proved too strong, and in 2011 the Cardinals returned to KMOX and those 50,000 watts that powered their flock.

"A Commitment to Heart"

1964 World Series: Cardinals Defeat New York Yankees 4–3

With less than a week remaining in the regular season and his Cardinals already having authored a surprise revival to reenter the pennant race, manager Johnny Keane pulled out a sheet of paper and began writing something unexpected of his own. He would later ask his wife to turn his longhand into a typewritten letter—an official memo to the owners of the ballclub, notifying them of his resignation. He slipped it into his jacket pocket and went to the ballpark.

There it would stay through a dozen more games, through a last-day clinching of the pennant, and through a seven-game World Series against the dynasty that was Mickey Mantle's New York Yankees. Keane's carefully crafted letter was untouched, unopened, and, to many, utterly unnecessary.

The Cardinals entered the 1964 season having gone 17 years without a pennant and playing for the first time in two decades without Stan Musial. The splendid outfielder had retired at the end of the 1963 season, when the Cardinals finished in second place, six games behind the National League–champion Los Angeles Dodgers. In early July 1964 the Cardinals fell 11 games behind in the league. They reached the All-Star Break at 39–40. Off the field, owner Gussie Busch and advisor Branch Rickey began organizing a shift in leadership. They planned to eject general manager Bing Devine, and a courtship of Gas House Gang member Leo Durocher had begun to replace Keane as manager. Despite the whispers growing to

Tim McCarver, Ken Boyer, and Bob Gibson celebrate the final out of the 1964 World Series.

rumblings and the heat rising on their positions, Devine and Keane orchestrated several key moves that jolted the team.

No move was bigger than the June acquisition of Lou Brock.

"Presto," pitcher Bob Gibson later wrote in his autobiography. "We were transformed."

Brock hit .348 with 33 stolen bases and 12 home runs after coming to the Cardinals in the celebrated trade with the Chicago Cubs. His presence energized a flagging lineup, but so too did the addition of rookie Mike Shannon in right field and the blossoming of Gibson as the pitcher who would come to dominate the league for the rest of the decade. On August 24, with the Cardinals trailing Philadelphia by 11 games, Gibson struck out 12 and raised his record to 11–10. That was the first of six consecutive complete-game victories pitched by Gibson and also the first of a run where the Cardinals would win eight of his final 10 starts of the regular season.

September of that season is often recalled for the Philadelphia Phillies' historic flameout. Treated almost as a footnote to their catastrophe, however, is how the Cardinals played almost flawlessly to catch Philadelphia, and how they did it under duress. On August 18, with the team nine games behind the Phillies, Devine was fired. With 13 games to play, the Phillies led the Cardinals by six and a half games, and Keane could tell what was coming. Even after sweeping a five-game series in Pittsburgh and watching the Phillies tumble toward a 10-game losing streak, Keane prepared his affairs. As Philadelphia arrived for a three-game series at Sportsman's Park with a two-game lead, Keane wrote that letter of resignation.

Then the Cardinals went and swept that series.

On the 179th day, the Cardinals took first for the first time. On the final day of the season, October 4, team captain Ken Boyer doubled in Brock to tie the New York Mets in the fifth inning. Boyer scored to help put the Cardinals ahead for good. Gibson pitched four innings in relief to clinch the victory, his 19th—and the unexpected league pennant. Keane, his letter still pocketed, had delivered the franchise's first league championship in 18 years and now was going to guide the Cardinals into the World Series against the October juggernaut, the Yankees.

The Yankees were appearing in their fifth consecutive World Series, and Mantle was making his 12th World Series appearance in just his 14th season in the majors. It was also his last. At the time, the '64 Series had a familial overtone. Yankees first-year manager Yogi Berra, like Keane, was a St. Louis native. The third basemen for both teams were part of the talent-rich Boyer clan, of Alba, Missouri. Clete played third for the Yankees; Ken played third for the Cardinals. Together, they became the first brothers to homer in the same World Series, and they did so in the same game, Game 7.

The series became an exchange of key home runs, from the Boyer boys and others. To win Game 1, Shannon drilled a two-run shot off Whitey Ford in a deciding four-run sixth inning. To give the Yankees a 2–1 lead in the best-of-seven series, Mantle crushed a home run in the ninth inning of Game 3 to take what had been a pitcher's duel between Jim Bouton and Curt Simmons. With the scored tied 1–1, entering the bottom of the ninth at a packed Yankee Stadium—67,101 were attending— Keane brought in veteran Barney Schultz to face Mantle. The knuckleballer appeared in seven of the Cardinals' final nine games in the regular season and did not allow a run. In 52⅔ innings, including 3⅓ already in the World Series, he had allowed just one home run.

On his first pitch to Mantle, Schultz gave up his second.

Mantle's walk-off home run into the third deck of the right-field stands gave the Yankees a chance to seize a commanding lead in the series with strikeout-leader Al Downing and Yankee Stadium at their backs in Game 4. Cardinals starter Ray Sadecki didn't survive the first inning, as the only out he got from four batters was on the base paths. The Yankees took a 3–0 lead in the first inning, and Downing took a shutout into the sixth. Singles by Carl Warwick and Curt Flood sparked the only rally the Cardinals would get in the game. Captain Ken Boyer made sure it was enough. With the bases loaded, thanks to an infield error, Boyer hooked a change-up deep into left field to upend the Yankees' lead with a grand slam.

Gibson controlled Game 5, pitching all 10 innings and receiving the win when catcher Tim McCarver laced a full-count, three-run home run in the tenth. McCarver's homer sent the series back to St. Louis with the Cardinals one win away from the championship. Back-to-back home runs by Roger Maris and Mantle in Game 6 were part of what became a rout as the Yankees forced both a Game 7 and a tricky decision for Keane. He elected to start Gibson on two days' rest, and Gibson responded with five shutout innings to protect a 6–0 lead built, in part, by a homer from Brock and McCarver's steal of home. The 28-year-old began to fray in the sixth when Mantle cleaved the Cardinals' lead in half with a three-run homer, his 18th career home run in a World Series. But Keane stayed with Gibson through the sixth, through the seventh and eighth, too, and into the ninth when solo home runs by Clete Boyer and Phil Linz whittled the Cardinals lead to 7–5 and put the tying run on deck in Maris.

Three days earlier Gibson had pitched 10 innings, and he was nearing the end of his 27th inning of this series. Including the 20 innings he threw in the final week of the regular season, Gibson had made six appearances in 18 days and thrown 46⅔ innings. He was one out away from a world championship. He was exhausted.

After a meeting on the mound, Keane stayed with his ace, and Gibson got Bobby Richardson to pop out and cinch the Cardinals' first World Series victory since 1946. Keane said later that he let Gibson finish because "I had made a commitment to his heart."

That was not the only commitment Keane kept.

Having guided the Cardinals through a tumultuous year that included backroom rumors of his own demise and the Phillies' implosion, Keane found himself the day after the World Series being whisked to a press conference. It was scheduled to announce an extension for Keane. Outside the press conference, Keane handed owner Busch an envelope. He implored Busch to read it immediately. He wasn't going into a press conference. He was finally handing in that letter of resignation.

"I've made other plans," Keane told Busch.

They included a different press conference. The next day the Yankees announced a new manager. It was Keane.

The Cardinals' World Series MVPs

Although it is now a staple of October, the World Series Most Valuable Player award was not a regular feature until 1955. Originally awarded by the editors at *Sport Magazine*, the trophy is now decided upon by journalists covering the World Series in a vote during the final game of that World Series. The 1964 Series was the first that saw a Cardinal win the MVP. Here are the five players who received the official award and the Cardinals who *should* have won MVPs in the six World Series victories before the advent of the award:

2011 David Freese

After three years of injury complications, Freese bloomed on baseball's biggest stage, going from hero to household name in two nights. Down to his final strike in Game 6, Freese struck a two-run triple to tie the game in the ninth. Two innings later, the St. Louis native forced a Game 7 with a walk-off home run. He tied Game 7 with an RBI double in his first at-bat, giving him 14 extra-base hits in October. Freese finished the postseason with MLB postseason records in RBIs (21), total bases (50), *Tonight Show* appearances with Justin Bieber (one), and, unofficially, marriage proposals. The newly crowned king of St. Louis was the first position player since Cardinals catcher Darrell Porter to win the World Series and NLCS MVP awards.

2006 David Eckstein

The scrappy shortstop underwent hours of treatment and was wrapped in yards of bandages just to play through injuries. Like the team he guided, Eckstein was a surprise—hitting .364 with a team-best four RBIs and a tie-breaking double in Game 4.

1982 Darrell Porter

He didn't lead the Cardinals in batting average, RBIs, slugging, or home runs in the series. All he did was lead the Cardinals. Porter, who caught all but one inning of the Series, hit .286 with five RBIs in the Series after batting .556 in the NLCS.

1967 Bob Gibson

In one of the most dominant pitching performances in any World Series, Gibson won all three games he started, pitched a complete game in every start, and held Boston to 14 hits against his 26 strikeouts in 27 innings. Ten of those strikeouts came in the decisive Game 7.

1964 Bob Gibson

Thumped by the Yankees in his World Series debut, Gibson recovered and won the MVP with a brilliant and gutty start in Game 7. Three days after pitching 10 innings to win Game 5, Gibson struck out nine and pitched a complete-game victory in Game 7.

1946 Harry Brecheen

In two starts, Brecheen allowed one earned run in 18 innings, including a four-hit shutout in Game 2. Two days after winning Game 6, the lefty pitched two shutout innings in relief during Game 7 for his third victory of the series.

1944 Ray Sanders

In the offensively challenged Streetcar Series—the two St. Louis clubs combined to score 28 runs in nearly 110 innings of play—Sanders wins for consistency. He had hit in every game, and led the Cardinals with five runs scored and a .429 slugging percentage. His home run proved the winner in the Game 5 that broke a Series tie.

1942 Johnny Beazley

In a Series noted for the defensive play of the upstart Swifties and Whitey Kurowski's title-clinching homer, it was right-hander Beazley who deserves the MVP. Beazley won both games he started, including the clincher in Game 5. A sign of the times: the rookie received a telegram from the Marines recruiting office after his complete-game win in Game 5.

1934 Dizzy Dean

The Deans—gregarious Dizzy and younger brother Paul—combined to win all four games against Detroit, two apiece. While Paul was impressive, Dizzy was dominant. After going 1–1 in his first two starts, Dizzy pitched a six-hit shutout in the winner-take-all Game 7, striking out five and backing his boast that his family would win the Series.

1931 Pepper Martin

A 27-year-old rookie who sat on the bench during the '28 World Series, Martin was a bolt of unbridled energy against the favored Philadelphia Athletics. Martin led the Cardinals with a .500 average, 12 hits (five for extra bases), five runs scored, and five steals.

1926 Grover Cleveland Alexander

Three Cardinals batters had 10 hits on the way to the franchise's first World Series title, but it was the clutch pitching of Alexander that won the championship. Alexander won both of his starts with complete games. A day after allowing two runs to the vaunted Yankees in Game 6, Alexander came out of the bullpen in Game 7 to strike out Tony Lazzeri with the bases loaded and a one-run lead in the seventh. Decades before baseball knew of such a thing, Alexander had the Fall Classic's finest save.

 Jaster Zeroes In on the Dodgers

In 1966 the Los Angeles Dodgers followed their World Series victory with a third National League pennant in four seasons, a rotation fronted by Cy Young Award–winner Sandy Koufax, and a confounding inability to solve an otherwise little-known Cardinal named Larry Jaster.

The Cardinals' rookie left-hander tied with Koufax, teammate Bob Gibson, and several other pitchers for the NL lead that season with five shutouts. All five of Jaster's, however, came against the Dodgers. Jaster, 22 at the time, made five starts against the Dodgers and blanked them in all five. Over 45 shutout innings, Jaster walked eight, struck out 31, and allowed just 24 hits, all of which were singles. His first two shutouts of the Dodgers that season were separated by a six-week stint to fine-tune in the minors. "I don't see any reason why we can't hit him—it's weird," L.A. second baseman Jim Lefebvre said.

Jaster was an all-state quarterback in Michigan when he signed with the Cardinals for a $60,000 bonus. He made his major league debut in September 1965, and his first three big-league starts were three consecutive complete-game victories. In 1968 he flirted with a perfect game against the New York Mets, was 6–4 at the All-Star break, and seemed on the cusp of channeling his talent into stardom. But he stumbled. Jaster went 3–9 after the break and was thumped brutally in a World Series appearance. Montreal selected him in the expansion draft that winter, ending his career as a Cardinal with a 32–25 record in four seasons. Five of those wins made history.

Jaster's 1966 Game-by-Game vs. L.A. Dodgers

Date	Score	IP	H	R	ER	BB	K	L.A. starter
April 25 at L.A.	2–0	9	7	0	0	0	7	Claude Osteen
July 3 at L.A.	2–0	9	3	0	0	1	5	Don Drysdale*
July 29	4–0	9	5	0	0	2	8	Don Drysdale*
August 19 at L.A.	4–0	9	5	0	0	3	7	Claude Osteen
Sept. 28	2–0	9	4	0	0	2	4	Don Sutton*

Future Hall of Famer

A few days after his fourth shutout of the Dodgers in 1966, Jaster received a letter from Grover Cleveland "Pete" Alexander's widow. Years before his star turn as a Cardinal, Alexander shut out Cincinnati five times in the same season. The letter wished Jaster luck as he attempted to tie the record, adding, "I know it isn't easy." Jaster's fifth shutout came in his final start of the year, and his recipe for riddling the Dodgers hadn't changed. The first two hitters—speedsters Maury Wills and Willie Davis—combined to reach base once in eight plate appearances. Five of Jaster's first six innings were perfect, and the Dodgers had four hits with only two runners reaching third base the entire game. "They got frustrated," Jaster later told the *Sporting News*. "It works in your corner."

The lefty Jaster was the Expos' starter in their first ever home game, which came against the Cardinals. His last pitch in the majors was in 1972. A souvenir from his '66 season—a ball from his fifth shutout of the Dodgers—sits at the National Baseball Hall of Fame. On it, his season of shutouts is scrawled.

"I guess I'm on a lot of trivia things," Jaster told the *Post-Dispatch* on the 25th anniversary of his record-tying feat. "I was an average pitcher, but a trivia-type of guy."

Trivia, sure. But not trivial.

66 The All-Star Games

At the ceremony to unveil the logo for the 80th All-Star Game, a Major League Baseball official said the only town that could follow the retirement party the sport threw for Yankee Stadium in 2008 was one steeped baseball, like St. Louis. It did have four decades to prepare. After going more than a generation without visiting the Gateway City, Major League Baseball's midsummer classic returned in 2009 to showcase the new downtown ballpark, Busch Stadium III. The logo announcement alone had city officials dropping malaprops, calling the game the "Midwestern classic" and saying St. Louis would welcome the "baseball galaxy" to town. Although "galaxy" may have been accidentally apropos. The event has changed since they played at noon in a one-day, barnstorming visit to St. Louis in 1966. These days, it's no longer an All-Star Game, it's an All-Star invasion. The fifth All-Star Game in St. Louis was scheduled to feature a festival for fans, the annual Home Run Derby, and a Futures Game for top-flight prospects. Despite its absence from the city, St. Louis is intrinsically linked to the game. Stan Musial made a record 24 consecutive appearances as an All-Star. Seven NL-vote leaders have been Cardinals. Four of the first five All-Star Game starting pitchers were Cardinals (Bill Hallahan in 1933, Bill Walker in '35, and Dizzy Dean in '36 and '37). "New York went about the business of being New York [in 2008]," said Bob DuPuy, Major League Baseball's president. "St. Louis won't be going about the business of being St. Louis. It will be about the All-Star Game. It will be four days of celebrating the city." Here are the days that the city celebrated the All-Star Game:

8th All-Star Game, July 9, 1940, Sportsman's Park: NL 4, AL 0

A native of Dexter, Missouri, down in the boot-heel of the state, Max West made the most of his first and only All-Star Game at-bat. West, of the Boston Bees, started in right field and batted third for the National League lineup in the midsummer classic's first visit to his home state. Leadoff hitter Arky Vaughan (Pittsburgh) singled, followed by a single from Billy Herman (Cubs), and up came West to face New York Yankees ace Red Ruffing, an eventual Hall of Famer. West drilled a three-run home run, all the runs the NL would need in the first shutout in an All-Star Game. Five NL pitchers, including starter Paul Derringer (Cincinnati), who began his career as a Cardinal, combined to throw a three-hitter. West had just one at-bat in the game because in the second inning he injured himself chasing Luke Appling's double.

Cardinals All-Stars: *Johnny Mize* (1B), 0-for-2; *Terry Moore* (CF), 0-for-3. (Italicized names denote Cardinals who started in the All-Star Game.)

15th All-Star Game, July 13, 1948, Sportsman's Park: AL 5, NL 2

The St. Louis Browns were the hosts, but the Cardinals were poised to be the stars. The heart of the National League's All-Star starting lineup was loaded with three Cardinals and one former Cardinal—from No. 2 hitter Red Schoendienst, No. 3 Stan Musial, No. 5 Enos Slaughter, and cleanup hitter, former Cardinal Johnny Mize. In the first inning, Musial ripped the first of his six All-Star Game home runs and gave the NL a 2–0 lead. Those were the only runs the league would get in the game. Despite Joe DiMaggio and Ted Williams being limited by injuries to pinch-hit appearances, the AL rallied with five unanswered runs. Vic Raschi, the New York Yankees' right-hander, pitched three scoreless innings and hit himself to the win with a tie-breaking, two-run single in the fourth inning.

Cardinals All-Stars: *Stan Musial* (LF), 2-for-4, HR; *Red Schoendienst* (2B), 0-for-4; *Enos Slaughter* (RF), 1-for-2; Harry Brecheen (P), DNP; Marty Marion (SS), injured.

24th All-Star Game, July 9, 1957, Sportsman's Park: AL 6, NL 5

A crush of votes from Cincinnati fans carried eight Reds into the starting lineup for the National League. Before commissioner Ford Frick stepped in and unilaterally replaced two Reds with Willie Mays (New York Giants) and Hank Aaron (Milwaukee), the only non-Red voted to start the game was hometown hero Stan Musial. Batting third, Musial doubled in the game and scored in the ninth on Mays' triple. Musial's leadoff walk sparked what almost was a game-winning rally. Musial and Mays scored before Cubs shortstop Ernie Banks' RBI single sliced the AL's lead to 6–5. Gil Hodges (Brooklyn) came up with the tying run at second, and Banks, the winning run, at first. The AL countered with pitcher Bob Grim, the Yankees' reliever. Hodges launched a fly ball to deep left-center, and Minnie Minoso, just into the game for his defense, tracked it down in full gallop to cement only the second All-Star victory in eight years for the AL.

Cardinals All-Stars: *Stan Musial* (1B), 1-for-3, 1 2B; Wally Moon (OF), 0-for-1; Larry Jackson (P), 2 IP, 1 H, 0 R; Hal Smith (C), DNP.

37th All-Star Game, July 12, 1966, Busch Stadium II: NL 2, AL 1

The game was a taut classic, but it's the heat that is remembered. Barely a few weeks after the multipurpose Busch II opened, it and a crowd of 49,936 hosted the 37th All-Star Game in sweltering afternoon heat. Reports of the temperature that day ranged from 103 degrees to 105 degrees, depending on one's constitution. The scorcher gave birth to an oft-repeated critique of the new ballpark. "It certainly holds the heat," Casey Stengel grouched in the dugout. It almost didn't hold the game. Delays in construction nearly moved the game to Houston, and airline strikes made it difficult for players to get to St. Louis. Runs were as rare as a breeze that day. Brooks Robinson started his MVP afternoon with a triple off Sandy Koufax (Los Angeles), the first of his three hits. He scored on a wild pitch to give the American League a quick 1–0 lead that lasted through Detroit pitcher Denny McLain's three perfect innings. Ron Santo (Cubs) singled in Mays to tie the game in the fourth inning. Thirty-five outs passed with the score still tied and the heat still tyrannical. More than 40 fans, many in the upper deck, had to be treated during the game for extreme heat-related problems. In the bottom of the tenth, hometown catcher Tim McCarver singled to right. A bunt moved him to second, and Maury Wills' single off Pete Richert scored McCarver for the NL's fourth of eight consecutive All-Star victories.

Cardinals All-Stars: Tim McCarver (C), 1-for-1; Curt Flood (OF), 0-for-1; Bob Gibson (P), injured.

80th All-Star Game, July 13, 2009, Busch Stadium III: AL 4, NL 3

After more than four decades away, the All-Star Game returned to St. Louis to find Busch Stadium II had fallen and a new civic treasure had risen next door. Not the spiffy new ballpark, but the Cardinals' first baseman: Albert Pujols. For two days, Pujols welcomed the world to his yard and served as host and de facto mayor of St. Louis for the midsummer classic. Said teammate Ryan Franklin, a fellow All-Star: "This is Albert's show." It was also Albert's year. He received nearly 5.4 million votes from the fans to set a National League record, trailing only Ken Griffey Jr.'s 6.1 million in 1994 for the overall record. Pujols arrived at the break leading the NL in homers and RBIs and flirting with a Triple Crown. On the eve of the All-Star Game, New York Mets third baseman David Wright said: "He's having a typical Albert season. He's head and shoulders above everybody else. He's really broadened that gap between him and the rest of the league. As a peer, it's fun to watch the show he's putting on."

Pujols was the star of a constellation that descended on St. Louis. President Barack Obama attended to throw out the first pitch—to Pujols. Stan Musial was fêted before the game, and the All-Star there to greet him was Pujols. Pujols went hitless in the game and still asserted his place as the game's most prominent, as Ozzie Smith put it that week, "megastar."

The game itself gave way to another Cardinal: hometown catcher Yadier Molina drove in the NL's first run with a two-out single and keyed a three-run rally. The NL nursed its 3–2 lead into the fifth inning before the AL tied it. In the seventh Colorado's Brad Hawpe smoked a drive to deep left field. The ball was certain to clear the fence and give the NL the lead back, until Tampa Bay's Carl Crawford skied above the padded lip to steal Hawpe's home run. Detroit's Curtis Granderson tripled and scored on a sacrifice fly in the eighth, and Mariano Rivera collected his fourth All-Star save to push the AL's unbeaten streak to a record 13 years. The MVP award that is usually given for what a player does with the bat or a pitch went to Crawford for what he did with the glove.

Cardinals All-Stars: *Albert Pujols* (1B), 0-for-3; *Yadier Molina* (C), 1-for-2, 1 RBI; Ryan Franklin (P), 1 IP, 0 H, 0 R.

67 Putting "Lonborg and Champagne" on Ice

1967 World Series: Cardinals Defeat Boston Red Sox 4–3

The morning of Game 7, the St. Louis Cardinals woke up in Boston to a headline proclaiming their imminent and bubbly demise. The Red Sox and their overdue, overwrought nation sensed their "Impossible Dream" season was about to end in euphoria. Borrowing on a quote from Red Sox manager Dick Williams, one of the Boston morning papers, in blaring red and in a font size normally reserved for earthmoving news, asserted:

"LONBORG AND CHAMPAGNE"

The Lonborg was Jim Lonborg, the Red Sox's right-hander, a 22-game winner during the regular season and already a winner in Games 2 and 5. The champagne was what Lonborg's teammates planned to spray at each other after winning Game 7 with their ace on the mound. Hours before the headline was tacked up in the clubhouse, most Cardinals had already seen it over their coffee that morning.

"That didn't sit too good with my breakfast, I can tell you that," third baseman Mike Shannon said years later. "But we had Gibson."

For much of the 1967 season, the Cardinals did not have Gibson. The right-handed ace of the Cardinals, Bob Gibson won 60 games the previous three seasons and was one of the cornerstones of a would-be dynasty built on the 1964 World Series win. Gibson missed eight weeks of the regular season because of a fluke injury. On July 15, at Busch Stadium, Roberto Clemente scalded a line drive off Gibson's right leg and fractured his fibula just above the ankle. It was the first hit Gibson allowed in the game. He pitched to three more batters before leaving the game, and he didn't pitch again until September 7.

At the time of Gibson's injury, three teams were within four and a half games of the league-leading Cardinals. By the time Gibson was back, the Cardinals had pulled away, leading by 11½ games and eventually winning the league by 10½. In Gibson's absence, lefty Steve Carlton won five games. Nellie Briles took Gibson's spot in the rotation and won his last nine decisions of the season. Dick Hughes won 16 of his 20 career victories that season, had a top-10 ERA, and finished second in the Rookie of the Year voting. A young pitching staff that was asked just to survive without Gibson actually arrived.

Hall of Fame Scribes

Besides delivering the most famous ham-and-egg sandwich in Cardinals history, sportswriter Bob Broeg wrote the first (and lasting) drafts of Cardinals history during his decades as beat writer, columnist, and eventually sports editor at the *St. Louis Post-Dispatch*. He also continued a trend. Since J. Roy Stockton traveled to Cuba to cover spring training for the St. Louis Federal League club, professional baseball in St. Louis has been covered, uninterrupted, for nearly a century by Hall of Fame baseball writers. The St. Louis baseball writers inducted into the scribes' wing of the National Baseball Hall of Fame in Cooperstown, New York, are winners of the J.G. Taylor Spink Award. They are:

- **J.G. Taylor Spink.** Publisher of the *Sporting News*, 1914–1962. Inducted 1962.
- **J. Roy Stockton.** Covered the Cardinals for the *St. Louis Post-Dispatch*, 1917–1958. Inducted 1972.
- **Red Smith.** Famous for work in New York, Smith, a Pulitzer Prize winner, covered the Browns in 1929 and joined the Cardinals beat in 1930. Writer for the *St. Louis Star* and *Star-Times*, 1928–1936. Inducted 1976.
- **Bob Broeg.** Joined the *Post-Dispatch* in 1945, popularized nickname "Stan the Man," and served on the Hall's board of directors for nearly 30 years. Inducted 1979.
- **Rick Hummel.** Began covering the Cardinals in 1973 and was lead writer during the heyday of the 1980s and home runs of 1990s. Inducted 2006.

It helped that a lineup of veterans kept the runs coming, the clubhouse light, and gave a fiercely talented roster a charismatic swagger. At its epicenter was Orlando Cepeda.

Acquired in May of the previous season, Cepeda gave the Cardinals their MVP in 1967 and their nickname. It was Cepeda who dubbed this team "El Birdos," and it was Cepeda who would lead a postgame chant about "El Birdos" being the finest team in the league. Cepeda backed up his bravado with a .325 average, 25 home runs, and 111 RBIs. He fit snugly among Lou Brock (21 homers, 52 steals), Curt Flood (.335 average), Roger Maris (55 RBIs in 125 games), and Tim McCarver (.295 average). A year later, the Cardinals stalwarts would be featured in an iconic *Sports Illustrated* cover that folded out to show the Cardinals' stars, dressed nattily and sitting at their lockers. The accompanying text showed how 10 of their salaries added up to $607,000. The magazine called them the "highest paid team in baseball history."

They were because they played like it.

Boston knew it.

Led by Carl Yastrzemski's Triple Crown season in 1967, Boston had rebounded from a ninth-place finish in 1966 to its first American League pennant in 21 years. Emboldened by their backstretch sprint for the pennant, Yastrzemski announced that he thought the Red Sox would win the World Series "in six." Lonborg had 10 more victories than any other Red Sox pitcher, yet he couldn't start Game 1 because he was needed to clinch the pennant on the season's final day. The Cardinals had Gibson for Game 1, and the MVP of the 1964 World Series held Boston to one run—a solo homer by the pitcher—and struck out 10 in a complete-game win.

Lonborg returned for Game 2 and pitched a one-hit shutout. He was back in Game 5 with Boston trailing 3–1 because of Gibson's shutout in Game 4. Echoing Gibson, again, Lonborg held the Cardinals to one run and three hits in Game 5. Lonborg was able to win because he could do what other Red Sox pitchers could not—keep Brock off base. Brock was 0-for-8 against Lonborg through five games, but 8-for-12 with five runs scored in the three games Lonborg did not start. Brock reached base 14 times in the series, stole seven bases, and scored eight runs.

Having won Game 6, 8–4, at Fenway Park, Boston manager Williams announced that his lineup for Game 7 was "Lonborg and champagne." Lonborg was starting on two days' rest, and he was facing Gibson for the first time in the Series. The Cardinals pounced on him in the third for a 2–0 lead. In the fifth Gibson drove a Lonborg pitch deep to center field for a solo home run. Brock followed with his first hit of the series off Lonborg and then promptly stole second and third. When Julian Javier cranked a three-run home run off Lonborg in the sixth, the Cardinals led 7–1, and it was clear the Red Sox's Impossible Dream was getting its wakeup call. Gibson was fueled in part by a ham-and-egg sandwich, one purchased for him by baseball writer Bob Broeg. Gibson authored his third complete game of the Series and had 10 strikeouts to go with his homer in Game 7. A double play, turned by Shannon and Javier, brought the Cardinals to the verge of the championship, and Gibson's strikeout of George Scott ended it. Gibson was named the MVP of the Series, and while the only champagne Lonborg had that day was in the headlines, El Birdos celebrated at Fenway the same way they had all season. They sang.

"Lonborg and champagne! Hey! Lonborg and champagne! Hey!"

68 Gibby's 17-K October

It took a pitching great to give perspective to one of the greatest seasons to be a pitcher and the duel for the ages that climaxed the Summer of '68. Sandy Koufax, just two seasons removed from retiring, came to call the 1968 World Series as part of the radio broadcast team, and was greeted by a Game 1 at Busch Stadium that pitted the season's Cy Young Award winners, Detroit ace Denny McLain against the Cardinals' World Series hero Bob Gibson. McLain had won 31 games that season, and 40 years later no pitcher had since won more than 27. Gibson won 22 games, but his 1.12 ERA was the lowest anyone had thrown since 1920. Koufax weighed these two pitchers, their historic numbers, and came to a succinct conclusion about the pending Game 1 matchup. As Bob Broeg recalled, Koufax predicted Gibson would dominate the Tigers and outclass McLain.

He was more right than he could know.

Gibson whipsawed through Detroit's lineup—easily besting McLain, who allowed three runs (two earned) and three hits in five innings—and then took aim at Koufax himself.

Decades before the advent of regular-season interleague play, the American League champions had scarce experience against the best pitcher in the National League. And this was Gibson at his best. Overpowering fastball. That sinister slider. A blend of power, control, and biting movement made all the more imposing by Gibson's fierce presence. Gibson struck out six of the first seven batters he faced, and few even had a sporting chance against the break of his slider. When he froze Bill Freehan with a slider to open the third inning, Gibson had struck out five consecutive— plowing through the heart of the Tigers' lineup. In order, he struck out Al Kaline, Norm Cash, Willie Horton, Jim Northrup, and Freehan. Four of the five had at least 20 home runs during the pitcher-friendly season, and three of them had at least 84 RBIs. The one who didn't have 20 homers was Kaline. The Hall of Famer was limited to 102 games because of a broken arm. Gibson struck out Kaline three times in Game 1, and Kaline would go on to hit .379 in the World Series as Detroit rallied from a Game 1 humbling to win in seven games. Kaline was one of two Hall of Famers that Gibson K'd in the game, as he got pinch-hitter Eddie Mathews swinging to open the eighth in one of the final at-bats of Mathews' career.

Mathews was Gibson's 14th strikeout of the game, putting him one shy of the World Series record, set five Octobers earlier by Koufax. With the Los Angeles Dodgers in 1963, Koufax struck out 15 to set the record. Gibson learned he was close to Koufax from catcher Tim McCarver, and that a dazzling ninth would not only claim his fourth consecutive World Series complete game but the record. Awaiting him in the ninth were the Tigers' No. 2, 3, and 4 hitters. "I'm never surprised at anything I do," Gibson said after the game.

The Pennant Years

No National League team has won as many World Series as the Cardinals' 11, and though they trail the Dodgers and Giants in total NL pennants won, only the Cardinals can boast 18 while playing in the same city. Here are the seven pennants that didn't result in titles:

2004 World Series: Boston Red Sox Sweep 4–0

The Red Sox exorcised their curse and ended 86 years of baseball futility with the franchise's first World Series win since 1918. Still steamrolling after their unprecedented rally from a 0–3 deficit in the ALCS, the Red Sox knocked the wind from the 105-win Cardinals quickly. Busch Stadium opened its gates at the end of Game 4 to welcome any fans outside so they could see history—for the visitors.

1987 World Series: Minnesota Twins Win 4–3

With whirling, swirling Homer Hankies urging them on, the Twins' four victories all came at home, where they outscored the Cardinals 33–12. The closest game was the final game, won by Series MVP Frank Viola after holding the Cardinals to two runs in eight innings.

1985 World Series: Kansas City Royals Take I-70 Series 4–3

The Interstate-70 Series began with two quick wins for the Cardinals and a chance to eliminate the Royals in Game 5. But the crumble began when Bob Forsch struggled in Game 5 and when umpire Don Denkinger whiffed on a call at first base in Game 6. The Royals routed the Cardinals 11–0 in Game 7 for the title.

1968 World Series: Detroit Tigers Win 4–3

Again denied winning consecutive titles, the Cardinals spoiled a Series best known for Gibson's 17-strikeout game. Lou Brock decided not to slide home and was tagged in a key play in Game 5, and in Game 7 Curt Flood misplayed a fly ball into a triple that led to three decisive runs.

1943 World Series: New York Yankees Win 4–1

In a rematch of the previous year's classic series, the Yankees quickly doused any notion the 105-win Cardinals had of repeating. With Joe DiMaggio and Phil Rizzuto serving in the military, the Yankees turned to 20-game winner Spud Chandler. He allowed one earned run and went 2–0 in the Series.

1930 World Series: Philadelphia Athletics Win 4–2

The A's became the first team to win consecutive World Series for a second time, led by pitchers George Earnshaw and Lefty Grove, who helped hold *(continued)* the Cardinals to a .200 average. Earnshaw won Game 6, backed by seven runs and seven extra-base hits, including Al Simmons' homer.

1928 World Series: New York Yankees sweep 4–0
The treacherous duo of Lou Gehrig and Babe Ruth punished the Cardinals. Gehrig ripped two homers in Game 3, Ruth a record three in Game 4. Combined, the Yankees greats had 13 RBIs, 14 runs, and 11 extra-base hits.

Outfielder Mickey Stanley led off with a single and didn't move past first. Gibson tied Koufax's record by blowing a 1–2 fastball past Kaline. He struck out Cash for the third time in the game to set a new record. The scoreboard flashed with the news as an ovation coursed through the crowd of 54,692, most of whom had been standing from the start of the inning. Horton didn't have a prayer. Gibson spun a backdoor slider by the right-handed hitter, catching him looking at strike No. 3, out No. 3, and strikeout No. 17. Gibson struck out the final three batters he faced in the 4–0 victory, and the record still stood 40 years later.

Koufax called that, too.

"Well there's no way for me to ever get it back," the lefty reportedly said. "I think Bob has put it beyond anyone's reach."

69 Too Grand: Tatis' Big Inning

Los Angeles Dodgers broadcaster Vin Scully, the velvet voice who has called more baseball history than most have read, didn't even bother to reach for the record book.

Cardinals third baseman Fernando Tatis, that night's replacement cleanup hitter, was digging into the box for his second at-bat of the third inning on April 23, 1999. Eight batters earlier, Tatis had sparked the Cardinals' scoring rally with his first career grand slam, and here he stood with the bases loaded again. As he called the action and described what was possible with Tatis' next swing, Scully didn't need to double-check the numbers. What Tatis was about to do, everyone knew had never been done.

Tatis launched two grand slams in the same inning to become the first and so far only player in major league history to do so. With three on and none out, Tatis drove a 2–0 fastball from Chan Ho Park some 450′ into the bullpen at Dodger Stadium. In his 225th game, that was his first career grand slam. The shot erased the Dodgers' 2–0 lead, and by the time Tatis came to the plate later in the inning, the Cardinals led comfortably 7–2. With Park still pitching and the bases loaded, slugger Mark McGwire flew out to shallow right field for the second out of the inning. The bases remained loaded. The pitcher remained Park. Tatis took aim. On the sixth pitch of the at-bat, Tatis hammered a breaking ball over the left-field wall for history.

"I get goose pimples just thinking about it," manager Tony La Russa said that night. "What have they? One hundred years of baseball? And this is the first time it's ever been done? Wow."

Los Angeles was the final stop on a numbing, four-city, three-time zone, 11-game road trip in April. The Cardinals had won six of the first eight and knew packed houses would await them at Chavez Ravine. It was, after all, native son McGwire's first business trip home since obliterating the single-season home-run mark with 70 the year before. The fans may have come to applaud history. Instead, they saw it.

Before the Cardinals arrived at Dodger Stadium that night, 4,777 grand slams had been hit, but no two had ever come from the same player in the same inning. No Cardinal had ever hit even two home runs of any kind in any one inning. Tatis became the first to do both with two swings. Then only 24 and in his second year as a big-league regular, Tatis had hit 23 home runs to that point in his career. On the road trip, Tatis had batted cleanup only once before, but he was thrust back into the spot because of an injury to Eric Davis' left hand.

Tatis' eight RBIs in one inning set a record. Park tied a record with his final pitch of the game, the one deposited over the left-field wall, by becoming the second pitcher ever and first in 100 years to allow two grand slams in one inning.

"I didn't think I had enough explosion," Tatis said of the second grand slam later to Hall of Fame baseball writer Rick Hummel. "It just happened. I thought, *I'm going to fly.* My mind is in other worlds right now."

Tatis was the 10th player in major league history to hit two grand slams in one game, but only the second National Leaguer with two in one game. Atlanta's Tony Cloninger did it in 1966, a game he started—as the pitcher. Over the next 24 games, Tatis hit seven more home runs and drove in 22 runs. He finished the season with career highs in homers (34), runs scored (104), RBIs (107), and average (.298). In August of that same season Tatis slammed again, ripping Philadelphia pitcher Billy Brewer for a 431' grand slam. Tatis' third grand slam of the season tied a franchise high set in 1925 by Jim Bottomley and answered in 1977 by Keith Hernandez. Tatis shares that record, but it may take a while before someone matches the grand fashion in which he got there.

The Big Mac Attack

Mark McGwire's shortest home run of his record-shattering season was also his biggest, and the one that would resonate longest for baseball. On September 8, 1998, McGwire scalded a first-pitch fastball for a line drive that barely cleared the wall in left field, some 341′ away. The bolt was his 62nd of the season, breaking Roger Maris' treasured single-season home-run record and climaxing a captivating season for baseball and the Cardinals.

That summer felt too good, too magical to be believed.

Years later, baseball learned that it was.

The hulking slugger, St. Louis' own Big Red Machine, had already won the heart of his new hometown before taking a swing in 1998. General manager Walt Jocketty gambled at the trade deadline by dealing three prospects to Oakland for McGwire. Jocketty risked losing him to free agency unless the Cardinals could sway him to stay in the next nine weeks. It took seven. The Cardinals and the former Oakland Bash Brother agreed on a three-year deal worth $28.5 million. Jocketty heralded the extension as the beginning of "the Mark McGwire era." A teary-eyed McGwire explained how $1 million a year of his salary was going to a foundation to help abused children and how St. Louis fans had won him over. That night, in his first at-bat, he nailed a 517′ homer, the longest yet at Busch Stadium II, and trotted around the bases to a thunderous ovation.

He had them at home run.

A decade after his successful pursuit of Maris' record, one of the most hallowed in the game, McGwire described that summer as "so spiritual, so universal," in an interview with the *Post-Dispatch*. McGwire had hit a career-high 58 home runs the year before, including 24 in 51 games with the Cardinals. With talk of a Maris Chase swirling in spring 1998, McGwire began the season with a blast: an Opening Day grand slam against the Dodgers and homers in his first four games of the year. Records fell consistently after that. In June Sammy Sosa unexpectedly joined the race and stayed on McGwire's heels all summer. Together, they elevated baseball back into the headlines and salved a fan base embittered by the 1994 strike.

Mark McGwire tied Roger Maris' single-season record with his 61st home run off the Cubs' Mike Morgan in 1998.

It was hip to dig the long ball again. McGwire's batting practices became must-see events, once covered live by the *opponent's* radio station.

Sports Illustrated called 1998 "The Greatest Season Ever," and stated that though there would be no October for the Cardinals, St. Louis "was the epicenter" of this season. McGwire busted the franchise record for homers in a season easily. On consecutive days in September he became the record-holder in homers by a National Leaguer and then, with two more on September 2, the all-time leader for right-handed hitters. McGwire hit his 61st on September 7, his father's 61st birthday. Spiritual, indeed. And the next night he made history. With the Maris family in attendance and a national television audience of an estimated 43.1 million—in modern rating metrics it was one of the highest-rated shows ever for local St. Louis, second only to the finale of NBC's sitcom *Cheers*—McGwire came through in the fourth inning. Fittingly, Sosa was in right field as McGwire launched Steve Trachsel's pitch into history. The Cubs' infielders congratulated McGwire as he rounded the bases.

"The whole country has been involved in this," McGwire said that night. "If people say it's bringing the country together, I'm happy to bring the country together."

Sosa would actually take the lead briefly—for all of 45 minutes one day—before McGwire finished with a flurry. He hit five home runs in his final 12 at-bats to not just set the record but redefine our notion of it. McGwire transcended the 60s and finished with 70.

The red-headed slugger's career was all but over by the time his record was, too. Barry Bonds hit 73 homers in 2001, and McGwire faxed his retirement announcement a few weeks later. McGwire had hit 220 home runs for the Cardinals but walked away from $30 million when nagging injuries eroded his ability to play. His career was over. The chase wasn't.

Seven years after delighting the nation, McGwire was subpoenaed before Congress. Baseball's performance-enhanced culture had been called before the government, and McGwire was asked to answer for newspaper reports and allegations that he had used banned performance-enhancing drugs. His previous denials faded into a refusal to answer the congressional panel's answers. A friend described McGwire as "too lawyered-up" for the hearing. The slugger, who zealously guarded his privacy in retirement, repeatedly answered questions with a phrase as familiar as his jog around the bases after No. 62.

"I'm not here to talk about the past," he said.

If McGwire had led a disenchanted fan base back from the strike with his big swings and vulnerable-though-congenial personality, his performance before Congress left many disillusioned. Viewed as a surefire, first-ballot Hall of Famer on the day he retired, McGwire failed to get more than 24 percent of the vote in his first three appearances on the ballot. It takes 75 percent for induction. In 2010 Big Mac finally came clean and admitted he had used steroids throughout his career as he prepared to re-enter baseball as the Cardinals' hitting coach.

On the way out of St. Louis on Interstate 70, there is an aging sign that designates a stretch of asphalt once named for Mark Twain as the "Mark McGwire Highway." In the delirium of 70, many other things were about to be named for McGwire—bridges, streets, highways—and this one was. Years later, it remains as a sign of one unforgettably thrilling summer for a slugger and his city. Like the sign, the summer hasn't aged well.

71 The Mad Hungarian's "Controlled Hate"

His signature Fu Manchu moustache framing a famous scowl, Cardinals reliever Al Hrabosky would snatch the throw from the third baseman at the start of an inning and go about earning his nickname, the "Mad Hungarian." Hrabosky stomped to the back of the mound, stewing over the next pitch, building himself to a boiling point. Cheers or jeers from the crowd would swell with each movement. He'd imagine his "herky-jerky delivery" coming together to unleash a fastball that sizzled by the hitter, fueled as much by his arm as all the rage he could muster. Finally, he'd slam the baseball into his glove, turn to face the batter, and huff his way to the rubber.

He says his calling-card routine was all about pinpointing his thoughts, harnessing his temper. But it did as much for his persona as it did for any of his pitches.

"I had an uncontrolled temper," Hrabosky says. "I just got into a rage and I became useless. I felt this adrenaline surge and this energy, but I didn't know how to channel it. I started specifically trying to get myself into what I called a 'controlled hate.'"

Hrabosky, the left-handed fireballer, was the Cardinals' first-round pick (19th overall) in 1969. He pitched in 44 games in 1973, but in 1974, as the team's Opening Day closer, he heard whispers he was headed to the minors or elsewhere. He knew the problem: his mind wandered on the mound; he could not channel his adrenaline; he was, in his words, "struggling mentally." He felt he was throwing on what he called "borrowed time."

On June 11, 1974, the inspiration for controlled hate struck. Necessity was the mother of the madness. In a game that night against the Los Angeles Dodgers, Hrabosky entered in the ninth inning with a 1–0 lead, two runners on, and two outs. He was brought in to face left-handed-hitting outfielder Bill Buckner, but L.A. sent up a right-handed pinch-hitter, Tom Paciorek. All-Star Steve Garvey, on his way to the league MVP award that summer, loomed two batters later—if the game got that far. Hrabosky paused behind the mound and talked himself into a frenzy, steeling for the moment emotionally even as he envisioned it mentally.

Hrabosky spun. Stormed up the mound. Leered at Paciorek. Fired three pitches, all strikes. Paciorek watched a fastball zip by to end the game and cinch Hrabosky's second save of that summer.

Controlled hate was born.

"The ball went exactly where I wanted it to go," he said. "There was a swing and a miss. And it seemed like I had a lot more life on my pitches, too. It was real dramatic, and I was like, *Wow*."

Al Hrabosky led the NL in saves in 1975 and became a fixture in the Cardinals' broadcast booth after his retirement.

Over 41 innings from July 14 through September 17 of that season, Hrabosky allowed one run and finished the year fifth in Cy Young Award voting. During the season, he grew the famous Fu Manchu to add to his menace. Any bit of facial hair or antic that gave the perception he was slightly unhinged was a bonus to the Mad Hungarian guise. He spent the next three seasons as the Cardinals' closer, and in 1975 led the National League with 22 saves to complement a 13–3 record and a 1.66 ERA. His pre-pitch histrionics guided him the whole way. Hrabosky finished third in the Cy Young voting that year and won the *Sporting News'* Fireman of the Year award. At midseason, he received a salute to all things Hrabosky from the Cardinals' faithful.

In response to Hrabosky not being selected to the '75 All-Star Game, the Cardinals held "We Hlove Hrabosky Hbanner Day" on July 12 against the Dodgers, led by All-Star manager Tom Lasorda. The Cardinals won 2–1 in the tenth inning, giving Hrabosky the victory after retiring all six batters he faced. He has often referred to that day as his "personal All-Star Game."

Hrabosky would go on to pitch for Kansas City and Atlanta before retiring after the 1982 season. He returned to St. Louis and has become a fixture on Cardinals broadcasts. Hrabosky agreed that the Mad Hungarian took on a life of its own, one that Hrabosky at times cultivated and, just as often, flaunted. While with Kansas City, Hrabosky entered a game at Cleveland only to have hitter Horace Speed mimic the "controlled hate," much to the delight of his home crowd. The next day, Speed called Hrabosky's hotel room to apologize for what he had been told was disrespectful.

"Horace, there is no need to apologize to me," Hrabosky said, soothingly. "If you think you need to apologize to somebody, you need to apologize to the Mad Hungarian—*and he doesn't talk to anybody!*"

Hrabosky slammed the phone down, grinning furiously.

Not all messages are sent from the mound.

72 Mini-Mac's Three Big Whacks

Keith McDonald was a journeyman minor leaguer, an accomplished and valuable if not exceptional catcher to whom the Cardinals once entrusted their precious and fragile jewel of a pitcher—Rick Ankiel—on a rehab assignment. Drafted out of Pepperdine in the 24th round of the 1994 draft, McDonald had very little contact with the majors in his 13-year professional career. But he made history with every swing.

McDonald retired with three major league hits, and all three were home runs. He hit two home runs in his first two major league at-bats, the first and only other player to do so since St. Louis Browns outfielder Bob Nieman hit two in his 1951 debut. During

First-Hit Wonders

No team in the majors has had more debut homers than the St. Louis Cardinals, and it's not just the club's hitters who have the honor. Of the 18 pitchers in history who have homered in their first major league at-bat, three are Cardinals and two did so as relievers. The first-hit wonders:

Name	Pos.	Date	Opp.	Of Note
Eddie Morgan	OF	4/14/36	Cubs	Opening Day, first pitch. Morgan appeared in eight games that season; his only MLB homer in 66 AB.
Wally Moon	OF	4/13/54	Cubs	Opening Day. Won Rookie of the Year that summer, later an All-Star with Cardinals and L.A.
Keith McDonald	C	7/4/00	Reds	Pinch-hit. Second player in history with two HRs in first two ABs, all three hits were HRs.
Chris Richard	OF	7/17/00	Twins	First pitch. Spent six games with Cardinals before trade to Baltimore for Mike Timlin.
Gene Stechschulte	P	4/17/01	D-backs	Pinch-hit, first pitch. Right-hander went 8–7 with six saves in 116 relief appearances with Cards.
Hector Luna	IF	4/8/04	Brewers	Second pitch. Rule 5 pick hit .285 that next season, spent two and a half summers as utility infielder.
Adam Wainwright	P	5/24/06	Giants	First pitch. Won that game in relief, and his 1.167 SLG in '06 led the league (in six AB).
Mark Worrell	P	6/5/08	Nationals	First pro HR. Pitched four games in '08 before winter trade to San Diego for Khalil Greene.

the Independence Day series in 2000, McDonald debuted with a pinch-homer on the sixth pitch he saw in his first big-league at-bat. Two nights later, while catching his minor league teammate Ankiel, McDonald homered in his first at-bat of the game. The crowd of 43,287 erupted with a standing ovation that coaxed McDonald, sheepishly, from the dugout for a cap tip. "I'm the most surprised of anyone," McDonald told reporters that night. "The fans are probably going to expect it every time, but it may be a long time before I hit the next one." Nine days and three at-bats later, he hit No. 3.

McDonald got a September call-up the next year and meandered through the minors until 2006, catching for affiliates with the Cubs and New York Yankees, among others. His last at-bat came in 2006, six years after his first and final major league hit. He retired as the third of four players in history to have three hits in a season and all of them homers, joining Ed Sanicki (1949), Clem Labine (1955), and pitcher Jorge Sosa, who did it in 2006 with Atlanta before joining the Cardinals later that season. At the plate, as opposed to behind it, McDonald saw 42 pitches in nine plate appearances. The three that he put in play all went over the fence.

73 Torch a Glove Like Reitz

Nicknamed "the Zamboni Machine" for his ability to suck up groundballs off the rigid turf of Busch Stadium, Ken Reitz would win a Gold Glove and set and reset records for fewest errors by a third baseman. But once he was so incensed by committing two errors in one inning that he stormed into the clubhouse, grabbed a bottle of lighter fluid, and torched his glove.

On July 18, 1974, Reitz's second full season in the majors, he flubbed two groundballs in the seventh inning of a game against

Houston at Busch. He committed another fielding error in the ninth. That was enough.

"Made sense," he said, "to go and burn my glove."

Reitz raced to the clubhouse, grabbed the materials made for destruction, and in a corner just off the dugout doused his glove in lighter fluid. With no remorse, he dropped a match on it. Several stories have Reitz shouting at the glove as he lit it on fire: "You're no good!" One of the clubhouse managers raced over to put the fire out, but Reitz resisted and pushed back the usher. The Zamboni insisted he needed the purification ritual.

The slightly built infielder's reputation as a slick fielder grew in the years to come. He was the last National Leaguer to win a Gold Glove at third base before Hall of Famer Mike Schmidt won nine consecutive at the position. In 1977 he set a record for fewest errors by a third baseman with nine errors in 450 chances. In 1980, as an All-Star, he reset his own record by committing just eight errors during 150 games. That was his last year with the Cardinals before being dealt to the Cubs in a deal that netted closer Bruce Sutter.

That 1974 game in which he went pyro on his glove was the only three-error game of his career, and he had just two multi-error games in 1,321 at third base. He said it didn't take long after he burned his glove that he committed another error, but there weren't many afterward. "I figured it out that it was me," Reitz said, "and not the glove."

74 Bake's Early-Morning Run

Countless pitches had already been thrown that night at Shea Stadium, a total of 13 pitchers would record at least an out, and the Cardinals and New York Mets used 50 players who combined for

202 plate appearances. But it was in the twenty-fifth inning that a throw to first base did what no pitch to the plate had done for hours—it decided the longest night game in baseball history.

Bake McBride, the Cardinals' rookie center fielder, led off the top of the twenty-fifth with an infield single in his 10th at-bat of the game. Long-legged but weary from nearly seven hours of baseball, McBride took a generous stride off first base as Hank Webb steadied to face Ken Reitz. Webb, in his first inning of work that night, wheeled and fired to first baseman John Milner.

Webb's throw was wide.

McBride was off, racing more the daylight.

The game began on September 11, 1974, and commissioner Bowie Kuhn and his wife came to catch quite a pitching matchup, pitting Cardinals right-hander Bob Forsch against the Mets' Jerry Koosman. Five days earlier the rookie Forsch had out-dueled Koosman for his second major league shutout. The veteran Koosman lasted the nine innings this time, long enough to still be in the game when Reitz ripped him for a game-tying, two-run homer in the top of the ninth inning.

The Cardinals had 18 hits in the 25-inning game, and Reitz's home run was the only one that wasn't a single. Their roster beefed-up by September callups, the Cardinals used 26 players—Jack Heidemann, acquired that June and traded that December, came into the game in the twelfth to play shortstop and still had time to go 3-for-6. The Cardinals used six pitchers in relief of Forsch, none more effective than lefty Claude Osteen. Osteen pitched just 22⅔ innings in his Cardinals' career, and 9⅓ of them came as September 11 faded to September 12 and the game kept going.

Osteen did not allow a run and gave up only four hits. From the fourteenth to the twenty-first inning, he allowed just two hits, and the Mets didn't get a runner into scoring position against him until the twenty-second inning. Mets reliever Jerry Cram matched him zero for zero through eight innings, and as the twenty-fifth inning arrived, the teams had gone scoreless for 15 innings—a combined 90 outs without a runner coming home.

The longest game in National League history was a 26-inning affair between Brooklyn and Boston in 1920. The game was called because of darkness as a 1–1 tie. The Cardinals and Mets had already played the longest night game by the time McBride reached base in the twenty-fifth and were now about to play the longest game to reach completion.

McBride would steal 30 bases and hit .309 in 1974, speeding away with the NL Rookie of the Year award. When Webb's throw went wild, it skipped into the right-field corner. McBride peeled around second, sprinted through third-base coach Vern Benson's stop sign, and blazed for home. Mets catcher Ron Hodges, who came in at the start of the twenty-fourth inning, dropped Milner's throw as McBride slid by for the go-ahead run. Two errors were assigned on the play.

After a scoreless inning from Sonny Siebert—the 19th thrown that night by a Cardinals reliever—the Cardinals won 4–3. The game ended at 3:13 AM, 7 hours, 4 minutes after the first pitch.

The Cardinals won later that same day at Shea and would construct a six-game winning streak that pushed them into first place. Two days later McBride delivered the tie-breaking run in the seventeenth inning of a win at Philadelphia. The winning streak ended after a 13-inning win at Pittsburgh. And the season ended with the Cardinals slipping to second place in its final weekend.

75 Musial's Accidental 3,000th Hit

Stan Musial wasn't supposed to play the day he got his 3,000th hit. On a brief two-game road trip to Chicago to face the Cubs, Musial

Sweet Lou's 3,000th

A little more than 21 years later, the Cardinals' home crowd finally got to see a 3,000th career high. On August 13, 1979, Lou Brock's second hit of the game was the 3,000th of his career. Brock's historic hit—and one of the last of his career (he finished with 3,023)—came off Cubs pitcher Dennis Lamp, quite literally. The Cardinals' outfielder laced a line drive up the middle that glanced off Lamp's hand and was scooped by the third baseman. There was no play. Brock was the 14th player to reach 3,000 hits. He called the career milestone a "star in that crown."

got a base hit in the first game of the series to give him 2,999 in his career. After the game, he told coach Terry Moore that he'd like to save 3,000 for the home crowd. Why do it at Wrigley Field when a homestand at Sportsman's Park was just a day away? Manager Fred Hutchinson agreed, and Musial wasn't in the lineup on May 13, 1958. But he wasn't long for the bench.

Musial entered the 1958 season 43 hits shy of a mark he'd been privately eying for a decade. It had been 16 years since Paul Waner reached 3,000, and it would be 12 more before Hank Aaron and Willie Mays did it in 1970. Musial was an island—the lone 3,000 hitter in nearly three decades of baseball. From Opening Day of '58, he sped toward the milestone. Musial had 42 hits in his first 87 at-bats of the season, a .483 average. Not really the kind of bat that can stay shelved in a close game against a rival. With the Cubs leading 3–1 in the sixth and a runner at second, Hutchinson sent Musial up to pinch-hit for pitcher Sam Jones. The Hall of Famer with the screw-top swing lashed Moe Drabowsky's pitch to the left-field corner for a stand-up double. The shot keyed a rally, and the Cardinals won 5–3. Musial became the only member of the 3,000-hit club to reach in a pinch-hit at-bat.

"I never knew that hitting a little ball around could cause so much commotion," he said after the game.

While Musial had envisioned a 3,000th-hit celebration special for the hometown fans, what he got was a chance to share the career achievement with the region. The train trip back to St. Louis became a congratulatory tour, stopping a couple times in Illinois so crowds could cheer and serenade the Man. When the train reached Union Station in St. Louis, a crowd was waiting—even past midnight. Musial saw the number of kids there to greet him and yelled, "No school tomorrow!" But there was a game the next day, and Musial gave the home crowd the promised show. His 3,001st hit was a home run, and he didn't stop there, hitting Nos. 3,002 and 3,003 before ending that game with a .500 average so far that season.

76 Visit Class A Quad Cities River Bandits

Modern Woodmen Park in Davenport, Iowa

Set on the banks of the Mississippi River, many hours upstream from where the prospects hope to play, Modern Woodmen Park is one of the oldest and most picturesque minor league ballparks in the country. The 5,024-seat ballpark was built in 1931, was renovated in 2002, still has its classic brick façade, and features a soaring view of the Centennial Bridge across the Mississippi. The atmosphere at games is enlivened even as it is endangered by its proximity to the river.

In 2001 the river leapt into the ballpark and washed out most of the season. Other rising waters have forced the team to move its games to other Midwest League locales. In 2008, when water flooded the area, Modern Woodmen Park's playing field was an island in the Big Muddy. The city of Davenport constructed a 375' walkway—one big plank—to take fans from an elevated parking lot on the opposite side of the street from the ballpark into the field. A total of 9,000 fans attended two games on their personal baseball island.

The riverfront ballpark opened on May 26, 1931, with a crowd of 3,000. In 1971 the park was christened John O'Donnell Stadium, the name it had until 2007. In 2002 work began on a $14 million overhaul, fitting the ballpark with 20 climate-controlled suites, new batting cages, a team store, a video scoreboard, and a large lounge for entertaining. The upgrades continued before the 2008 season, with a hot tub and a Tiki Village on the right-field berm, nestled in the shadow of the Centennial Bridge. Prospect Mike Folli hit the first home run into Tiki territory, a shot nicknamed a "Tiki bomb." The team planted a cornfield in left field, and in July 2008 finished the Iowa homage by having players emerge from the corn during introductions.

Come for the atmosphere, stay for the baseball. Quad Cities is the Cardinals' lowest full-season affiliate, where premium draft picks often make their debuts. And try a Bandit Dog. The signature concession is a hot dog, sliced down the middle and stuffed with melted cheese before being wrapped in bacon and doused in chili sauce. If the Bandit Dog is meant to be devoured, the Modern Woodmen Park's view is to be savored. After dusk, in time for late innings, the Centennial Bridge lights up and the river shimmers, creating a backdrop city administrator Craig Malin wanted—a scene, he said, "so beautiful grown men will weep."

Address: 209 South Gaines Street, Davenport, Iowa

Web site: www.riverbandits.com

Visit the Farm

The brightest gems of the Cardinals' minor league system of affiliates are fittingly situated along the two main lines of commerce to St. Louis. Class A Quad Cities and its majestic ballpark and Triple A Memphis and its novel relationship with the community both sit along the Mississippi River. Double A Springfield, owned by the Cardinals, is just down Interstate 44, a short trip deeper into Cardinals Nation. All talent flows toward Busch Stadium.

77 Visit Double A Springfield Cardinals

Hammons Field in Springfield, Missouri

From the posh clubhouse to the vast indoor training facility that shames a few major league ballparks, the Cardinals' Double A affiliate's home ballpark is about a four-hour drive away from the big leagues, but it feels much closer. The state-of-the-art Hammons Field is outfitted with every major league amenity $32 million can provide, and several gentle touches to commemorate not only the history of the minor leagues in Springfield, Missouri, but a steeled bond with the big-league Cardinals up a ways on Interstate 44.

"But have you seen 'The Rumble'?" one executive asks a visitor after a tour of the ballpark.

"The Rumble," as it's nicknamed for the sensation it causes as it echoes around the 7,500-seat ballpark in downtown Springfield, is a visual and audio bouquet bursting from the scoreboard. It's a mix of highlights and graphics and zooming images and thumping music that welcomes a standing-room-only crowd to every Springfield Cardinals home game. Installed at the ballpark shortly after the Cardinals' affiliate arrived, the $1 million scoreboard is a 20' x 36' screen that boasts the ability to project 4.4 trillion colors.

The scoreboard's eye-catching "Rumble" is one of myriad reasons Hammons Field won consecutive Texas League "Field of the Year" awards in 2007, 2008, and 2011 and, in its first year of use, was considered by several different critics as one of the finest in the minor leagues. Not bad for a ballpark that opened with only the hope of a tenant.

In 2004 Springfield developer and philanthropist John Q. Hammons opened his namesake ballpark with the promise to host a minor league team by the next spring. Phone lines were crippled under the weight of season-ticket requests before the town had a team. What followed was even harder on the phones: the Cardinals, who have deep roots in the area, purchased an affiliate and moved it to Springfield, bringing a longtime fan base back under their wing. The Cardinals saw the proximity of the ballpark as a plus and its facilities as ideal for, among other things, rehabbing major leaguers. The Texas League is seen as a weed-out level for top prospects, and players have been known to skip ahead from it to the majors, like Cardinals pitcher Kyle McClellan did in 2008.

In its first year, the ballpark opened to early crowds nearing 10,000. The inaugural season drew 526,630 fans, among the top 20 totals in the minors and an average of 7,523, or more than the advertised capacity. Because of the Cardinals' ownership, the ballpark is loaded with Redbird allusions, right down to having the big club's game playing on television sets around the ballpark. In the years that followed the opening, the "S-Cards" put the big-league Cardinals' retired numbers up as ornaments, added bar stool–like seating called "Rail Birds," and finalized a boardwalk that connects the outfield hill in center to the right-field corner. Concessions include an ice creamery that offers a beer float, made from Anheuser-Busch products, of course.

Springfield has a deep history with minor league baseball, as a team was there in 1887. From 1902 to 1950, Springfield sporadically hosted different affiliates, including a Cardinals affiliate from 1930 to 1942. A rose garden planted past the outfield at Hammons Field pays tribute to the rose bushes at White City Park, home of many of those minor league clubs. The other nod came during the big-league Cardinals' first visit. A ballplayer who hit 26 homers in 1941 for a team that called White City home came with the

Cardinals and pulled out his harmonica to serenade the new jewel. The player's name: Stan Musial.

Address: 955 East Trafficway, Springfield, Missouri
Web site: www.springfieldcardinals.com

78 Visit Triple A Memphis Redbirds

AutoZone Park in Memphis, Tennessee

Hours before the game begins, its sounds waft from the striking plaza that serves as the entryway to AutoZone Park. At the corner of Union Avenue and Third Street in downtown Memphis, AutoZone Park's "Nostalgia Man" welcomes visitors to what's advertised as the minor league ballpark that is, like the prospects who play there, closest to the majors.

The 12,000-seat stadium is nestled near the landmark Peabody Hotel and is just a few blocks away from the famous Memphis strip, Beale Street. The entire area is a concert of music and history, and as soon as you pass under the giant, old-time ballplayer icon whom locals know as Nostalgia Man, the soundtrack is baseball. The plaza is designed like a baseball diamond, complete with life-sized players, one frozen in the act of delivering a pitch to another. And from under the bases comes "sound art," recordings of baseball's distinctive noises.

At a total price tag estimated at around $80 million, AutoZone Park is reportedly the most costly ballpark not in the majors. It celebrated its 10th anniversary in 2009, and for all 10 years it has been host to a Cardinals affiliate. In 1998 the Redbirds came to Memphis as the first Triple A team there since 1978. In 2000 they moved into their palatial ballpark, and in 2008 they had a record ticket sale of 18,620 for one of the last games of the season.

The ballpark has big-league inspirations, often big-league crowds, and big-league details, done with a minor league flair. The guts of the ballpark include indoor batting cages and separate weight rooms for the teams. The concourse is a 360-degree band that offers an open view of the playing field. The outfield wall in right and center is purposefully 7'8" high because the founders wanted fielders to be able to scale the wall and pull back home runs. The specialty concession smacks of Memphis: BBQ Nachos. It's made like it sounds, with a choice of chicken or pork, and slathered in the world-famous Rendezvous sauce.

Tucked in the back of the souvenir shop is a mural not to miss, Michelangelo's David, dressed in a Redbirds uniform and clutching a baseball in that famously cupped hand. Overwhelming the field is a scoreboard that cannot be missed—the largest video board in the minors, looming 13 stories over the field.

As distinguishing as Nostalgia Man and as refreshing as tunes on Beale Street is the Memphis Redbirds' relationship with the city. Founder Dean Jernigan and his wife Kristi established the group that runs the affiliate, the Memphis Redbirds Baseball Foundation, as the only non-profit group in the country that owns and operates a baseball team. Revenue from the baseball team funds charities, such as RBI (Returning Baseball to the Inner City) and STRIPES (Sports Teams Returning In the Public Education System). Jernigan spoke of the team being part of his city's "soul," and in the first three years of existence the Foundation brought baseball and softball to 34 inner-city schools, according to a 2000 report in *Fast Company*. In 2007 AutoZone Park established a prominent role nationally as the host of the first Civil Rights Game. Pitting the Cardinals against Cleveland, the game was established to honor and increase awareness of baseball's role in the Civil Rights Movement, and it was played in the shadow of the National Civil Rights Museum. As part of the game, the teams, like many visitors to the area, take a tour of the museum.

When the Redbirds moved out of the Memphis ballpark that bore his name, Cardinals great Tim McCarver told the *Commercial Appeal* that AutoZone Park was a welcome fixture because "Memphis needs something to be proud of, other than Graceland." The city has it.

Address: 200 Union Avenue, Memphis, Tennessee
Web site: www.memphisredbirds.com

79 Meet Fredbird

For a fair-feathered fan who earned a lifetime contract with the Cardinals for how he flew around Busch Stadium, flying out of Busch Stadium didn't seem too difficult for a publicity stunt. Then the storm rolled in.

As part of a sponsored pregame ceremony at Busch II in the mid-1990s, Fredbird, the beloved mascot, climbed inside the Re/Max hot-air balloon for takeoff and was set to become the first fan ever to fly the coop, so to speak. With ominous weather lurking, it was supposed to be a short trip. Up from the turf, over the crown of arches, and then a few blocks' flight to a gentle landing in an Anheuser-Busch parking lot. Once the balloon emerged from the ballpark, the wind caught it and whisked it out of downtown and over the Mississippi River. Fredbird didn't miss home games, and here he was, adrift and soaked with rain.

The pilot turned to Fredbird, pointed to a bean field on the Illinois side of the river, and said, "I can land it there. I need you to hop out when we land and stop the carriage, or else we're going into the Mississippi."

Just another night for baseball's best fans' biggest fan.

Born in April 1979, Fredbird prepared himself to reach the big 3-0 during the 2009 season. The brainchild of Marty Hendin, the Cardinals' longtime vice president of community relations, Fredbird has become one of baseball's most recognizable and longest-serving mascots. Local lore says that Fredbird hatched in the kids' corner of Busch II, the red-feathered son of Mom Bird and Dad Bird. As a chick, Fredbird frolicked with the players, but his attempts to play the game failed. One day, a close friend said, he improvised a clap, and other fans joined in. He jumped on the dugout, and other fans cheered him on. At five, the story goes, Fredbird bought season tickets, and he didn't miss a game, not once, not even narrowly, not until a hot-air balloon marooned him in an Illinois bean farm.

Fredbird does 600 or so events a season. He'll visit fans in hospitals, attend other mascots' birthday parties, and go on the team cruises. (Fredbird is big in Jamaica.) He also hosts a weekly television show for the Cardinals' kid fan club and visits schools for his "Doin' it Right" program, an effort to encourage children to stay in school and stay fit. But games, oh games…games are Fredbird's lifeblood. That's where he poses for pictures and lives by a simple code: "You can take their nachos," the media shy mascot wrote in a rare interview for this book, "but you have to give the nachos back." Fredbird's favorite move is "beaking" fans. So many fans, mostly kids, beg to be "beaked." There's something about having the bobble-bellied bird clamp his floppy yellow beak on your head that makes for a good picture. "One million beaked and more to come," Fredbird writes.

"I think he's the ambassador for all of the fans, young and old," said Tim Falkner, one of Fredbird's handlers through the three decades. "Fredbird is out there in the community when the Cardinals are not playing. He's the face of the team when and where the players aren't."

Born in 1979, Fredbird has become a beloved part of the Cardinals' game-day experience.

Fredbird told friends, including former handler Tony Simokaitis, that his role was never more important than when coming out of the players' strike in 1994. Fans were disenchanted, and Fredbird had to reinvigorate Cardinals Nation. It was then that Fredbird upped his antics, started teasing the umpires, and, one day, asked manager Joe Torre if he could fire T-shirts into the crowd from center field. It's been a tradition ever since.

It was just as baseball was emerging from its post-strike fog that Fredbird found himself alone, pelted by rain, stranded in a field somewhere in Illinois, and separated from the game by the Mississippi River. Two or three hours later, rescue came and took him, mud-covered, dripping wet, and disappointed he missed the game, back to the ballpark. It was there, handler Simokaitis said years later, that Fredbird learned he didn't miss a game at all. The storm that swept him away also delayed the game until he returned.

"But what about that farmer?" said Joe Strohm, who organized the fateful balloon event. "He wakes up and sees those big foot prints in his field. There was no way to know it was only Fredbird."

80 The White Rat: Whitey Herzog

Manager…Inducted into Hall of Fame, 2010….Number retired, 2010

On the eve of the 1980 Winter Meetings, *Post-Dispatch* baseball writer Rick Hummel arrived at the Wyndham Anatole Hotel in Dallas thinking he'd drop off his bags and head to a football game. Cardinals general manager—and soon to be manager, again—Whitey Herzog met him in the lobby.

"Where ya been?" the White Rat chomped. "I've got trades to make."

Just Rewards

Two Cardinals managers have won the National League Manager of the Year award, given each season by active members in the Baseball Writers Association of America. In 1985, Whitey Herzog won it for guiding the Cardinals to 101 wins and his second pennant in four years. In 2002, Tony La Russa won it with a 97–65 record and division title.

He wasn't kidding.

By the next morning he had sketched out an 11-player deal with San Diego, and by the end of the week Herzog had upended baseball and remade the Cardinals into a team, his team, that would come to dominate the 1980s, both in the standings and in style. In a dizzying Winter Meetings, Herzog made four deals that involved 24 players. Rollie Fingers was acquired in one deal, on December 8, and traded four days later in another. He started his moves by signing Darrell Porter, the MVP of the 1982 World Series, and punctuated them with a deal to get closer Bruce Sutter, who threw the fastball to Porter that ended the 1982 World Series. The next winter, Herzog was at it again, dealing malcontent shortstop Garry Templeton to San Diego for Ozzie Smith. He landed unheralded Willie McGee in another deal. Herzog was as cunning as he was itchy with his trade trigger finger. He knew the kind of team he wanted and was willing to trim and swap and sign his way to it.

"Yeah, I got a philosophy," Herzog once said. "It's run, boys, run."

It was a philosophy that now goes by another name: Whiteyball.

Dorrel Norman Elvert Herzog, an Illinois native, had made the majors as an outfielder, playing in 634 games but was once blocked by Mickey Mantle. In 1973, he skippered an awful Texas team and began a run of managing at three different teams in three years. He stayed with Kansas City from 1975 to 1979, leading the Royals to a 102–60 record in 1977. Even that wasn't enough to eclipse the Yankees. Shortly after he was fired on one side of the state, Herzog

Whitey Herzog led the Cardinals to three World Series during his 11 years on the bench in St. Louis.

was hired on the other, halfway through the 1980 season. He and Cardinals owner Gussie Busch immediately clicked, and Busch conferred on Herzog a tremendous autonomy with baseball decisions. "One man in charge," Herzog wrote in his autobiography, "no committees, no crap."

Many of the reasons Busch enjoyed Herzog are the same reasons Cardinals Nation embraced Herzog as a bosom pal and enduring folk hero. He was the barstool manager, the guy who shot straight, could tell a knee-slapper of a story, and would buy the next round unless he got you to do it first. He was a keen judge of talent and a players' manager. He let them go—run, boys, run. But he had a stern hand, as in 1981 when he jerked shortstop Templeton into the dugout by his jersey after Templeton made an obscene gesture to a home crowd. Herzog suspended him and traded him. He also piloted the team through the drug problems that polluted the mid-1980s. Herzog, with his high-and-tight haircut, tailored his lineup to his ballpark. Herzog saw the vast expansions of Busch Stadium II's outfield and its fast-track turf field and decided to stress defense, speed, and the bullpen. All the buttons he pushed had to do with winning tight ballgames.

In his first full season with the Cardinals, 1981, he led the club to the best record in the division, though a strike-split season kept them out of the playoffs. In 1982, Herzog won the first of three pennants and defeated Milwaukee, one of his trade partners during the December 1980 dealapolooza, for the Cardinals' first World Series title since 1967. While the players Herzog landed powered that lineup—15 of the 25 on the '82 roster were acquired in the White Rat's wheeling and dealing—it was Herzog's imprint as their manager that also drove the baby-blue Cardinals.

In 1990, Whiteyball lost its momentum. A team picked to contend instead was mired in last place when, on July 6, Herzog resigned. He cracked: "I came here in last place, and I leave here in last place. I left them right where I started." Hardly. Including the three pennants, Herzog went 822–728 as Cardinals manager. Just as importantly he reared a generation of Cardinals fans on hit-and-runs and steals and brilliant defense. Nearly two decades after Herzog resigned, Whiteyball remains a widespread doctrine of Cardinals Nation. Many grew up on it, and Herzog's presence as a St. Louis resident, ballpark icon, and local pitchman only reinforces the devotion.

Herzog may have left the Cardinals.

The Cardinals never left Herzog.

Steal Home with Glenn Brummer

Even 25 years after he boldly broke for home and the most unexpected stolen base ever by a Cardinal, Glenn Brummer still finds himself fielding the same question, sometimes several times in the same day: "What were you thinking?" Affable, quick to grin, quicker to guffaw, and comfortable in his Illinois country-boy skin, Brummer through the years has coined a ready answer that fits his personality even as it serves his place in Cardinals lore.

"It was a long ballgame," he explains, "and I wanted to get off the field as soon as possible."

On August 22, 1982, a couple months away from their dash to the World Series title, the Cardinals were thick in the back stretch of a pennant race. Ozzie Smith, Willie McGee, Keith Hernandez, and company paced the National League East, keeping the Cardinals ahead of Philadelphia and eventually winning by three games. Somewhere low on a roster loaded with names that even made baby-blue look good was Brummer. He was one of three catchers on the roster, had a grand total of 64 at-bats that year (none in the playoffs), and was about to appear in the 50th of the 178 big-league games he'd have in his career. Never a regular, the Olney, Illinois, native's career season came in his last season when at 30 he hit .278 in 108 at-bats for Texas. Brummer entered that August 22 game against San Francisco at Busch II in the eighth inning as a pinch runner, but no runner was he. Built like a catcher, Brummer successfully stole a base only four times in 12 attempts in his career. And yet with one 90′ shock he was about to join Enos Slaughter's dash and any of Lou Brock's thefts as one of the famous runners in Cardinals history.

In the twelfth, Brummer singled and needed singles by McGee and Smith to make the 180′ trek to third base. With the bases loaded, two outs, and David Green at the plate, Brummer had an idea. Giants pitcher Gary Lavelle, a lefty, was throwing from the stretch and never bothered to peek at Brummer. He was quite literally turning his back on the runner at third, and why shouldn't he? Brummer was a station-to-station runner and no threat to do anything but win the game if Green got a base hit. Brummer was a mitigating circumstance; Green was the threat. On the 2–1 pitch, Brummer wanted to go home but got talked out of it. On 2–2, he was gone. He had an exceptional lead, knew he had the pitch beat, and his only worry was whether Green would swing to avoid strike three. San Francisco catcher Milt May caught the pitch and lunged to make the tag. Umpire Dave Pallone called Brummer safe and the game over, a 5–4 victory in 4 hours, 1 minute. However, he never called the pitch. Had it been a strike, the inning would have been over, and Brummer's chutzpah would have been forgotten, or maybe chided. Instead, it adds to the legend: Brummer may have stolen home on strike three. "I beat the ball, I know I beat the ball there," Brummer said at the 25th anniversary celebration of his steal. "I caught them all by surprise. Every one of them. They had no idea I was going. Even years later, it is still a surprise I went."

Brummer was the toast of the clubhouse after the victory that put the Cardinals two ahead of Philadelphia—their largest lead in the division since early July. Renowned St. Louis sports cartoonist Amadee, who drew the *Post-Dispatch*'s Weatherbird for decades, got a whitewashed home plate and sketched a caricature of Brummer, dressed in prison stripes and behind bars, "wanted" for theft of home. His teammates signed the plate all around the sketch and presented Brummer with it as the spoil of his daring. "I knew I had a chance to make it," he insisted years later. "I said I could do it. And I did it. That's what I was really thinking."

Whiteyball Runs Away with Title

1982 World Series: Cardinals Defeat Milwaukee Brewers 4–3

As he took his position for Game 7 of the 1982 World Series, Cardinals shortstop Ozzie Smith dazzled with a special postseason twist on his usual acrobatics. First he did a front flip and then the signature back flip. Starting pitcher Joaquin Andujar had a flip all his own. To finish his warmup, Andujar flipped the ball up before firing it home for his last toss.

"We might need a big mustard jar by the time this day is over with all the hot dogs we have seen so far," St. Louis native Joe Garagiola said on the televised broadcast.

Welcome to Whiteyball, Joe.

The Cardinals spent most of the 1982 season hearing about how they couldn't win a World Series. They didn't have a slugger to build a lineup around. They didn't have one standout ace. They won by archaic notions like stealing bases and catching balls in the gap. But, man, did they have fun doing it, and did they have motivation. The club fumed over their absence from the previous postseason despite having the best record in the division. A players' strike led to a commissioner's ruling that the first-half leader would face the second-half leader in the playoffs. The Cardinals were the overall leaders, but finished second in both halves. Whitey Herzog's club came into 1982 buoyed by the addition of shortstop Ozzie Smith and the budding of Willie McGee, certain not to let a technicality keep them out of this October. They were a running, diving, and riverboat-gambling Reagan Era answer to the Gas House Gang. Said closer Bruce Sutter: "We expected to win."

The Cardinals never lost more than four consecutive games in 1982. They had a 12-game winning streak at the start of the season and an eight-game winning streak in the final weeks of the season, as they clinched the franchise's first postseason berth in 14 years on September 27. After dispatching Atlanta in the NLCS, the Cardinals faced the Milwaukee Brewers in the World Series, the so-called Suds Series between the two beer towns.

Now Milwaukee, there was a team built to win a championship. Harvey's Wallbangers—named for the manager Harvey Kuenn and his sluggers' ability to break barriers with homers—won 95 games and sported a fearsome lineup with five players who had at least 20 home runs, three of whom hit at least 30. Four Brewers had at least 100 RBIs. Combined, the Wallbangers had 216 home runs, 70 more than any team in the NL. The power was coupled with a bona fide ace in Pete Vuckovich, who won the Cy Young Award with an 18–6 record and 3.34 ERA. (A plot twist to the World Series was Vuckovich and Ted Simmons' return to St. Louis, where they had been Cardinals until Herzog's sweepstakes trading in 1980.)

The Cardinals had balance. Andujar and Bob Forsch both won 15 games, and only one position player had more than 12 home runs. The Cardinals hit 67 homers total and scored nearly 200 runs fewer than Milwaukee. Yet they stole 200 bases as a team, led the league in defense, and had the fewest runs allowed. As catcher Darrell Porter said later, the Cardinals' dominance was subtle—teams didn't realize they had "been dominated" until they were swept and sent home. Defense does that.

"Our pitchers meetings in St. Louis were simple—don't walk anybody and keep it in the park," Sutter said. "Watching those guys play every day was truly amazing."

Milwaukee skunked the Cardinals in Game 1, 10–0, with Simmons cranking the lone home run in the Brewers' 17-hit assault. The Cardinals won the next two games, seizing Game 3 with rookie Willie McGee's scene-stealing breakout. He took two home runs away from the Brewers with catches in center, and he hit two, both off starter Vuckovich. Milwaukee rallied, however, to take Games 4 and 5 and set up a chance to clinch in Game 6. The Cardinals, unbowed, returned the rout, however, winning 13–1. That set the stage for Game 7 at Busch. Smith's two flips followed by Andujar's one gave way to a taut game that went into the bottom of the sixth with Milwaukee leading 3–1. A bases-loaded single by Keith Hernandez tied the game, and George Hendrick followed with a single for the go-ahead run. Andujar yielded to Sutter for the two-inning save, and the right-hander clinched the World Series title with a fastball past Gorman Thomas.

Sutter had two saves and one win in the series. Smith, ever the emblem of that era's golden defense, turned five double plays and handled 39 chances peerlessly in the series. But it was catcher Porter, a .231 hitter in the regular season, who won the World Series MVP. Porter had five RBIs in the series and a .286 average. Only one of Harvey's vaunted Wallbangers had as many RBIs as Porter. In the champagne celebration, Porter reportedly hollered: "Hoo-eee, I been to county fairs and a goat roast—and I ain't never seen nothin' like this."

A crowd of 100,000 crammed into downtown St. Louis to fête the World Series champions in a noon parade the next day. Phone lines at the Cardinals' offices fried, handling so many calls after Sutter's strikeout clinched Gussie Busch's and the franchise's first title in 15 years.

Hot dogs. Mustard. Goat roasts. Slick defense. Fevered fan base.

Clearly, Whiteyball had arrived.

"I've never been happier in my whole life," Busch gushed after Game 7. "I was sure this team could win it, and it didn't let me down."

No-No Doubting Forsch

About the time in his no-hitter bid that teammates stopped talking to him, Cardinals starter Bob Forsch still defied tradition by keeping the radio on while he was back in the clubhouse. On the radio, *all* the broadcasters talked about was the no-no he was in the middle of authoring. "Leave that stuff to the superstitious," Forsch said. "Every inning I'd go back there, and you'd hear about it. Look, at that point, you're either going to do it or not. It won't make a difference if somebody talks to about it. You're either going to do it or not."

Forsch did it—twice.

On April 17, 1978, Forsch won a 5–0 no-hit shutout against Philadelphia at Busch Stadium. A little more than five years later, on September 26, 1983, Forsch echoed that performance with a 3–0 no-hit shutout of Montreal. He will always be the only player, Cardinal or competitor, to throw a no-hitter at Busch Stadium II. Forsch, a right-hander, spent longer with the Cardinals than all but three pitchers, logging 15 seasons, 163 wins, and 455 games for the team. He won more games than Dizzy Dean, had a 20-win season in 1977, and claimed a World Series in 1982. He had better times, but not a better game than either of the two that made him the 25th pitcher in baseball history with two no-hitters.

In 2011, the Cardinals chose Forsch to throw out the ceremonial first pitch of the World Series' decisive Game 7. Less than a week later he collapsed and died at age 61. His ceremonial appearance celebrated his place in Cardinals history. The no-hitters cemented it.

Cardinals No-Hitters

Pitcher	Date	Opp.	Score
Ted Breitenstein	Oct. 4, 1891	vs. Louisville	8–0

Rookie and St. Louis native wins for American Association Browns.

| Jesse Haines | July 17, 1924 | vs. Boston | 5–0 |

Second-longest tenured Cardinals twirls one on "Tuberculosis Day" at Sportsman's.

| Paul Dean | Sept. 21, 1934 | at Brooklyn | 3–0 |

Rookie and Dizzy's younger brother completes dazzling doubleheader for bros.

| Lon Warneke | Aug. 30, 1941 | at Cincinnati | 2–0 |

Faced the minimum 27 batters in win that pushed Cardinals into first place.

| Ray Washburn | Sept. 18, 1968 | at San Francisco | 2–0 |

Day after Gaylord Perry no-hit Cardinals, Washburn answers with no-hitter.

| Bob Gibson | Aug. 14, 1971 | at Pittsburgh | 11–0 |

At 35, three years removed from MVP, Gibson K's Willie Stargell for no-no.

| Bob Forsch | April 16, 1978 | vs. Philadelphia | 5–0 |

Only 11,495 saw this brisk 1-hour, 52-minute jewel.

| Bob Forsch | Sept. 26, 1983 | vs. Montreal | 3–0 |

Second no-hitter thrown at Busch Stadium, and both were by Forsch.

| Jose Jimenez | June 25, 1999 | at Arizona | 1–0 |

Righty outduels Randy Johnson to be first NL rookie in 27 years with no-no.

| Bud Smith | Sept. 3, 2001 | at San Diego | 4–0 |

Rookie struck out seven, a year after throwing two no-hitters in Class AA.

In Forsch's first no-hitter, a sharp grounder in the eighth inning glanced off third baseman Ken Reitz's glove and was ruled an error. Forsch promptly got a double play and pitched a perfect ninth. Fourteen of his outs came on grounders. "Good location," he explained, "and everything was hit right at people." It was the same recipe five years later. Lumbering toward the end of a disappointing season, Forsch had just been told he should learn a knuckleball to prolong his career. He answered by striking out six in a brisk 96-pitch no-hitter. After an error in the second inning, Forsch retired 22 consecutive batters to complete his second no-no.

Bob Forsch tips his cap in 1983 after pitching the second no-hitter of his career.

As the perfect innings mounted, his teammates began avoiding him in the dugout. They stopped talking to him completely. He sought peace in the clubhouse, where the radio chattered away about what he was doing.

"Not once did I go in thinking I had no-hit stuff," Forsch said in 2008. "Not in either of them. One was at the beginning of the season and the other was the end. One, my arm wasn't yet at full strength, and the other my arm was tired from a full season. They

just sort of happened. They felt like every other game until at the
end you knew they weren't like any other game."

Clark Clinches in the Clutch

NLCS Game 6: October 16, 1985

Leading the Cardinals by one run and choosing to ignore the one
base he had open, Los Angeles Dodgers manager Tommy Lasorda
decided to pitch to Jack Clark.

It was one decision he'd like to have back.

Showing signs of recovering from Ozzie Smith's go-crazy, game-
winning home run two days earlier, the Dodgers had retaken a lead
on Mike Marshall's home run in the eighth and were an inning
away from forcing a Game 7 in the 1985 National League
Championship Series. Closer Tom Niedenfuer, who had a 2.71
ERA and finished 43 games that season, came in for his third
inning of work. He had one out and an 0–2 count on Willie
McGee when the Cardinals' center fielder poked a single. McGee
stole second, and Niedenfuer walked Ozzie Smith. A groundout by
Tommy Herr moved the runners over—but also moved the
Dodgers an out closer to Game 7 and opened first base for Clark.
The hulking first baseman had been acquired by the Cardinals for
just this kind of at-bat, and he had rewarded them so far with 22
homers and a top-10 finish in the MVP balloting that season. Two
innings earlier, however, Niedenfuer had fed Clark a series of sliders
and struck him out to squelch a Cardinals rally.

Lasorda could have intentionally walked Clark and had
Niedenfuer or a lefty specialist pitch to Andy Van Slyke. Many on
the field and around it expected the Dodgers' manager to fire four

fingers into the air and be done with Clark. He didn't flinch. Lasorda wanted the right-handed Niedenfuer to face the right-handed-hitting Clark and did not want the bases loaded. "It was my fault," he later told his team. On Niedenfuer's first pitch, Clark drove a bolt deep and long gone to left field. "It was serious Star Wars," Van Slyke told reporters.

The enduring image of the shot that catapulted the Cardinals into the 1985 World Series isn't the jubilation at home plate after Clark's three-run homer or the champagne-spritzing after the 7–5 victory. No, it's Dodgers left fielder Pedro Guerrero not even moving as the ball soared over his head, save to turn and spike his glove into the grass.

The enduring question is all about pitching to Clark.

"Why?" Cardinals manager Whitey Herzog said years later, settling back into a chair. "I don't know why they pitched to him."

The Call

World Series Game 6: October 26, 1985

There was little else Don Denkinger could do when presented over and over again with photographic evidence of his botched call on baseball's biggest stage than sign off on it. Some 19 years after one of the finest umpires in the American League became one of the foulest words in Cardinals Nation, that umpire slipped into St. Louis to appear at a memorabilia show. A good sport, he signed his name over and over again on pictures of the play immortalized—and agonized—as "the Call."

Denkinger's only role in the Interstate 70 Series should have been bit player, a nameless official who is out of focus in the swirling snapshots of the victorious Cardinals. Buoyed by a brilliant Game 6 start by Danny Cox—seven shutout innings and eight strikeouts—and Brian Harper's RBI single when pinch-hitting for Cox, the Cardinals held a 1–0 lead going into the ninth inning. A postseason that had featured the homer heroics of Ozzie Smith and Jack Clark and the killer tarp that ate Vince Coleman was three outs away from Whitey Herzog's second championship in four seasons.

The Tarp That Ate Vince

The Cardinals' slowed offense in the '85 World Series was traced back to a bizarre incident before Game 4 of the NLCS. As rookie Vince Coleman left the field a couple hours before game time, a light rain began to fall. Busch Stadium II had an automatic, push-button tarp—and Coleman wasn't watching it as the tarp cranked up its march across the diamond. The tarpaulin caught the outfielder's foot and gobbled his leg, rolling up past his hip and pinning him for 15 or so seconds. Coleman yelped and sustained bruising and a bone chip before being rescued. The rookie who stole 110 bases that season didn't appear again in the postseason. The mechanical tarp had some staying power, at least another decade, before the grounds crew went back to the old-fashioned roll-by-hand tarp.

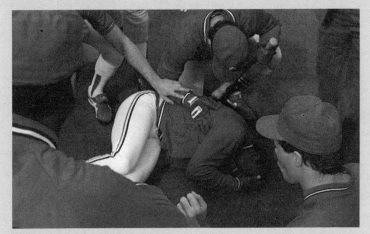

The speedy Vince Coleman was knocked out of the 1985 playoffs after an automatic tarpaulin injured his leg.

That all changed when Denkinger said one word: "Safe."

Cardinals reliever Todd Worrell started the ninth inning at Royals Stadium, facing pinch-hitter Jorge Orta. The two-time All-Star was a bench bat for the Royals, getting three plate appearances total. He chopped Worrell's fourth pitch to the right side of the infield. First baseman Jack Clark charged to field it. Worrell raced to cover the bag. Clark's throw was wide left, but Worrell's reach was true, and he caught it while keeping a foot on the bag. The throw beat Orta by a half stride. First-base ump Denkinger swiped his hands through the air in the universal sign for "safe" and instantly morphed from umpire to a derisive verb. To Denkinger was to blow it.

There wasn't an angle that supported Denkinger's safe call. Television replays showed the throw beating Orta to the bag. Still photographs—even one that later inspired a ubiquitous painted print in the St. Louis area—showed the ball in Worrell's glove before Orta's foot hit the bag. One picture clearly shows Orta's cleat snagging and pulling off the heel off Worrell's right shoe as he touches the bag. If Worrell's shoe is under Orta's shoe as they both hit the bag: "How could he [beat the throw] if he stepped on Worrell's foot?" Herzog asked after the game.

"We had the damned World Series won," he added.

Instead, the Cardinals crumbled.

From the moment Denkinger became a pariah in St. Louis, the Cardinals self-destructed. The hitter after Orta, Steve Balboni, skied a foul popup toward the first-base dugout and Clark and catcher Darrell Porter allowed it to drop between them. A passed ball three batters later moved two runners into scoring position and forced an intentional walk to Hal McRae. Pinch-hitter Dane Iorg, a former Cardinal, then roped a single to right field to score both runners and force a Game 7 with a 2–1 victory.

The Cardinals' meltdown continued the next night as they lost 11–0. Herzog was ejected—by Denkinger, behind home plate for Game 7, no less—and the Cardinals' 101-win season imploded.

There were many culprits besides Denkinger's blown call. The Cardinals hit .185 in the seven-game series, scored just 13 runs, and the trio of Ozzie Smith, Andy Van Slyke, and Tommy Herr combined for one more hit in 60 at-bats than the six Clark had in 25. The cross-state rival Royals used just six pitchers in the seven games, and the Cardinals still had a lead after Denkinger's call. "There were a lot of mistakes made in the latter part of that inning," Denkinger told the *Post-Dispatch* a year later, "and they weren't all made by an umpire."

Though fans could be hostile in the years that followed, Denkinger remained humorous, even self-deprecating, about the Call. When the umpire returned to unfriendly territory in 2004 for the show, a fan passed him something other than a picture of Worrell at first and Orta lunging. The fan wanted him to autograph an eye chart.

Denkinger signed it cheerfully.

86 Laga Has Left the Building

A few days before Mike Laga and his famous foul ball became the answer to a beloved standard of St. Louis trivia, the .199 career hitter all but predicted that no ballpark, not even the cement monolith of Busch Stadium, could hold him. "It's a more forgiving park for pitchers, but I think it will make me a better hitter," Laga told reporters when he first joined the Cardinals in September 1986. "But if I hit it right and get it up in the air, I can hit it out of any ballpark."

It's unlikely he meant it as literally as it happened.

Less than two weeks before he stepped in for his third-inning at-bat against New York Mets starter Ron Darling, Laga was finally named as the player to be named later in a deal between Detroit and the Cardinals. It was a break in what had been a precipitous fall for the former first-round draft pick. Laga had averaged 26 homers and 83 RBIs a season in five full seasons in the Tigers' minors, but he couldn't get such traction in the majors. Four years after debuting in Detroit, he'd never been able to echo his three homers and 11 RBIs in 88 at-bats that summer. Whitey Herzog, however, saw latent power that just needed a jumpstart. If you're going to swing, Laga once reasoned, "you might as well swing hard." And so on September 2, 1986, Laga became a Cardinal to complete a deal that also brought pitcher Ken Hill from Detroit for catcher Mike Heath. Instantly confirming Herzog's hope, Laga homered in his first at-bat at Busch Stadium. He doubled off Darling in the second inning when he started at first and hit cleanup that next day, the now infamous September 15, 1986.

The multipurpose ballpark in downtown St. Louis—officially Busch Memorial Stadium, but also the second Busch Stadium—had so many features that were indistinguishable from the other cookie cutters of the time. From Pittsburgh to Cincinnati to St. Louis, the only reliable way to identify the slab of stadium was asking the name of the river closest to it. Well, that and the crown. Sometimes called the "bottle cap" for how Busch ballpark had a top similar to cap on many Busch products, Busch Stadium's "crown of arches" was a ring of mini, scalloped arches circling the stadium, a wink to the landmark Gateway Arch that was built at the same time. The crown leaned out over the last rows of the upper deck, some 130' above the playing surface.

The geometry of hitting a ball hard enough and high enough to actually clear the crown was so implausible that it had to be impossible. Or so was thought until Laga arrived.

The first baseman would play parts of three seasons with the Cardinals, and he could have been the starting first baseman in 1988 if not for separating his shoulder when he stepped on his glove during a spring training drill. He returned from injury to receive a

Longest Home Runs, Both Legendary and Legitimate

During 2005, the last summer Busch II stood, outfielder Larry Walker took batting practice with an aluminum bat, and while he shelled the deepest reaches of the right-field stands (and shattered one luxury-box window) not even then could he do what Mike Laga did in 1986. No one did. It took a new ballpark for the boundary to be broken again. Since the design of the new ballpark went public, a break in the stands—different from the complete circle of Busch II—got people to wondering if a ball could literally (finally) leave the ballpark. Albert Pujols proved it's possible. On April 2, 2006, the Cardinals took a pit stop in St. Louis for a private workout at their new ballpark before jetting to the season opener in Philadelphia. During his first batting practice, Pujols drilled a shot that cleared the stands in left-center field and hit an open concessions area before, allegedly, bouncing out of the ballpark and onto Clark Street. That's what witnesses, the few that were present, said that evening. "If it bounced much," manager Tony La Russa said a few hours later, "it certainly did." The longest homers exist mostly in legends; here are the ones in the record books.

Longest Home Runs at Busch II (1966–2005)

Est. Distance	Player (Team)	Date	Opponent
545 ft.	Mark McGwire, Cardinals	5/16/98	Florida
Nailed *Post-Dispatch* sign in center; Band-Aid was placed there to mark shot			
527 ft.	Mark McGwire, Cardinals	5/12/98	Milwaukee
Reached left-center upper deck			
517 ft.	Mark McGwire, Cardinals	9/16/97	Dodgers
First-inning shot off of left-field façade			
514 ft.	J.D. Drew, Cardinals	5/16/03	Cubs
Hit top of Diamondvision screen in right field			
511 ft.	Mark McGwire, Cardinals	7/17/98	Dodgers
Landed in left-field upper deck			

Longest Home Runs at Busch III (2006–2008)

Est. Distance	Player (Team)	Date	Opponent
465 ft.	Albert Pujols, Cardinals	8/14/11	Colorado
Took NL lead in homers with a bolt that cleared the bleachers behind the visitors' bullpen in left			
452 ft.	Lance Berkman, Cardinals	7/5/11	Cincinnati
The first-pitch homer went deep to right field and was the 350th of his career			
450 ft.	Ryan Ludwick, Cardinals	7/22/08	Milwaukee
First-inning shot creamed to grassy batter's eye in center			
449 ft.	Dan Uggla, Florida	8/29/06	Cardinals
Landed in "Big Mac Land", second deck of left field			
448 ft.	Josh Willingham, Florida	8/23/07	Cardinals
Marlins slugger had two homers in this game, including a grand slam			

Source: St. Louis Cardinals media relations and St. Louis Post-Dispatch *research*

career-high 100 at-bats that season and responded with a career-low .130. He was with San Francisco the next season and out of the majors after 1990. Such was his career. Big swings. Bigger misses. He retired with 16 homers in 423 at-bats and one Bunyanesque foul ball that became legend. In the third inning of that game on September 15, Laga dug into the left-handed hitter's box and with one mighty chop did as he nearly predicted. Laga launched a ball with such force and such height that it cleared the crown and vanished. The ball was found later, sometime after the 13-inning 1–0 Cardinals' victory ended, in a flower bed outside of the ballpark, near the employees' parking lot. No hitter had ever done it before and none since, leaving Laga as the only Cardinal ever to hit a ball completely out of Busch II. The crowd stood and roared with applause—even though the blast was 150' foul, down the first-base line.

Laga stepped back into the box for the next pitch.

And he struck out.

87 The Secret Weapon

The night Jose Oquendo pitched his way late into the early morning, the organization's super-sub outlasted even last call.

On May 14, 1988, the Atlanta Braves and Cardinals played a 5-hour, 40-minute game that included 11 scoreless innings between the time Atlanta tied the score and won the game with Ken Griffey Sr.'s double in the top of the nineteenth inning. Three of those innings were pitched by Cardinals utilityman Oquendo, the eventual losing pitcher. Fans had time to leave the game, stay at the bar 'til close, and come back to grab a beer and watch the final few innings of Oquendo pitching. A steady trickle of fans funneled into Busch after midnight, and while they may have come for the beer and stayed to see some bonus baseball, what they didn't know at the time was they were watching National League history.

Oquendo had already played first base in the game and had appeared at five other positions already that season, including his debut in center a night before. Less than a month later he'd play left, and on September 24, for the first time in his professional career, he caught the seventh inning of a blowout loss. Nicknamed the Secret Weapon for his ability to play adeptly anywhere at any time, Oquendo spent his youth playing mostly in the outfield. During a Little League tournament, the Puerto Rico native moved to shortstop and there he stayed, from signing at 16 to debuting in the majors at 19. The switch-hitter switched positions regularly. He was the starting third baseman early in 1988 and played 156 games at second in 1989. The next year he set a franchise record with a .996 fielding percentage.

With any other team, Oquendo could have been the finest fielder on the roster, but his 10 years with the Cardinals overlapped Ozzie Smith's heyday. Oquendo became a master of all positions, starter of none. That's why after throwing four innings in a 19-inning game one night, Oquendo was playing center field the next. His arm felt "like Jell-O," he said. His back, toes, and shoulder all ached, and he had to throw virtually underhand from center because he couldn't raise his elbow above his shoulder. But he was in the field, and that's all that mattered.

"I enjoy being in the game, and whatever it takes to be in the game needs to be done," says Oquendo, who retired to become a gifted infield and third-base coach for the Cardinals. "For me, I didn't care where I was. I don't have a favorite position. My favorite position is in the game."

88 Meet Ernie Hays, the Organist

When he got the tip that the local baseball club was going to audition musicians to play its posh new organ at games, Ernie Hays already had an in—first-hand experience. The organ being installed at Busch Memorial Stadium was the same model that Hays had been paid to play at the same store doing the installing. "We already had a working relationship," Hays cracked decades later. Hays, a University City kid and music fan before baseball fan, first tickled the keys at a Cardinals game in 1971; he retired in 2010 after 40 seasons. When he first sat down, the Cardinals gave him simple rules: "rah rah" for home team, "raspberries" for the visitors, and not a peep about the umpires. Through the decades, Hays adopted a rule of his own: "I don't do any Top 40."

Born on New Year's Day 1935, Hays caught the music bug as a boy who would "smudge up his nose by pressing it up against the screen door" to listen to his U-City neighbors play away the night. He started with piano lessons—at $1 a lesson—and cultivated the talent through his youth while playing for fun, playing for family, and playing for a paycheck at the music store that supplied the Cardinals' organ. In his three decades, he has composed the incidental music for Cardinals' history and seen the organ become a technical marvel, exchanging pull stops for programs. The instrument has changed. His music did not.

Hays specialized in what he calls "clap chants"—the foot-stopping, crowd-pleasing tunes that stir a silent ballpark. He turned many tunes into clap chants, like TV themes, but none as well or as lasting as "Here Comes the King." The Cardinals' unofficial theme song has its roots in soccer. Hays played at professional indoor soccer games and in the late '70s broke out the Budweiser tune, "Here Comes the King," to great effect. Encouraged to take the song with him to the ballpark, Hays played it into a tradition. It is the song that now welcomes the parade of players on Opening Day. The song has come to define the ballpark in St. Louis so much that it transcends the ballpark. Hays has been hired to play it at weddings, often as the groom enters.

In February 2006 Hays had a heart valve replaced—sort of fitting for an organist—and still he was in his new box for Opening Day at the new ballpark. He stands out for his Cardinal-red suspenders and his jokes. He had a feel for when to play, and sometimes—in the case of heroics—when to let the crowd do the work. So that he could keep playing as he approached 80, Hays pumped iron. Sure, the fingers have to be nimble, but his abdominal muscles had to be fine-tuned, too. For proof, Hays points to his years of blasting out those clap-chants and the marathon "King" anthems—and, he says grinning, "no lower back trouble" from always carrying the tune.

89 The Big Numbers: Rogers Hornsby's .424

On Opening Day 1924, Cardinals second baseman Rogers Hornsby had two hits in five at-bats and finished a 6–5 victory against the Chicago Cubs with a .400 batting average. It would only go up from there. As part of Hornsby's run of six consecutive National League batting titles, the Cardinals' second baseman set what was long viewed as a modern record with a .424 batting average that summer.

In a season with an unremarkable record and a sixth-place finish, the Cardinals stood out for individual achievements, from Jesse Haines' no-hitter and Hi Bell's two-win doubleheader to Jim Bottomley's record-setting 12-RBI game. In each game, Hornsby provided the complementary hits. He had three hits in Haines' no-no, raising his average to .410. He had three hits total in the doubleheader games started and won by Bell, and Hornsby scored two of Bottomley's 12 RBIs. Hornsby had won his 1923 batting title at home, having finished the season suspended by manager Branch Rickey. The two feuded over a take sign, and Rickey fined the future manager $500 and released a statement that Hornsby had been sent home.

Back for 1924, he led the league in runs (121), slugging (.696), on-base percentage (.507), walks (89), doubles (43), and, of course, hits (227). He went hitless in just 24 of the 143 games he played, batted .509 in August, and his .424 average was .049 better than the second-best in the league and .141 better than the league average. Both he and American League star Nap Lajoie died believing Hornsby had the highest average in baseball since 1900, but Lajoie's average in 1901 underwent some revising and correction as late as the 1980s. Set at .422 for most of the 20th century, Lajoie's average is now accepted as .426, edging Hornsby for the title. It was another second-place finish from 1924 that really gnawed at Hornsby. Brooklyn pitcher Dazzy Vance won the league MVP that season, finishing 12 points ahead of Hornsby in the vote of writers. Hornsby offered a simple explanation for his average on the final day of the season: "Hustled on everything I hit."

90 The Big Numbers: Bob Gibson's 1.12

There have been countless baseball legends who have changed the games in which they played, but few can claim what Bob Gibson can after his epic 1968 season. He changed the way all games are played.

The same season that Denny McLain won 31 games in the American League and pitchers were exceedingly successful, Gibson redefined dominance and forever changed the landscape of pitching with his 1.12 ERA that summer. Gibson's '68 ERA is the fourth-lowest in history, and in a 135-year span of professional baseball records, Gibson's 1.12 in the only single-season ERA in the top 40 of all time that came after 1920. Only one pitcher since has had a half season with an ERA lower than Gibson's (Roger Clemens' 0.97 in the second half of 1990). On his way to both the National League Cy Young Award, his first of two, and the NL MVP, Gibson went 22–9 with 304⅔ innings and a league-best 13 shutouts and 268 strikeouts. The next season Major League Baseball altered the dimensions of the mound to diminish a pitcher's edge and inspire more offense. "You don't sit down and go, 'Hell, I was pretty good,'" Gibson said on the 40th anniversary of the 1.12. "I didn't ever think that I wasn't going to finish a ballgame. You think when you give up a run or two, that's it. Or if you give up four, that's it. That's the way you have to look at it.... Everything has to go just right, just right, for a year like that. Great defense behind you. Get good calls from the umpire. All of it."

In his first 10 starts of the season, Gibson had a 1.52 ERA but only a 3–5 record. His teammates scored two or fewer runs in eight of Gibson's losses in 1968, and twice he lost 1–0—including San Francisco ace Gaylord Perry's no-hitter. Eleven of Gibson's 34 starts were opposite pitchers who would later join him in the Hall of Fame, and he went 5–5 with a 1.45 ERA in those games. After one such game—a 1–0 shutout of Atlanta against Phil Niekro—Gibson's own teammate, outfielder Bobby Tolan, chirped, "Don't you ever get tired of getting people out?"

That summer, Don Drysdale pitched 58⅔ consecutive scoreless innings, a span that included a duel with Gibson, in which the Cardinals' right-hander allowed one hit and Drysdale got the shutout. But Gibson had a stretch that rivaled—if not surpassed—Drysdale's. From June 6 to July 25, Gibson started and finished 10 games that included eight shutouts against eight different teams. He allowed two earned runs total in the span of 90 innings for an ERA of 0.20. Of the two runs, one scored on a bloop double down the line and the other, the one that kept his scoreless streak from trumping Drysdale's, came on a wild pitch. "Well, it wasn't," Gibson said. "It was a passed ball." On September 2, Gibson won his 20th game, and his ERA was still less than 1.00. The major league average that summer was 2.98, and the next spring the mound was lowered from 15 inches to 10 inches. The bats began to take over.

"It lowered the mound and literally took a lot of those sinker-ball guys out of the game. Not too many people can do that," said Joe Torre, who became a teammate and friend the next season. "You can do things in other sports that change the rules. Aren't too many times they've changed the rules in this game. What'd he lose—nine games that year? Think about losing nine games with a 1.12 ERA. He caused a change in the game."

91 The Big Numbers: Steve Carlton's 19

Perhaps it was a sign of things to come that Lefty's stirring and record-setting start with the Cardinals ultimately ended as a disappointment. Steve Carlton, the left-handed starter so good and eventually such a recluse that his nickname "Lefty" became an excuse as much as a moniker, was still ascending as one of the game's most enthralling pitchers when he faced the New York Mets on September 15, 1969, at Busch Stadium. The 24-year-old starter had gone nine consecutive starts without allowing more than three earned runs. His record was just 1–3 in his previous five starts, but he'd plunged his ERA down to 1.92 after allowing seven earned runs in his previous 37⅔ innings. He'd also struck out 10 for the fifth time that season just four days earlier. He was primed to do what no modern-day pitcher had ever done.

Carlton's first six outs of the game were strikeouts. He also struck out the final four batters he faced, including three expedient whiffs in the ninth for a complete game. When he struck out Amos Otis for the fourth time in the game and the final out of the top of the ninth, Carlton had set a major league record with 19 strikeouts. He bettered the modern-day record held at 18 by Sandy Koufax, Bob Feller, and Don Wilson. He had made history.

He had also lost.

Bracketed between his first and his major league record 19th strikeout, Carlton gave up two two-run home runs to Ron Swoboda, and the Mets won 4–3. "I'm very elated to have done something no other pitcher had ever done," Carlton said after the

game. "Superswat got me. I got him twice and he got me twice."
Lefty added later, "I kept challenging everybody. It cost me the ballgame." Carlton's record dropped to 16–10, and his ERA actually
rose to 2.00. He'd finish the year with a 2.17 ERA, the second-best
in the National League and his lowest as a Cardinal.

Carlton flew to St. Louis as a college pitcher to try out for the
club and sell them on signing him as a free agent. They did for what
would become an ironic bonus of $5,000. By 20 he was in the
majors. He was a regular at 22, a pivotal member of two pennant
winners. At 24, he was a major league record-holder. At 26, a 20-
game winner. And, at 27, a Phillie. Like one of his most dazzling
games, Carlton burned bright as a Cardinal only to end as a loss.
Recognizing the salary clashes between owner August Busch Jr. and
the stubborn, quirky left-hander had become irreconcilable, general
manager Bing Devine dealt Carlton to Philadelphia for right-
handed pitcher Rick Wise. Later, it was revealed that the difference
was a puny $5,000. Carlton went on to win the first of his four Cy
Young Awards in 1972, the year after the trade. He become one of

Lefty Haunts Cardinals

The Cardinals slogged through a difficult decade after trading Steve Carlton to
the Philadelphia Phillies, and before winning the 1982 World Series, leaving
some to wonder if Carlton's absence upset the club's karma. It didn't help that
Lefty routinely reminded the Cardinals of his ability, firsthand. Since 1957, no
pitcher has more than 30 wins in his career against the Cardinals save Carlton.
He was 38–14 against his former club with five shutouts—including his first
game against the Cardinals—and a 2.96 ERA. Moreover, his pivotal milestones
came against the Cardinals. In June 1983 Carlton struck out Cardinals outfielder
Lonnie Smith for his 3,522nd K, moving ahead of an injured Nolan Ryan into the
all-time lead, however briefly. In September of that same season Carlton, age
38, returned to Busch Stadium to strike out 12 in eight innings and win the 300th
game of his career. That prompted *Post-Dispatch* sportswriter Kevin Horrigan to
muse a few days later in the paper: "I wonder what Rick Wise is doing right this
minute."

the game's most exceptional starters, sometimes at the expense of the Cardinals, using a fastball that singed in the 90s and a slider he refined while touring Japan with the Cardinals. Carlton retired in 1988 with a 329–244 record and 4,136 strikeouts. As a Cardinal, he collected 77 of those wins and 951 of those strikeouts.

Once the all-time leader in strikeouts, he now sits fourth overall, and Randy Johnson pushed by him as the all-time leader for lefties. His 19 strikeouts has also been echoed and surpassed. Four different pitchers have combined for five 19-K games since Carlton's, and two pitchers—Kerry Wood and Roger Clemens—have reset the record at 20 Ks.

After the deal to Philadelphia, Carlton began to distance himself from a public eye he distrusted. He stopped talking to the media. He became known as an eccentric. And he attempted to pull a J.D. Salinger—authoring brilliance and then fading into anonymity. The Hall of Fame wouldn't let him. Despite cutting off the media shortly after leaving St. Louis, the voters lauded what Lefty did on the field. In 1994 he set another record with a tidier ending—receiving the most total Hall of Fame votes of any player inducted at the time.

92 The Big Numbers: Lou Brock's 118

A few days after Hank Aaron electrified baseball by eclipsing Babe Ruth and being crowned as the new home-run king on April 8, 1974, the Cardinals cruised into New York for just the second series of the young season. Lou Brock dashed by the league offices and was presented with a plan. Years later he described how an official suggested a way to piggyback on the excitement created by Aaron's race for Ruth's 714 home runs. "Maybe," Brock recalled the official saying, "you ought to go after Maury Wills' record." Wills' record was 104 stolen bases in one season, and it stood for 12 years and still remained 30 more than Brock had ever taken in a season. About to turn 35, Brock, the "Base Burglar" in St. Louis, didn't know if his legs could keep up with the league's idea. Still, the official persisted. "They wanted to hitch their wagon to me," Brock told the *Post-Dispatch* a couple decades later.

The chase was on.

Brock stole his first base of the season on April 13, a couple days after leaving New York, and he sprinted to a remarkable 38 steals in his first 40 attempts. Manager Red Schoendienst planned to urge his Cardinals to run, run, run for the pennant, and Brock set the pace. With nine consecutive seasons with at least 50 steals as his tailwind, Brock scoffed later at the idea he had any element of surprise on his side that late in his career. He likened swiping a base to a clandestine operation, but done in broad daylight. "You have taken a piece of territory behind enemy lines," Brock said, adding that he had to do it when everyone knew he was going to try. At the All-Star break he had 60 steals. On August 6, with baseball eyeing his every swipe, Brock broke his personal best with his 75th steal of the season in the Cardinals' 110th game. On September 1, he stole four bases to reach 98, and within two of being only the second player since 1900 to steal 100 in a season. "When he got around 80," Wills told reporters that season, "it became very obvious." On September 10 at Busch against visiting Philadelphia, Brock tied Wills' record when he stole second in the first inning and broke it when he stole second in the seventh for his 105th of the season. (He did, after all, steal second 112 times that summer.) As Brock dusted off the dirt from his right shin, Negro League great James "Cool Papa" Bell marched onto the field as part of an immediate ceremony. Bell took the base and handed it to Brock, saying "he could take it home [because] he'd steal it anyway." Brock would go on to steal 13 more bases and reset the record at 118. It would last seven years until a brash young speedster named Rickey Henderson would burn by it with 130 in 1982, and then nearly nine years later eclipse Brock's major league best career total of 938, too.

From the moment he arrived in the majors, Brock was chasing the Dodgers' Wills, either inspired by his steals or, in 1974, a challenger for his record. "It was always we wanted to do what Maury Wills does," Brock said three decades later. And he did. Only better.

93 Hard-Hittin' Mark Whiten

The crowd at Cinergy Field on September 7, 1993, had already been treated to an eyeful of offense when the Cardinals and hosting Cincinnati Reds—two going-nowhere teams—began limbering up for Game 2 of a late-season doubleheader. The Reds rallied in the bottom of the ninth of Game 1 to win 14–13, concluding a game that included a combined 36 hits, 49 base runners, 15 pitchers used, and 3 hours, 41 minutes of artificial turf baseball.

The second game started at 9:46 PM local time. The crowd had thinned out. There was little reason to tune in, drop by, or stay up.

And then history happened.

Mark Whiten, a switch-hitting outfielder in his first season with the Cardinals, announced his intentions with his first swing of the evening. The sixth hitter of the first inning, Whiten got ahead 2–0 against Reds starter Larry Luebbers and then ripped a pitch 408′ for a grand slam. He was just getting started. Whiten would tie two major league records that night—launching four home runs and echoing Cardinals great Jim Bottomley with 12 RBIs. They are the only two players ever with a dozen RBIs in one game.

Whiten's Hard Hittin' Game Stats

Inn.	Opposing Pitcher	HIT	RBIs
1	Larry Luebbers, RHP	HR	4
4	Larry Luebbers, RHP	FO	0
6	Mike Anderson, RHP	HR	3
7	Mike Anderson, RHP	HR	3
9	Rob Dibble, RHP	HR	2

Whiten, 26 at the time, had been on a prolonged power outage entering the late-night game. Traded to the Cardinals at the end of spring training that year, Whiten was on his third team and had barely 1,000 at-bats in the majors. His first turn in the National League, however, agreed with him. Whiten had yet to hit 10 home runs in any big-league season before 1993, leaving him with a nickname built more on its rhyming than on Hard-Hittin' Whiten's actual hard hittin'. But he had 11 home runs by the All-Star break in '93 and 16 by the end of July.

The brownout started in August, as Whiten came to the plate against Luebbers that night without a home run in about a month, a span of 80 at-bats. In the offensive display of Game 1, only two starting position players on the field didn't get a hit—Cincinnati's Hal Morris and Whiten. He, instead, got flummoxed by a sinking liner in the ninth that allowed the winning run to score. Whiten made up for Game 1 quickly in Game 2.

Bounding toward career highs in homers (25) and RBIs (99) that season, Whiten feasted on three different Reds pitchers. He opened with the grand slam, followed with two three-run shots off reliever Mike Anderson, and closed with a two-run launch off "Nasty Boy" fireballer Rob Dibble. His fourth and final home run traveled 441' as it made him the 12th player in major league history with four in a game.

"Man, what a blast that was," Jack Buck said in the KMOX broadcast that night. "What a blast this is…. Wow! Excuse me while I applaud."

The total distance covered by Whiten's home runs in his record-tying night was 1,634′. He would go on to hit three more home runs that season and drive in as many runs in his next 24 games as he did that one night. Coming out of the 1994 strike, the Cardinals swapped Whiten for a third baseman, Scott Cooper, and Whiten really only had one more year as an everyday player before leaving the majors in 2000. The night he hit four, his teammates improvised a red carpet of team-issue equipment bags and left him two bottles of champagne in his locker. All four balls were retrieved and delivered to Whiten.

"I don't have words to explain this," Whiten told reporters that evening. "Every time I hit it, I was kind of amazed."

94 One Pitch, Four Steals

Chicago Cubs right-hander Scott Sanderson flirted with whiplash before he dared throw the pitch to the Cardinals' No. 3 hitter, Tommy Herr. At least four times he snapped his head back to peek at second base. There, Vince Coleman, liquid speed in rookie form, was easing off the base. Willie McGee, racing toward an MVP award, was at first. There were no outs, and Sanderson didn't need to look back to know what Coleman was thinking. He was thinking what he was always thinking: *90′ ain't so far.*

Once Sanderson stopped looking and threw his next pitch, Coleman wouldn't stop at a mere 90′, and the Cardinals would do something that confounded the official scorer even as it tested the record book.

On August 1, 1985, the Cardinals concluded their longest road trip of the season with a 9–8 loss to the Cubs at Wrigley Field. The game was decided in the fourteenth. It was memorable in the first. On one pitch, the Cardinals stole four bases—two by Coleman, including home, and two by Willie McGee. It was the kind of swift thievery that was the hallmark of the go-go Cardinals in the 1980s. That season, they stole 314 bases, the most by any one club in any season that decade. No other club stole 190 in that season. The summer of '85 was the fourth of seven consecutive years that the Cardinals would lead the league with more than 200 steals.

Just as he paced the play, Coleman set the tempo for the season. A rookie who came up from Triple A to absorb playing time in Tito Landrum's absence, Coleman ran away with a starting job and sprinted toward the Rookie of the Year award. He stole 110 bases that season, shattering the previous rookie record of 73. His 110 remains the second most in franchise history, second to Hall of Famer Lou Brock. In an article about the man nicknamed Mercury Swift, *Sports Illustrated* wrote that he covered "the 90′ between bases quicker than an opposing catcher can say 'Lou Brock.'"

When Sanderson did finally deliver the pitch to Herr in the first inning that Thursday, Coleman and McGee were off. Coleman beat catcher Jody Davis' throw to third but he slid—head first, of course—by the bag. Toast if he turned back to third, Coleman scrambled to his feet and raced for home. Third baseman Ron Cey threw to Davis. The catcher ran Coleman back toward third and flipped to Cey. At the same time, McGee streaked behind the Cubs' third baseman to take third. Cey's momentary hesitation allowed Coleman to dart back toward home, pass Davis on the third-base line, and cruise into an uncovered home. Sanderson had chosen to cover third instead of the plate.

The Cardinals' lead was short-lived, but the research was just starting. The press box placed a call to the Elias Sports Bureau to find out how to score the play. There was no error. There were mistakes, but no error. The ruling: four steals. "Four bases on one pitch," Coleman told reporters after the game, during which he tripled twice to go with the two steals that gave him 74 in his first 88 big-league games. "That's a record. That goes in the *Guinness Book of Records*."

Musial's Dynamic Doubleheader

While Stan Musial was on a power tear to start the 1954 season, a May edition of the *Saturday Evening Post* hit newsstands with a painting of the Cardinals great on its cover, capturing "the Man" and his reputation even as it helped to promote it. In the painting, done by John Falter, Musial is standing near the bat rack and studiously signing autographs for several teen boys. It's a painting that would later hang in the Hall of Fame and add to Musial's off-field reputation.

Its published date was May 1, 1954.

A day later he added to his on-field legend.

In a doubleheader against the New York Giants at Sportsman's Park (then called the first Busch Stadium), Musial became the first major leaguer to hit five home runs in a doubleheader. He cranked three in the first game—the first three-homer game of his career— and hammered two in the nightcap. Rain had washed out that day's batting practice and, in his biography, Musial recounts a visit that day by a New York reporter asking around about the best player in baseball. Cardinals manager Eddie Stanky jerked his thumb Musial's way, answering, "Number 6."

Number 6's day started innocently enough with him limping off a walk in the first inning of the first game. In the third he ripped lefty Johnny Antonelli's curve for a solo home run onto the pavilion roof. He homered onto the roof in the fifth. In the eighth with the scored tied 6–6, Musial jacked a Jim Hearn slider to the roof for his third homer of the game and enough to boost the Cardinals to a 10–6 victory.

In his third plate appearance of the second game, Musial had his hardest hit of the day—a blast that traveled 410 or 420′, depending on the memory of the witness. At either distance, everyone knew its destination: Willie Mays, the Giants' slick center fielder, tracked it down less than a stride from the wall in center field. His next at-bat he launched a Hoyt Wilhelm curve where no one could reach it—over the stands and out onto Grand Avenue. Wilhelm would ride his knuckleball all the way to Cooperstown and so he tried to flutter one by Musial in the seventh only to have that soar over the roof in right-center field.

Musial got one more at-bat, in the ninth inning of a 9–7 loss, and thinking homer, itching for a homer, and swinging mightily for that sixth homer. "I had one more time at bat, and that's the only time that day I really tried for a homer," Musial said years later. "You know what I did? I popped up."

Musial, who also had an eight-hit doubleheader back in 1946, would go on to hit 35 home runs that season, the third-highest total of his career, and he would drive in 126 runs, his second-highest total. The Cardinals would finish a disappointing sixth in the National League, leaving Musial's early power as the signature of the season.

Musial's Five Doubleheader Home Runs

Game	Inn.	Opposing Pitcher	RBIs
1	3	Johnny Antonelli, LHP	1
1	5	Antonelli	2
1	8	Jim Hearn, RHP	3
2	5	Hoyt Wilhelm, RHP	2
2	7	Wilhelm	1

Eighteen years later his five-homer feat was matched. On August 1, 1972, San Diego first baseman Nate Colbert, on his way to the only 100-RBI season of his career, cranked five home runs against Atlanta. Colbert had his three-homer game in the nightcap, and afterward the St. Louis native revealed an uncanny coincidence. He was an eight-year-old fan, glove in hand, at the doubleheader in which Musial set the record he had just tied.

"Stan was my idol after that day," Colbert told the *Los Angeles Times* in 1989. "Now when I see him, he says, 'We're the only ones to do it.'"

96 La Russa Leaves on Top

In the champagne-soaked afterglow that followed making good on his pledge to win the Cardinals franchise its 10th World Series championship, manager Tony La Russa sought a quiet corner of the clubhouse. It was October 2006, and La Russa needed a moment to reflect after more than a decade on the job. But Bob Gibson followed him. The Hall of Fame pitcher extended a hand to La Russa and said simply, "Welcome to the club."

Fewer phrases have resonated more with La Russa.

A manager who believes the highest compliment one can get or give is to be called "a baseball man," La Russa has a keen appreciation for history. Yet for much of his early years in red he felt detached from the history of the organization he managed. He was with the Cardinals, but not a part of the Cardinals—not even when he piloted the team to annual October appearances, two 100-win seasons, and a National League pennant in 2004. He knew something was missing: a World Series ring. Any Cardinal who is a true Cardinal has one.

La Russa's Right (and Left) Hand Man: Dave Duncan

La Russa repeatedly said during his career that baseball is mostly about pitching, and for three decades La Russa took pitching cues from one man—Dave Duncan. A former All-Star catcher, Duncan served as pitching coach longer than anyone in major league history. The 2011 season was his 32nd and likely last as he took a leave of absence to aid his wife's fight against cancer. Duncan mentored eight Cy Young Award winners and was renowned for an ability to rebuild scuffling veterans or redirect wayward talents. His scouting reports were encyclopedic, his grounded philosophy proven. La Russa said Duncan's title could be "the perfect pitching coach." "What else needs to be said?" the manager explained.

"When you're around here," La Russa said, "you just don't feel you can join the club unless you can say you won a World Series."

He retired with two as a Cardinal.

Less than 48 hours after the Cardinals won the 2011 World Series, La Russa gathered his players into the weight room for what many thought was going to be his annual send-off speech. Instead, La Russa cleared his throat and said, "I'm done." In hindsight, some of the players said they should have seen the retirement coming. Pitcher Adam Wainwright said on the eve of World Series Game 1 that La Russa seemed to be "managing every game like it was his last." He left a 33-year career that included six league pennants, three World Series championships, a record 1,408 wins with the Cardinals, and 2,728 wins overall, 35 shy of second place all time behind only Connie Mack.

"I think this just feels like time to end it," he said. "No regrets."

Before coming to St. Louis, La Russa had already won one World Series while managing the Oakland Athletics. He earned a reputation that was often distilled into a single label he despised—"genius." La Russa was far more comfortable being known as a baseball lifer, a bonus baby whose career stalled and crashed as a .199 hitter and then revived and soared as a manager.

On October 23, 1995, La Russa joined the Cardinals having already established himself as a manager on a Hall of Fame track, one that included innovation (the modern-day closer, for one) and three consecutive American League pennants. La Russa embraced the Cardinals' perennial expectations to play in October, even explaining at the time that he would wear No. 10 to remind him of that purpose—winning a 10th championship for the Cardinals.

The Cardinals went to the playoffs in seven of his first 11 seasons with the team, including an unprecedented run of six appearances in seven years. Yet St. Louis was slow to embrace La Russa. After the years of Whiteyball, there was some initial coolness toward "TLR." He was a lawyer, a vegetarian, and most of all he didn't take root in St. Louis, migrating each winter back to his Bay Area home. One club official called La Russa an "outsider" for his first decade.

La Russa fueled some of the criticisms with his prickly press conferences and his perceived brainiac approach to baseball. He irked the locals when he feuded with icon Ozzie Smith. But to fixate on his quirks—like batting the pitcher eighth—is to miss how many steps ahead he was as a manager. Meticulous in everything he did from lineup cards to spring training workouts, he never wanted to "miss an edge."

After the 2004 NL pennant, the fan base warmed to a manager who is now inextricably linked with the identity of the club. He is a reflection of the Cardinals as much as the modern Cardinals became a reflection of him. La Russa shepherded the team through tragedy and triumph, most notably when his tender guidance helped a playoff-bound club through the stunning death of teammate Darryl Kile. In 2004, La Russa busted through an annual barrier by taking a 105-win team into the World Series, and in 2006 he and an 83-win club won it.

"So," a fan asked La Russa at a Cardinals Nation fanfest in 2007, "what can we do to get you to change your number to 11?"

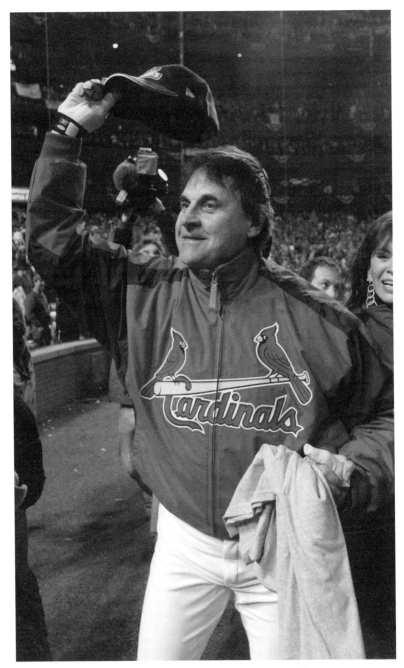

Tony La Russa became one of only two managers in baseball history to win a World Series in both the American and National Leagues in 2006.

La Russa and the Leaders

In 16 seasons with the Cardinals, Tony La Russa did more than bound to the top of the organization's list of managers in total wins; he joined the elite ranks of baseball's all-time managers in terms of total wins. Upon his retirement in 2011 after 33 years in the dugout, La Russa left as one of the winningest managers in history:

Manager	Games
1. Connie Mack	7,755
2. Tony La Russa	5,097
3. John McGraw	4,769
4. Bobby Cox	4,508
5. Bucky Harris	4,410
6. Joe Torre	4,329
7. Sparky Anderson	4,030
8. Gene Mauch	3,942
9. Casey Stengel	3,766
10. Leo Durocher	3,739

Manager	Wins	Pct. (all-time rank**)
1. Connie Mack	3,731	.486 (88)
2. John McGraw	2,763	.586 (7)
3. Tony La Russa	2,728	.536 (34)
4. Bobby Cox	2,504	.556 (18)
7. Joe Torre	2,326	.538 (32)
5. Sparky Anderson	2,194	.545 (25)
6. Bucky Harris	2,158	.493 (85)
8. Joe McCarthy	2,125	.615 (1)
9. Walter Alston	2,040	.558 (17)
10. Leo Durocher	2,008	.540 (29)

None of the managers listed above were active as of the 2011 season. Ranks reflect ranking among managers with at least 1,000 games.

He didn't change his number, but La Russa did deliver No. 11. In 2011, La Russa refused to surrender to the standings and willed the Cardinals to the biggest comeback in baseball history, from 10½ games out in August. La Russa spent 16 years with the

Cardinals, and his 2,591 games with the club rank third among players and managers behind only Red Schoendienst (3,794, player and manager combined) and Stan Musial (3,026, all as a player). La Russa notified ownership of his intent to retire two months before the World Series win. The "fire in his gut" that he followed throughout his career, in his office and from the dugout, had started to flicker, and that was all the sign he needed.

A few days after meeting with his players, La Russa walked past that spot where Gibson had found him five years earlier and out the door. He was no longer a part of the clubhouse.

He will forever be a part of the club.

He has two rings to prove it.

"Very Hollywood-esque," outfielder Matt Holliday said. "He's a Hall of Fame manager, and he gets to ride off into the sunset on possibly the highest note of them all—Game 7 of the World Series, at home, in a postseason that we were supposed to have no chance to get into. It's fitting for Tony."

Rick Ankiel's Second Act

The day everything went haywire for Rick Ankiel as a pitcher and he decided to reinvent himself for another swing at the majors, he stood at his locker as perplexed as anyone. His mechanics were off. His control was scattered. He was so self-destructive on the mound that all pitching coach Dave Duncan could do was end the workout after Ankiel walked five of six batters on 23 pitches.

"Frustrating. Disappointing," Ankiel said, reciting his litany of emotions after the aborted appearance. "You put it behind you."

He went home, melted into his couch, and decided that's exactly what he would do.

A once-in-a-generation talent tortured by injuries and fickle mechanics, Ankiel decided that afternoon to walk away from baseball. He thought maybe he'd coach, maybe he'd fish.... Then the phone rang. Cardinals general manager Walt Jocketty was calling with an unexpected alternative: Ankiel could hit. On March 9, 2005, instead of throwing his last bullpen before his first start of spring training, Ankiel retired as a pitcher, picked up a bat, and said he was going to attempt the improbable—return to the majors as an outfielder.

"This makes me freer to be myself, I'd imagine," he said. "There's no telling what I could have done as a pitcher. It fits my personality better being able to play every day as opposed to once a week."

The Cardinals selected Ankiel in the second round, 72nd overall, in the 1997 draft. The left-handed pitcher had pyrotechnic ability and was widely considered one of the top high school pitching prospects in the country. His fastball sizzled in the mid-90s and his curveball was sinister. Mark McGwire would nickname it "the snapdragon" when the two were teammates. In his first 390⅔ innings in the minors, Ankiel struck out 578 batters. He was the organization's top prospect, debuted at 20, won 11 games in his first shot at the rotation, and earned billing as a can't-miss ace. He was a fan favorite for that vicious curve, the quirky No. 66 he wore, and a personality as beguiling as it was magnetic. But things started to unravel in October 2000 during the National League Division Series.

Manager Tony La Russa attempted to deflect attention from his media-shy youngster by sending up veteran Darryl Kile for a press conference even though he planned to start Ankiel in Game 1. Ankiel pitched two shutout innings before crumbling in front of a national audience, throwing a record five wild pitches in the inning and allowing four runs before being removed.

His pitching career was a fight from there. Ankiel's arm was like a live wire—electric but untamed. He was optioned to the minors in May 2001 and did not return for three years. When he did, it was front-page news. And it didn't last. Ankiel reported to spring training the next season believing he could win a spot in the rotation. Before making his first start, he was through pitching.

"One of the reasons I retired from pitching, it was affecting me on and off the field," he said. "It was changing who I was."

Within a few days of his retirement, Ankiel had borrowed Jim Edmonds' glove and had thrown himself into a reinvention as an outfielder. Always a gifted athlete, he wowed teammates with his power during a rehab in the lower minors that included, for grins, turns at designated hitter. In 2007, eight years after he went 7–3 as a pitcher in Memphis, he led Triple A with 32 home runs in 102 games. He returned to the majors that fall, adding 11 more homers and 39 RBIs as he nearly powered the Cardinals into the postseason.

Ankiel became the only player in big-league history other than Babe Ruth to win 10 games as a pitcher and later hit 10 home runs as a position player. Consider the additional degree of difficulty in moving to a defense-intensive position like center field and Ankiel's second act is unprecedented. It's as a minor league manager once said: "I learned to never put anything past Rick Ankiel."

98 A Stay of Execution

The shot that saved Busch Stadium for another night of baseball was so stunning it also silenced the city of Houston.

On October 17, 2005, in Game 5 of the National League Championship Series, one strike separated the Houston Astros from their state's first visit to the World Series. That's when the Cardinals mounted a comeback that ended with Albert Pujols' epic home run off closer Brad Lidge. What the homer lacked in restorative power—the Cardinals would lose the pennant two nights later—it made up in timing, distance, and drama. Pujols' launch toward Minute Maid Park's left-field railroad trestle left former First Lady Barbara Bush's mouth agape as she watched from a front-row seat not 40' away from Pujols. And it was best captured by Astros pitcher Andy Pettitte, who was caught mouthing this in the Houston dugout: "Oh…my…god."

Brought in to protect a two-run lead and claim Houston's first National League pennant, Lidge struck out the first two batters he faced on nine pitches. Such was his MO against the Cardinals, who had managed little but a collection of Ks against the right-hander in two consecutive National League Championship Series. Lidge fired two called strikes against leadoff hitter David Eckstein to put the Astros one pitch away from the World Series. That was when Eckstein threaded a base hit through the left side of the Astros' infield. Jim Edmonds followed with a five-pitch walk.

Pujols hadn't gotten the ball out of the infield in his first four at-bats of the evening, and he swung awkwardly at Lidge's first pitch. Pujols' next swing, however, would propel a comet no field could contain. Conservatively estimated as a 412' shot, the only thing that stopped Pujols' three-run home run from streaking into downtown Houston was the glass wall on Minute Maid's retractable roof.

As soon as Pujols made contact, the raucous, ear-blistering crowd of 43,470 went instantly, eerily quiet. There were two sounds: the ball's melon-like thump on the glass and the cheers of the Cardinals' dugout. Pujols later said he could hear the crunch of his cleats on the dirt as he rounded the bases.

A 5–4 win sent them home for one more game before Busch fell.

"I'm a big believer," Pujols said after the game. "I put my batting gloves on knowing that if I have the opportunity…that hopefully I might be the last guy to make the out."

Back in St. Louis, a funeral was postponed. A wrecking ball was posed to descend on Busch Stadium II the moment the postseason ended, and Pujols' swing delayed the demolition. Bob Costas told the *New York Times* that the home run was "a reprieve from death row. It's a call from the governor." In the middle of the night in downtown St. Louis, two days before the Cardinals would be eliminated, fans gathered spontaneously at Busch II. Near Gate 5, a fan penned a number sign by the big "5" and scrawled: "Pujols Brought Us Back Here!" Another drew a silhouette of a player with Pujols' No. 5 bent into Superman's emblem.

Others just wrote their name, the date, and the time they were there—trusting that everyone who was anyone in Cardinals Nation would know what that date meant for their ballpark. Said one message: "My date with the wrecking ball was postponed due to the heroic efforts of Phat Albert."

He gave the fans one more day to say…

Farewell to Busch

Saying good-bye began with an inspired act of vandalism.

In the final weeks of the beloved ballpark, Busch Stadium, some fan at some time during some game picked up a pen and started a trend. The fan scrawled a farewell on the concrete cathedral that Cardinals called home for 40 seasons, and then another fan followed, and another—until an entire mural of memories and moments blanketed the walls and pillars. The graffiti spread, odes merging with signatures wrapped around poems and the best wishes that covered the inside and outside of the old multipurpose stadium. One read: "Best nest ever." Another was in French, a few more were written in Spanish, and another simply explained: "I raised my son at Busch." Several places carried proposals ("Will You Marry Me?"), acceptances ("We got married at Busch on July 3,

2003"), and announcements ("I received the best news ever!!! Baby Eade is on the way. I can't wait"). A fan's life chronicled on a column, generation to generation.

Pens were left at the scene of these crimes for co-conspirators. A few ushers later admitted to carrying an extra pen or two for fans. Messages were written after games, during games, by fans attending games, by fans who couldn't get into games. The writing was on the wall. On the stalls. On the seats. On the bleachers. On signs. Not even the two school-bus yellow foul poles were safe as fans wrapped each in the ink-black good-byes. By the time the wrecking ball arrived, most flat surfaces within an arm's reach were painted in loving tribute.

More than a high school yearbook passed around town for quick, frivolous jots, Busch Stadium became a living canvas for Cardinals Nation.

Near Gate 5, one fan crafted a eulogy:

Around here, baseball players are gods.
Brock, with the speed of Mercury.
Gibson with the lightning of Zeus.
Musial with the hammer of Thor.
McGwire with Herculean power.
And Jack, Harry, and Mike were the oracles who told their
legendary tales nightly.
Keep us tuned in to our transistors. Let's give one last toast to
Busch Stadium. For it is much more than a building. And when
the wrecking ball has come and gone, it will live on in memory
with the glory of Mount Olympus.

As the first scribbles began appearing on the ballpark, the Cardinals, led by stadium manager Joe Abernathy, ordered the staff not to scrub clean the notes. The club had been braced for people trying to take something from the ballpark in its final days, but it decided to embrace the fans giving something to the ballpark. Even a few employees penned farewells, including a column set aside for a group of ushers to sign for time served. "I guess it's not against the law," Cardinals shortstop David Eckstein told reporters, "when they're going to tear the place down."

On May 8, 1966, moments after the end of the Cardinals' 10–5 loss to San Francisco, a helicopter drifted down on Sportsman's Park—which was then also named Busch Stadium—and lifted home plate from its longtime address. The helicopter whisked it away, downtown to its new location. Four days later, Civic Center Busch Memorial Stadium opened with a Cardinals' extra-inning victory.

The ballpark, known chronologically as Busch Stadium II, was built for $26 million and was one of the first cookie-cutter stadiums that also took up residence in Philadelphia, Pittsburgh, Cincinnati, and elsewhere. Before it became the last of its stadium species to fall, Busch hosted an All-Star Game in 1966, welcomed six World Series, and boasted two World Series winners as tenants. In 2005, 3.5 million fans streamed through Busch, many on a last-season pilgrimage and all combining to bust a record set in 2000 by over 200,000 fans. In five of its final six seasons Busch II had October dates for playoff games. As iconic as its crown of arches— a ring of scalloped-cut openings at the top of the ballpark that some nicknamed "the bottle cap"—and the shadows those arches cast over the infield were, Busch II's legacy was simple: winning baseball. While its soul didn't change—"Good-bye Church," printed one fan on Busch's wall—the stadium's look and identity did.

In the 1970s the Cardinals swapped grass for turf and laid the foundation for Whiteyball and the Go-Go Cardinals of the 1980s. A facility that famously had The Beatles rocking in 1966 and Pele kicking in 1977 returned to its roots in the 1990s. Statues of Cardinals greats sprouted outside the ballpark in the mid-1990s and heralded a baseball-only renovation of the stadium. Natural grass returned in 1996. A manual scoreboard replaced seats in the upper deck above center field. The crown of arches remained, looming over fans and players, throwing its distinctive shadows and connecting the city's favorite sons with its international landmark, the Gateway Arch.

While the public view of the stadium reclaimed its charm, the guts of the stadium showed its age. Tigger and Snoopy, two cats found at the ballpark and adopted by the team as good-luck charms because of the two 100-win seasons that followed their discovery, lived in a nook of the stadium better suited for stalagmites than felines. The manager's office was a Hobbit hole toward the back of the Cardinals' clubhouse, and La Russa became so friendly with the groans and moans of the plumbing around it that he nicknamed the rusting beast "the Monster." He would joke that he could tell exactly what was being flushed from above by the pitch of the Monster's guttural strain. During his last day at Busch, La Russa halted conversations every time the pipes wheezed, paying silent reverence to a condemned friend and the acoustic beast that he was leaving behind.

"It's a bit of a bummer leaving Busch," said Cardinals pitcher Ken Dayley as he visited for the final regular-season weekend at the ballpark. "Because you come here now and you can say, 'There it is. Grandpa used to pitch here.' And now it will always be, 'There it was.'"

The final season of Busch II became a journey through the 40 seasons, a celebration of the moments and people and spectacles. At each home game, a member from Cardinals history would peel a number off the right-field wall to count down the regular-season games remaining. Ozzie Smith took down No. 1, ending a parade that included former All-Star and manager Joe Torre (No. 50); Vince Coleman (No. 29); the aforementioned Mercury, Hall of Famer Lou Brock (No. 20); and Mark McGwire (No. 3). No. 57 was among the most moving, as Darryl Kile's family joined two of the pitcher's teammates, Jim Edmonds and Matt Morris, to remove

The All-Busch Stadium Team

Position	Player	Years Played
Manager	Whitey Herzog	1980–1990
Starting Pitcher	Bob Gibson	1959–1975
Relief Pitcher	Bruce Sutter	1981–1984
Catcher	Ted Simmons	1968–1980
First Baseman	Albert Pujols	2001–present
Second Baseman	Tom Herr	1979–1988
Third Baseman	Scott Rolen	2002–2007
Shortstop	Ozzie Smith	1982–1996
Left Field	Lou Brock	1964–1979
Center Field	Jim Edmonds	2000–2007
Right Field	Roger Maris	1967–1968

the number. Current players shied away from participating in the number drill for awhile because the first three had awful performances in the same night. Nostalgia ultimately trumped superstition, and the players resumed their role, when requested.

As the ballpark's farewell tour neared an end, the Cardinals players were asked to sign so many last-year items—jerseys, baseballs, bases, the door to their locker's lockboxes—that outfielder Larry Walker went wild with a pen. He signed phones, trashcans, random walls, a bullpen phone, and, he boasted, the inside of a urinal. While Walker was writing all over the inside of the Cardinals' clubhouse, the story continued outside during the postseason. "For Grandma, who taught me the Joy of Cardinal baseball, keeping score," wrote one fan on a Busch pillar. Another: "Mrs. Hitz and her 7th grade class were here." And another: "Ozzie would have had that."

Out in Section 244: "I sat here for eight years and loved every minute."

Busch became its own memorial.

The club had planned to have Stan Musial be the last person out of the ballpark after the last game, closing the gate—possibly the one right by his statue—behind him, the final act at a stadium host to so many theatrics. But early on it became clear the loitering and the good-byes were going to go too late for Musial to be the last to leave. Despair has no curfew.

On October 18, 2005, buzzsaws began dismantling the dugout benches. The scoreboard was stripped. The large, red, universally known KMOX sign didn't last long in its fight with a wrecking ball. Several players drove their trucks onto the outfield grass and spun donuts around the positions they played. Employees grabbed armfuls of equipment and took their last swings at the place in an impromptu game. La Russa bid adieu to the Monster.

Outside, the sentimental vandalism continued.

The place began coming down a few days later.

Words written by the fans stayed until the final arch from the crown of arches fell. One faced the street that would take fans to the new place, Busch III, just down the block. Under an arrow pointing that way, someone wrote: "New Memories This Way."

100 Welcome to New Busch

As they prepared for its 2006 grand opening, the Cardinals designed their new downtown stadium with retro touches galore, a few knowing winks to the franchise's past, and even transferred the name from the old place for branding continuity. But it was Busch Stadium in name only, just another baseball field built out of red bricks and throwback coolness, until the team added a distinctive, house-warming touch.

Nothing christens a new ballpark like a championship.

Six months after it opened with a win on April 10, 2006, Busch Stadium closed for the season with a burst of fireworks and a parade to mark the team's 10th World Series title. The new ballpark was the

On April 10, 2006, the Cardinals beat the Milwaukee Brewers 6–4 in the inaugural game at the new Busch Stadium.

first since Yankee Stadium in 1923 to host a World Series winner in its inaugural season, and the Cardinals were the first franchise in nearly a century to clinch a title at a brand-new ballpark. The Boston Red Sox did it in 1912—at Fenway Park. The championship run infused the glitzy new field with the life and history that even the new-wave old-school architecture couldn't replicate. And that was the goal of Busch III, to take the shared memories of multi-purpose Busch, the classic feel of Sportsman's Park, the timelessness of the franchise's titles and transplant that blend into the function of the modern, retro ballpark.

The Cardinals began construction on their $365 million ballpark in January 2004, building it on an adjacent—and overlapping—plot while the club had consecutive 100-win seasons. New Busch's red-brick façade was a nod to nearby historic sites, the Wainwright Building and Cupples Station. The Musial Bridge, a walkway spanning Gate 3, was inspired by the ribbed steel archways of the Eads Bridge, which, when it opened in 1874, was the largest of its kind and an architectural marvel for spanning the Mississippi River. Borrowing from landmarks was only the start. The Cardinals' ownership wanted to open up the ballpark, break the isolation of the enclosed circle that was Busch II, and have the new place embrace the city's skyline. Look out to center field from inside the stadium and the Gateway Arch rises in the distance and the green-domed Old Courthouse stands in the foreground. There is now a visual link between the three famous landmarks of St. Louis.

Inside the ballpark, unofficially Busch III, there are details to be discovered. The gigantic hand-operated scoreboard from Busch II is hanging on the south wall of the new stadium, the inning-by-inning score from the final game frozen there. Scattered throughout the ballpark, there are stone medallions carved to reflect the evolution of the Redbird logo. (There used to be similar carvings behind home plate until a few balls ricocheted unpredictably off the logos.) Out in the left-field terrace a keen eye will notice a scoring in the concrete to designate where the right field from the old ballpark was.

A World Series title proved to be an exceptional decorator, as new Busch was dressed to impress by 2007. Pennants for all 10 of the club's championships were erected above the scoreboard, a sign trumpeting the 10 titles to the passersby on the nearby interstates was installed, and photos of the iconic players were emblazoned on the left-field wall near their retired numbers. (A pennant for the Cardinals' 11th championship will be added in 2012.) The improvements continued in 2008 with the unveiling of Musial Plaza.

Surrounding the relocated Musial Statue and sitting underneath the Musial Bridge at Gate 3, the Cardinals installed 3,630 personalized bricks, one for every base hit in his career. There are 1,815 on one side of an inlaid baseball with Musial's signature, and 1,815 on the other, just as Musial had 1,815 hits on the road and 1,815 at Sportsman's Park.

At the ceremony to dedicate the Plaza and rename a stretch of Eighth Street "Stan Musial Drive," the Man himself stood up and told the crowd why he walked so delicately. "The reason I have a bad knee," he said, "is I hit too many triples."

It's a fitting image, Musial posed at third base. Even at its new locale, on a pedestal above the Plaza, the statue honoring Musial remains the meeting place for the melting pot of Cardinals Nation. The bronze Musial acts as a guide, reminding all who come to see the self-described man who hit too many triples that they stand like he so often did—90' from home.

Selected Bibliography

A sizeable stack of books, newspaper clippings, and yellow legal pads accompanied me on this 100-step journey through Cardinals history. In addition to firsthand reporting, I attempted to pan through as many tributaries as possible for the best nuggets. Among the most essential vaults of information were newspapers, magazines, and their archives, especially those from the *St. Louis Post-Dispatch*, the *St. Louis Globe-Democrat*, the *Sporting News*, *Sports Illustrated*, the *Chicago Sun-Times*, the *Chicago Tribune*, the *New York Times*, the *Belleville News Democrat*, and various others from around National League cities. Baseball-Reference.com and Retrosheet.org are invaluable, nimble, and omniscient resources for the modern-day baseball writer, and there is no other place to go for game details and career statistics.

Here were the other resources that sometimes made for heavy travel companions and many of which were often within an arm's reach:

Barthel, Thomas. *Pepper Martin: A Baseball Biography*. Jefferson, N.C.: McFarland & Company, Inc., 2003.

Bissinger, Buzz. *3 Nights in August*. Boston: Houghton Mifflin Company, 2005.

Broeg, Bob. *The 100 Greatest Moments in St. Louis Sports*. St. Louis, Mo.: Historical Society Press, 2000.

Broeg, Bob. *Memories of a Hall of Fame Sportswriter*. Champaign, Ill.: Sagamore Publishing, 1995.

Broeg, Bob. *The Pilot Light and the Gas House Gang*. St. Louis, Mo.: Bethany Press, 1980.

Broeg, Bob and Stan Musial. *The Man Stan Musial: Then and Now*. St. Louis, Mo.: Bethany Press, 1977.

Chieger, Bob. *Voices of Baseball*. New York: Signet, 1984.

Eisenbath, Mike. *The Cardinals Encyclopedia*. Philadelphia: Temple University Press, 1999.

Feldman, Doug. *El Birdos*. Jefferson, N.C.: McFarland & Company, Inc., 2007.

Feldman, Doug. *Dizzy and the Gas House Gang: The 1934 St. Louis Cardinals and Depression-Era Baseball*. Jefferson, N.C.: McFarland & Company, Inc., 2000.

Flood, Curt. *The Way It Is*. New York: Trident Press, 1971.

Gibson, Bob and Lonnie Wheeler. *Stranger to the Game: The Autobiography of Bob Gibson*. New York: Viking, 1994.

Giglio, James N. *Musial: From Stash to Stan the Man*. Columbia, Mo.: University of Missouri Press, 2001.

Goldman, Steven. *Forging Genius: The Making of Casey Stengel*. Dulles, Va.: Potomac, Inc., 2005.

Golenbock, Peter. *The Spirit of St. Louis*. New York: HarperEntertainment, 2001.

Gregory, Robert. *Diz: The Story of Dizzy Dean and Baseball During the Great Depression*. New York: Viking, 1992.

Halberstam, David. *October 1964*. New York: Fawcett Books, 1995.

Hardy Chinn, Sandra. *At Your Service: KMOX and Bob Hardy, Pioneers of Talk Radio*. St. Louis: Virginia Publishing, 1997.

Haudricourt, Tom. *Where Have You Gone '82 Brewers?* Stevens Point, Wis.: KCI Sports Publishing, 2007.

Heidenry, John. *The Gashouse Gang*. New York: Public Affairs, 2007.

Hornsby, Rogers. *My War with Baseball*. New York: Coward-McCann, 1962.

Hummel, Rick. *The Commish and the Cardinals*. St. Louis, Mo.: St. Louis Post-Dispatch Books, 2007.

Lieb, Frederick G. *The St. Louis Cardinals: The Story of a Great Baseball Club*. Carbondale, Ill.: Southern Illinois University Press, 2001 (reprint).

Lowenfish, Lee. *Branch Rickey: Baseball's Ferocious Gentlemen.* Lincoln, Neb.: University of Nebraska Press, 2007.

McCarver, Tim. *Few and Chosen: Defining Cardinal Greatness Across the Eras.* Chicago: Triumph Books, 2003.

Peterson, Richard, ed. *The St. Louis Baseball Reader.* Columbia, Mo.: University of Missouri Press, 2006.

Rains, Rob. *Cardinal Nation.* St. Louis, Mo.: Sporting News, 2002.

Rains, Rob and Jack Buck. *Jack Buck: "That's a Winner!"* Champaign, Ill.: Sports Publishing LLC, 1997.

Rains, Sally and Rob. *The Mighty 'Mox.* South Bend, Ind.: Diamond Communications, 2000.

Ritter, Lawrence S. *The Glory of their Times.* New York: Harper Perennial, 1992.

Smith, Red. *Red Smith on Baseball.* Chicago: Ivan R. Dee, 2000.

Snyder, Brad. *A Well-Paid Slave.* New York: Viking, 2006.

Snyder, John. *Cardinals Journal.* Cincinnati: Emmis Books, 2006.

Stockton, J. Roy. *The Gashouse Gang and a Couple of Other Guys.* New York: A.S. Barnes, 1945.

Thomas, Joan M. *St. Louis Big League Ballparks.* Charleston, S.C.: Arcadia Publishing, 2004.

Ward, Geoffrey C. and Ken Burns. *Baseball: An Illustrated History.* New York: Alfred A. Knopf, 1994.

Will, George F. *Men at Work: The Craft of Baseball.* New York: Harper Perennial, 1992.